Women'sHealth

Healthy Meals
for One
(*or* Two)
Cookbook

A Simple Guide to Shopping, Prepping,
and Cooking for Yourself
with More Than 175 Nutritious Recipes

The Editors of **Women'sHealth**
with Katie Walker

Recipes by the Rodale Test Kitchen

© 2017 by Rodale Inc.

Rodale books may be purchased for business or promotional use or for special sales. For information, please e-mail: BookMarketing@Rodale.com.

Women's Health is a registered trademark of Rodale Inc.

Printed in the United States of America

Rodale Inc. makes every effort to use acid-free ♾, recycled paper ♻.

Photographs by Mitch Mandel/Rodale Images

Book design by Carol Angstadt and Jan Derevjanik

Library of Congress Cataloging-in-Publication Data is on file with the publisher.

ISBN 978-1-63565-085-3

Distributed to the trade by Macmillan

2   4   6   8   10   9   7   5   3   1   paperback

Follow us @RodaleBooks on

We inspire health, healing, happiness, and love in the world.
Starting with you.

Contents

1 Set Yourself Up for Success

2 Let's Get Cooking!

3 Plans & Resources

For Grammy and Poppi,
who were never in doubt.

Acknowledgments

FIRST AND FOREMOST, I WANT TO THANK MY FANTASTIC EDITOR, ALLISON JANICE. Without you, this book wouldn't exist, and your guidance and vision are an invaluable resource. Thank you to the staff of *Women's Health* magazine and the incredible Rodale Test Kitchen.

To my wonderful parents, Sally and Todd Whitchurch and Norman and Lynn Walker, I owe you absolutely everything. My grandparents and my siblings, Chris, Tyler, Haley, Leslie, and Jenny, have always been my cheerleaders, and my nieces, Claire, Amelia, and Addison, and my cousins, Judith, Elle, and Sylvia, are my constant inspiration. This book is also for my aunt Deborah and my cousin Savannah, whose strength inspires me every day even though they're no longer with me.

Thank you to my friends who contributed to, critiqued, and supported me through the process of writing this book: Bethy, Stephanie, Becca, Melissa, Mimi, Amy, Deb, Jen, Mary, and Peter. Your faith in my ability to do this work allowed me to think it was possible. And much appreciation to the Fishtown cafés, coffee shops, and bakeries that let me sit and drink coffee and soak up ideas from their amazing food.

Finally, thank you to you, dear reader, for picking up this book and taking the first step toward creating a healthier, happier life for yourself. This book exists to help you treat yourself the way you deserve to be treated—with care, love, and respect. I hope it does just that.

Kate Walker, 2017

Cooking *for* One

WHEN WAS THE LAST TIME YOU COOKED FOR YOURSELF? WE DON'T MEAN THE last time you heated up a microwaveable meal, or even the last time you threw together a stir-fry. When was the last time you really cooked *for* yourself—when you thought about what you *wanted* to eat, went out and bought the ingredients to make it, and put together a simple and complete meal for one?

It's a scary idea, making a meal for one. For many people, it's as daunting as eating out alone at a restaurant. And for women, it's particularly daunting. It's not because we're not capable of planning, shopping, and cooking—of course we are! And it's not because of money—cooking at home is cheaper and often faster than takeout. It's because we're just not used to putting that much energy into something that is just for us. Most of us will happily (if not skillfully) cook a fun meal for friends or roommates, but we're constantly putting ourselves on the back burner (so to speak!).

It doesn't help that most recipes out there in cookbooks and online serve four to six, or eight, or even ten! It's not uncommon to find a delicious smoothie recipe that serves four. Four! Who makes smoothies for early-morning parties of four (and if you are, we are going to need an invite!)? That means that when you find a great recipe to try, you either have to remember how to use fractions to work the recipe down to two servings, or you get to eat the same meal six times in one week. Would you ever serve someone else the same boring dinner six nights in a row? Of course not. So why would you do that to yourself?

All of these multi-serving recipes are particularly out of touch because more Americans[1] than ever before are living on their own. In fact, more women between the ages of 24 and 36 live alone than with roommates. And while living on your own is great—No sharing milk! Unlimited bathroom time!—it can take a toll on your health if you aren't careful.[2]

A recent study found that people who live on their own have low diversity in the food they eat; consume fewer fruits, vegetables and fish than people in multi-person households; and are more likely to have an unhealthy diet—popcorn for dinner, anyone? Since fresh fruits and veggies are the foods that go bad the fastest, and are harder to finish as one person, it's not a surprise they get passed over at the grocery store. And it doesn't help that getting dinner (or lunch, or snacks, or bagels) delivered is easier than ever. We'll get into the details of nutrition and cost of cooking for yourself later, but what's becoming obvious is that we really are treating ourselves worse than we treat others. Much worse.

This book is here to help. Whether you're a first time cook or a recipe addict who just needs to master cooking for one, we have 175 fabulous recipes to get you started on the path to better health, more money in the bank, and tastier food. This is a book about radical self-care, about focusing on what your body needs, what you want to eat, and how to support everything else you have going on by adapting and prepping for your week in advance.

So pull the sweaters out of your oven, Carrie Bradshaw, and embrace your inner Monica. You're going to get cooking and, after a few weeks of planning, prepping, and preparing food for yourself, much of it will become second nature. Like anything else, cooking for yourself is about establishing good habits. And we're not suggesting that you should spend hours in the kitchen slaving over a 5 course meal for yourself—in fact, this book's recipe section is broken up into dishes that can be prepped ahead of time, recipes that can be thrown together in a few minutes, and recipes that are slower and indulgent so you can adjust based on your schedule.

Let's Talk About "Diets"

It's a common misunderstanding that the word "diet" means an eating plan undertaken with the desire and intention to achieve weight loss. In fact, diet just means "the kind of food that a person regularly eats." In that spirit, what this book isn't is a "diet book"—we're not giving you calorie restrictions or eliminating food groups (unless you count "delivery pizza" as a food group). But the goal is to improve your diet. Add more fruits and vegetables back in, incorporate interesting protein sources (check out our Lamb Meatball Skewers with Tahini-Goat Cheese Sauce on page 183), and don't forget snacks and smoothies that power you through your toughest workouts.

Your new diet is not going to make going out with friends difficult, or keep you chained to your office microwave for 10 minutes per day. Cooking healthy meals that are planned around your schedule and needs will fuel your life and your #goals.

Cooking vs. Delivery

For the first time EVER, Americans are spending more money on food prepared outside the home than food purchased to cook and eat at home.[3] And why not, when we can tap on our phone for two minutes and have almost any dish appear at our door within an hour? It's enough to make us feel like Marie Antoinette! And why shouldn't we eat cake?

Both cost and calories, that's why. And it isn't just cake. A recent study found that 92% of restaurant meals contained more calories than recommended for a single meal (which we prefer to keep below 500 calories), with the average dish clocking in at a terrifying 1,200 calories.[4] And these aren't fast food restaurants—these numbers are from sit-down spots. What are the odds that you're eating the 8% of meals that are under the recommended amount of per-meal calories? And eating out will almost always cost more than making it yourself, even before adding in delivery costs if you want to stay in your pajama pants.

Don't just take our word for it—let's compare one of the dinners in our book to its restaurant counterpart. Our Yogurt and Parmesan Fettuccine Alfredo costs $1.75 for the ingredients, and clocks in at 342 calories. At a popular restaurant, Fettuccine Alfredo will cost about $15, and could pack close to a whopping 1,800 calories. We could do the math for you about how many calories and dollars you'll save in one week from eating at home, but you get the picture.

So let's get to it and build you the perfect cooking-for-one kitchen!

1

Set Yourself Up for Success

CRAFTING YOUR KITCHEN

HOPEFULLY BY NOW YOU'RE CONVINCED THAT COOKING FOR YOURSELF is something you *should* do, but be honest with us—are you convinced yet that it's something you *can* do? Well, that's what this book is here for! Consider us your gurus for the world of becoming an ace chef for one (or two!), and let this book be your guide. As with any new habit, it takes a little bit of prep work and repetition, but within a few weeks you'll be prepping and cooking for yourself without even having to think about it. Trust us—if we can break our food delivery habits and manage to chop carrots after spin class, you can, too!

So as your sherpas to success, we're going to take you step-by-step through everything you need to cook for yourself. We'll start with the actual *things* that you need in your kitchen (spoiler alert: an avocado slicer is not one of them) and move on to the habits for planning and shopping. Then we'll dig into the fun stuff—cooking! The secret to cooking quickly and efficiently is a word we'll be using a lot in the chapters to come—*prepping.* By taking some time one day a week to prep for your meals, you're going to cut average cooking time down to a manageable level and make it a lot more fun. So let's get started with our favorite part—shopping!

The 25 Tools Every Kitchen Needs

In spite of what most kitchen stores will tell you, you don't actually need to own 10 knives, 15 spatulas, and a greens stripper (look it up—it's not as fun as it sounds) to be a great cook. In fact, if you took a peek at the kitchens of most professional chefs, you'd find a few high-quality tools and almost nothing that has only one purpose. The majority of kitschy kitchen implements can actually be replaced with a good knife. The list below assumes you have a standard kitchen with an oven, stove, and microwave, and we hope we don't need to tell you that you should own plates, bowls, and utensils (unless you like to eat meals directly out of your pots and pans to save time washing dishes—you do you!).

So what do you actually need to be a successful cook? We've made a list for you of our favorite kitchen tools. You probably have most of these in your kitchen already, and with the full set, you'll be able to cook everything in this book. That's right—everything.

1. **Chef's knife**
2. **Paring knife**
3. **Cutting board**
4. **Mixing bowl set**
   (Get the kind with lids so that they can also double as storage.)
5. **Large spoon**
6. **Slotted spoon**
7. **Whisk**
8. **Spatula**
9. **Ladle**
10. **Tongs**
11. **4-quart pot with lid**
12. **1- to 2-quart saucepan with lid**
13. **Large skillet**
14. **Large baking sheet**
15. **Blender**
16. **Box grater**
    (Look for the kind with multiple sides for lots of varied uses.)
17. **Colander**
18. **Vegetable peeler**
    (You can also use this to make fettuccine-style veggie noodles without a spiralizer!)
19. **Can opener**
20. **Measuring cups and spoons**
21. **Muffin pan**
22. **1-quart baking dish or other small ovenproof dish**
23. **Instant-read thermometer**
24. **Food processor**
25. **Mason jars**
    (Pint and quart sizes are great!)

Cost versus Quality

The debate about how much to spend on kitchen tools comes up a lot, and it's more worrying the more expensive the tool is. Is a $500 blender worth the money if it makes beautifully smooth smoothies and soups? Is there a difference between $3 measuring cups and the $20 variety? Considering that our list of necessary tools could either cost $150 or $1,500 all-in, it's certainly worth discussing. So here are our rules of thumb:

- **GO CHEAP.** Is it nonmechanical, not sharp, and not a cooking surface? This category includes measuring cups and spoons, mixing bowls, cooking utensils, colander, can opener, and cutting boards. This is where you can really save money and go to the dollar store (literally—many of these tools are available for $1!). These tools are about as effective no matter how much you spend on them and won't break the bank if you have to replace them once a year. Just make sure they're all made of BPA-free plastic and are dishwasher safe, to save time and hassle.

- **TAKE THE MIDDLE OF THE ROAD.** This is the category of tools where the quality actually affects how your food cooks or is prepared, and where a little extra money (we're talking $10 instead of $2) can mean a big jump in quality. These tools are ones that cook food but don't take direct heat (baking pans, baking sheets, muffin pans), have a sharp edge but aren't knives (box grater, vegetable peeler), or have some kind of mechanical component without being electric (instant-read thermometer). Look for a good deal, but don't splurge too much on this part of your kitchen.

- **HUNT FOR A WARRANTY.** And now we come to the hard part, because this is where we tell you that you might want to spend a little bit of money—but trust us, it's worth it. Aside from making cooking easier and more productive, kitchen tools that cost a little bit more also come with lifetime warranties, either from the manufacturer or from the store. So it might be tough to shell out $150 on that blender now, but if it lasts for 20 years, that's a lot more bang for your buck than a $35 blender that wears out every couple of years. Do your homework: Some major home stores offer great warranties on their products and will even sharpen your knives when they dull or replace your pans if they warp. For pots and pans that take direct heat, we recommend good stainless-steel types—nonstick is nice, but it needs to be replaced fairly regularly, and you miss out on that delicious fond that makes pan sauces taste amazing. Knives with a lifetime guarantee are fairly easy to find for less than $100 each, and you'll be able to get them sharpened (usually for free, or you can do it yourself), which will keep them feeling brand-new. For mechanical kitchen appliances, go with your gut and your budget. You can splurge now for a tool with a lifetime guarantee, or you can spend a little less, have it for a few good years, and replace it when it eventually putters out.

And don't worry too much, because your kitchen already has the two most important tools it needs: you and this book!

PLANNING
&
SHOPPING

SO WHERE TO EVEN GET STARTED WITH YOUR NEW PLANNING, COOKING, and shopping routine? The first step is to pick a day when you'll take a couple of hours to set yourself up for the week. We like to do this on Sunday, when we're looking at the week ahead (and possibly ready to atone for the calories consumed over the weekend). But really, any day when you can set aside time will work.

Before you do anything else, take 5 minutes and clean out your fridge. It sounds daunting (because right now you probably do it twice a year!), but it will actually take a lot less time than you think, and the benefits of a clean, organized refrigerator are huge. Throw out old condiments, late-night pizza boxes, leftovers that you never got to, and anything that is just too old to consume. This quick process will also enable you to know what you have, so that when you're making your shopping list later, you won't get duplicates.

One of the benefits of cooking for yourself (and living on your own) is having an entire refrigerator to organize however you want. Whether it's a New York City mini fridge or a Miele double-wide, put your refrigerator to work for you. We love to use brightly colored plastic baskets from the dollar store to create a system. You could designate each basket as a day of the week, or a different food group. Play around with a system that works for you, and enjoy it! We've all done the fridge hang—leaning on the door, staring at a sad assortment of leftovers and turned fruit that ultimately leads us to bad decisions. But with a bright and beautiful fridge stocked with fresh ingredients, you'll be drawn to better choices.

With a clean fridge and a sense of the food you already have in stock, it's time to make your meal plan and shopping list. We like to use a small whiteboard on the fridge for meal planning—it saves the trees, and it keeps your plan front and center. Write out the week, with spaces for each meal and snacks. Once you get the hang of meal planning, it will take you only a matter of minutes. To get you started, we've created a collection of weekly plans to save you time (page 223), but if you want to create your own, there are some things you'll need to take into account.

Check the Calendar

Take a minute to look at your calendar app and see what you have planned for the week. If there are events that will affect your eating, take note of the event on your meal plan. Have a date on Wednesday night? Block out that dinner, and maybe plan for light foods throughout the day so that you can indulge a little in the evening. Long meeting on Thursday? Take note and plan for a slow cooker meal or a prepped salad that will take

QUICK CLEANING SPRAY[1]

For an extra-sparkly kitchen and refrigerator, keep this homemade cleaning spray on hand. During your Sunday clean-out, spray a little on a paper towel and give your refrigerator shelves a quick wipe. Making your own spray does more than just allow you to avoid chemicals in your kitchen and keep it sparkling—it will save you a ton of money! This combo costs about 4 cents per cup, or 77 cents per gallon of cleaner. Just grab a spray bottle from the dollar store and get mixing.

9 parts water
1 part white vinegar

Mix both ingredients in a spray bottle. For a nice scent while you clean, add 2 drops of your favorite essential oil for every 1 cup of cleaner (we enjoy lemon tea tree or lavender). Use anywhere that needs a quick clean.

only minutes when you get home. Things will always come up, but the more you plan your meals around your life, the easier it will be to keep cooking for one.

Shop the Shelves

Think of your kitchen as a free grocery store. Keep in mind the food that you already have when picking out meals for the week. This keeps food from spending weeks untouched in the fridge until it spoils. Are there frozen leftovers that you're ready to eat again? Or some grains in the pantry, waiting to be cooked? Working from what you already have will save you money, save food from being wasted, and make your grocery bags lighter for hauling home.

Make a Meal Plan

Here's the big secret about cooking for yourself (or being the one in charge of meal planning)—you get to eat exactly what you want! Your food should power your week, and good food has the ability to truly make you feel better and have more energy. When you're doing your meal plan, really take some time to take stock of how you feel and how you want to feel. Did you overindulge a little this weekend? Maybe stick with cleansing, low-sodium foods for the week. Are your mornings feeling sluggish? Add some protein to your breakfast. The foods you choose to eat have the power to truly change how you feel—take control of that power.

Pick out your meals for the week and add them to your meal plan. As you can see in the meal plans we created on page 223, we like to eat from similar ingredients through-out the week. This simplifies shopping and lets us use bulk vegetable and meat dis-counts even for small servings.

Organize the List

Once you've picked out your meals and made a plan, it's time to write your grocery list. There are lots of great premade lists that you can buy online that sort your items by store department. But for maximum speed and efficiency (and minimum impulse purchasing), try to make your own. Think through the path you take at the grocery store, and note each department in order. Then add what you need under each department, and don't forget to list quantities for yourself! You can even make yourself a fancy template to print out and use each week.

Make the Trip

Now you've arrived at the main event! Whether you're walking, driving, or biking to the store, try to make this a highlight of your weekend. When else do you get time completely to yourself, surrounded by delicious food, with only the goal of doing something healthful and helpful for your week? There are some very small tricks that can convert this chore into a treat.

First, make sure you're full and hydrated—the old adage about never shopping hungry exists for a reason. Then dress for the occasion, and no, we're not talking about a bodycon and heels. Just put on your favorite athleisure that makes you feel fit and healthy, the kind of look that makes you feel ready to run into an ex or a frenemy. If you feel confident, you'll make better choices. If you're feeling gross and grungy, that ice cream and frozen pizza are going to be a lot more tempting.

When you get to the store, pop in your favorite podcast or playlist to help you focus on the task at hand. Most stores put their flowers right at the front, and we love to grab a big bunch for the front of our cart—think of it as mini interior decorating. It's great to set aside $10 to buy yourself a fresh bouquet every week, but if you're budgeting, just enjoy the company of the flowers and then put them back at the end of the trip.

In most grocery stores, the produce section is your first stop. If you've planned for the week to eat a lot of one vegetable, maybe peppers, then a bulk bag might be a great option. But sometimes the bulk bags are home to the vegetables that are just about to turn, so try to inspect them closely. If the produce you need is out of season (you can know this by checking out our seasonality guide on page 236, but the quick rule of thumb is that if it's more expensive than normal, it's out of season), then don't be afraid of the freezer section! Frozen produce is a lot more nutrient dense and flavorful than out-of-season produce.

The trick to grocery stores is that most of what you really *need* to eat and cook healthfully is located around the perimeter. The center section is mostly filled with processed food, impulse buys, and soda. As you work through the store with your list, go around the perimeter. When you come to an aisle with a pantry item that you need, leave your cart at the end of the aisle and go get it. Without your cart, you're far less likely to add items that aren't on your list.

It might sound counterintuitive, but a small kitchen's best friend is the bulk aisle of the grocery store. Bulk, raw grains, oats, spices, and more are usually the same price or cheaper than prepackaged, and you can get exactly as much as you want for the week. Don't be afraid to make a ¼-pound bag! It's a lot more fun to have five different grains throughout the week instead of the same basmati rice over and over.

At the checkout line, save yourself a little time at home by not just dumping everything onto the belt in a heap. Instead, as you unpack your cart, sort your items into freezer, refrigerator, and pantry sections. When they're bagged, the like-items will keep each other cool and will be a breeze to unpack back at home.

SAFE EATING

All of this regular cleaning of your refrigerator means that you'll be looking at a lot of date labels, but what do they all mean? Should you throw something away after its sell-by date? We checked in with our friends at the USDA (the experts in safe eating), and here's what they say:[2]

BEST IF USED BY/BEFORE: This is only an indicator of flavor or quality; this date has nothing to do with safety.

SELL BY: This label exists only to help grocery stores maintain inventory, and again has nothing to do with safety.

USE BY: This is the trickiest date because it sounds like food will be dangerous after it, but it actually just means that the food is at its peak until this date. Except in the case of infant formula, most food is still safe after this date.

Thanks in part to these labels, an estimated 30 percent of the food supply is lost or wasted before it is eaten. So how can you know when to throw something away? Just trust your instincts! Spoiled food will be off in odor, flavor, or texture—basically, if it looks weird, don't eat it. But if it looks good, smells good, and, most importantly, tastes good—go ahead and enjoy!

THE PERFECT PANTRY

HAVING A WELL-STOCKED PANTRY MEANS THAT YOU DON'T HAVE TO grocery shop every day. You should be able to walk into your kitchen any day of the week and make yourself a meal out of what's already there. But a well-stocked pantry doesn't mean spending a week's paycheck and cramming your shelves to look like a mini gourmet foods emporium. For a deep dive, read more about the different parts of your pantry. If you're in a rush, skip ahead to the concise list we've compiled for you on page 15. And don't let the length of the list scare you—unless you're moving into your very first apartment, the odds are good that you already have many of the foods listed.

We believe that there are some items everyone should have on hand, and those include the ingredients you'll need to cook the recipes in this book. When you're doing your pre-shopping survey, make sure you restock items you're out of, even if they aren't on the meal plan for the week. Once you get into the habit of being well stocked, you'll never want to go back to having empty shelves.

Oils

While every oil has its specific uses, a few can act as your kitchen workhorses. For salad dressings or drizzling—places where you want flavor—a bit of good extra-virgin olive oil goes a long way. For cooking, choose something with a more neutral flavor and a higher smoke point (the temperature at which oil begins to burn and smoke). Pure olive oil and canola oil work for frying, grilling, and baking. If you're a fan of Asian cooking, consider adding toasted sesame oil to your arsenal. And don't forget a good nonaerosol cooking spray. Store all of these in a cool, dark place, like a kitchen cabinet.

Beans

High in protein and fiber, beans can get you through any meal. Choose canned beans for faster cooking and less prep, although they are notoriously high in sodium, so opt for low-sodium or no-salt-added varieties. We also recommend draining and thoroughly rinsing beans to remove as much of that salty canning water as possible. If you keep a few 15-ounce cans on hand, you'll be able to make most bean dishes in this book. Beans also freeze well, so be sure to portion out what you don't use into a freezer-safe container. Consider keeping a small bag of brown or green (French) lentils in your cupboard for a protein- and fiber-packed addition to soups or salads.

Grains

Nutrient-dense whole grains make us feel fuller longer. Pick your favorites to have on hand, as most whole grains in these recipes are interchangeable (though cooking times may vary). These days, many whole grains—such as brown rice, quinoa, and even farro—come precooked in shelf-stable, microwaveable pouches. Or, to spend less, buy bulk grains and cook a batch at the beginning of the week to save cooking time on busy weekdays. Also opt for a container of traditional rolled oats, rather than steel-cut or instant; they still contain a good deal of the nutrition of steel-cut, but they cook in far less time. You can store raw grains in the refrigerator to extend their shelf lives. And what's a well-stocked pantry without pasta? With so many healthful varieties on the market these days, there's no reason to eat nutrient-deficient white pasta. Keep a box of small (ditalini, elbow), medium (penne, rotini), and long (spaghetti, fettuccine) whole grain pasta on hand for whenever you want to bulk up a soup or salad—or whenever that carb craving hits.

Sweeteners

While many foods have carbs and calories, we strive to keep added sugars to a minimum, and when we do use them, we try to use natural sugars over the processed white stuff: honey, maple syrup, fruit, agave, and brown sugar. Each of these natural sugars can be used interchangeably in these recipes, and they each have long shelf lives.

Vinegars

Most dishes benefit from a small amount of acid—it breaks up rich food, balances the fat, and adds a bit of brightness. Strongly flavored vinegars like balsamic have specific uses, while many Asian dishes employ rice vinegar. Other vinegars, such as red wine, sherry, apple cider, or white wine/champagne, can generally be used interchangeably. Pick up red wine vinegar and apple cider vinegar if you don't have space to spare, since they have terrific shelf lives and can stand in for most vinegars called for in this book.

Nuts and Seeds

In addition to crunch, nuts and seeds add flavor, protein, and healthy fats to any dish. To get started with the recipes in this book, you'll want the nuts listed in the shopping list on page 16. Other nuts are called for in moderation, but generally, your favorite nut will make a fine substitute. For example, if you don't like (or don't want to spend the money on) pine nuts, substitute almonds. Some recipes call for unsalted nuts to keep the sodium of the entire dish in check, so consider stocking your pantry with unsalted versions of your favorite varieties—then simply adjust the salt in the recipe to suit your taste. When it comes to nut butters, look for creamy, natural varieties that don't contain added sugar. Feel free to swap almond butter or cashew butter for peanut, and they can all hang out in your cupboard. Make sure you store tahini (sesame seed butter) in the fridge to keep it from going rancid.

Herbs and Spices

Do we really need to tell you what a difference a good spice cabinet can make for your cooking? In addition to adding a ton of flavor, better spices usually mean less unhealthy salt and sugar. As tempting as it might be to buy that large, last-jar-of-this-spice-you'll-ever-need container, opt for smaller spice jars. Though less cost-effective, they will maintain their freshness longer and won't take up as much space in your cupboard. The only exception is salt: Buy the box of kosher salt and the canister of iodized salt. Keep bouillon cubes on hand for soup; they last longer and take up significantly less space than boxes of stock.

Baking Basics

Even if you don't consider yourself a baker—or own a single piece of bakeware—it's a good idea to keep some sort of thickening and leavening agent on hand. All-purpose flour and whole wheat flour can be used interchangeably in small amounts; most of the recipes in this book call for all-purpose. You can store flour in a cool, dry place, but if you're not using it frequently, consider finding a spot for it in the refrigerator. If you're gluten-free, any commercial flour mix that says it can substitute one for one for flour can be used. Items like baking powder, baking soda, and cornstarch have their place outside the muffin pan; opt for baking powder without aluminum sulfate. And don't be afraid of baking for one—it's possible, and we have great recipes, like our Spicy Peanut Butter Cookies (page 211) and Butternut Squash Soufflé (page 217), to do just that.

Everything Else

Tomatoes end up in all kinds of dishes, and we love the canned version because they're quick and always in season. Keep handy a 14.5-ounce can of diced tomatoes with juice, no added sugar, and a tube of tomato paste that you'll keep in the refrigerator once it is opened. If a recipe calls for crushed tomatoes, you can throw the diced ones in your blender or mash them in a pan. Portion and freeze any tomatoes you don't use.

Canned and jarred items store well in your pantry until you need to use them. Once you open jarred or canned food, use as much as you need and store the rest in the refrigerator after transferring it to a sealable glass or plastic container. When it comes to bread, it's best to store it in the refrigerator to make it last longer. Tortillas can be frozen by separating them with sheets of waxed paper or parchment, so you can take out just what you need.

Refrigerator Pantry

There are certain foods and sauces that last for a long time but need to be kept in the refrigerator. These sauces are great to have on hand and will most likely last for several weeks or even months. When you buy the more perishable items, like eggs and milk, check the sell-by or use-by date before buying—food on the same grocery shelf can have dates that vary by more than a week. Buy the one that will last the longest after purchasing; organic milk and nut milks last weeks longer than conventional milk sitting unopened in the fridge.

PANTRY STOCK-UP SHOPPING LIST

OILS

Canola oil

Coconut oil

Extra-virgin olive oil

Nonaerosol cooking spray

Sesame oil

BEANS

Black beans

Chickpeas or garbanzo beans

Lentils

Red kidney beans

White beans

GRAINS

Brown rice

Farro

Long whole grain pasta like spaghetti, fettuccine

Medium whole grain pasta like penne, rotini

Quinoa

Rolled oats

Small whole grain pasta like ditalini, elbow

SWEETENERS

Agave

Brown sugar

Honey

Maple syrup

VINEGARS

Apple cider vinegar

Balsamic vinegar

Red wine vinegar

Rice vinegar

(continued)

NUTS AND SEEDS

Almonds

Cashews

Ground flaxseeds

Peanut, almond, or cashew butter

Pepitas

Pistachios

Sesame seeds

Tahini

Walnuts

HERBS AND SPICES

Black peppercorns

Bouillon cubes

Chili powder

Crushed red-pepper flakes

Curry powder

Garam masala

Garlic powder

Ground cardamom

Ground cinnamon

Ground coriander

Ground cumin

Ground red pepper

Iodized salt

Kosher salt

Onion powder

Paprika

Vanilla extract

BAKING BASICS

All-purpose flour

Baking powder

Baking soda

Cornstarch

Unsweetened cocoa powder

Whole wheat flour

EVERYTHING ELSE

Almond milk or other nondairy milk

Diced tomatoes with juice, canned, no sugar added

Light coconut milk

Oil- or water-packed tuna

Plain coconut water

Plain, whole wheat bread crumbs

Pumpkin puree

Roasted red peppers

Tomato paste

Tortillas

Vanilla protein powder

White Miso or Shiro

REFRIGERATOR PANTRY

Asian-style hot sauce

Butter

Eggs

Fish sauce

Greek or regular yogurt

Hot sauce

Ketchup

Mayo

Milk

Mustard

Soy sauce

PREPPING FOR THE WEEK

PREPPING SOME OF YOUR INGREDIENTS IN ADVANCE CAN MAKE A HUGE difference in how easy it is to cook for yourself all week. Just like an assembly line, it's much faster to do the same task than to switch between jobs. Plus, it will save you a ton of time during the week. So put on a podcast or pump the jams, pull out the cutting board, and get ready to prep for a terrific week.

Grains

Grains are one of the best things you can prep in advance. They add lots of cooking time to recipes, but they store very well. Grains are also a healthful base for a very quick meal, but the healthiest grains are whole, and those take a lot longer to cook. So while you work on the meat and chop the veggies, get the grains you need for the week cooking on the stove.

Cooked rice and grains, like farro, will last in the refrigerator for 3 to 4 days in resealable plastic bags. You can also freeze them in freezer bags for longer storage. Cooked pasta should be tossed with a tablespoon of oil before storing it in the refrigerator—it will also last for 3 to 4 days.

Meat

There are a few different degrees to which you can prep your meat at the beginning of the week. It all depends on how much prep time you have, and how crazy your week is going to be.

At a minimum, it's really helpful to divide out your meat for each meal. Put each meal's portion into a resealable freezer bag, along with any marinade you might want for it, and be sure to label what day you packaged it. Raw meat is good for a few days in the refrigerator, and if you can't get to it before then, you can just throw it directly in the freezer. If the recipe calls for the raw meat to be cut, cut it up now. This will save you from extra meat knives and cutting boards later.

If you have a little bit more time, we recommend cooking meat on Sundays to get a big jump start on the week. Oven-roast a bunch of chicken breasts on a baking sheet to have a step up on salads and stir-fries. Make meatballs, roast a whole chicken and piece it apart for different meals, slow cook some pork or beef for tacos and quick sandwiches.

The only animal protein that we don't recommend cooking in advance is fish. Fish cooks very quickly, and the trade-off in flavor that reheating causes is definitely not worth the minimal amount of time saved. Saving time is important—but so is taste!

Vegetables

When we think about how annoying cooking a whole meal is, the image that usually pops in our heads is chopping onions, tears included. But prepping veggies is actually

PREP-ABLE PRODUCE			HANDS OFF	
This produce will slice and dice and store beautifully.			These delicate flowers are better prepared right before cooking.	
Broccoli	Garlic	Squash	Beets	Leafy greens
Cabbage	Onions	Tomatoes	Carrots	
Cauliflower	Peppers	Zucchini	Eggplant	Potatoes

KITCHEN REPS WHILE YOU PREP

As you wait between steps of a recipe, take a moment to do a few quick toning moves while you work so that not only do you get a week of food, but a stronger body and a calmer mind at the same time.

SINGLE-ARM DUMBBELL THRUSTER • While you're waiting between steps, grab the bottle of soy sauce or another small but slightly heavy bottle (beer, anyone?). Hold the bottle in your right hand next to your shoulder, with your palm facing in. With your feet shoulder-width apart, lower your body until the tops of your thighs are at least parallel to the floor. Push your body back to standing while pressing the bottle up directly over your shoulder. Lower the dumbbell back to the starting position. Repeat this move 5 times on the right, then switch to your left side. Repeat these reps until your soup is done simmering, your food is cooked, or you're done thrusting, whichever comes first!

GOBLET SQUATS • Grab the nearest heavy item in your kitchen (5 to 10 pounds is perfect—try a sack of flour or a milk carton). Stand with your feet hip-width apart and hold the item vertically in front of your chest, elbows pointing to the floor. Push your hips back and bend your knees to lower into a squat; let your elbows brush the inside of your knees. Push yourself back up to start. Repeat for as many reps as you can.

REVERSE LUNGE WITH PULSE • Get your legs engaged with this variation on a classic lunge. Stand with your feet hip-width apart and your hands on your hips. With your upper body still, flex your core. Then take a large step back with your left foot, and bend both knees to lower into a lunge. While you're lowered, press your heels up so you're on your toes, raising your body about an inch, then lower back down an inch. Press through your right heel to return to standing. Lunge again with your right foot, and continue alternating for 20 reps.

SQUAT JACKS • With your arms bent at 90-degree angles and held in tight against your body, take your feet hip-width apart, then lower your body until your knees are bent to almost 90 degrees. Then explosively jump your legs outward, and then immediately bring them back to the starting position. Repeat this quick movement until you're ready for the next step in your recipe.

DUMBBELL DEADLIFT TO ROW • While you wait for something to cook or bake, grab a couple of beer bottles to jack up your arms. With slightly bent knees, hold the beer bottles, one in each hand, at arm's length, palms facing your thighs. Bend at your hips and lower your torso until it's almost parallel to the floor. Bend your elbows to pull both bottles to the side of your torso. Pause and slowly lower. Then raise your torso back to the starting position. Repeat.

really fun and will give you a *huge* head start on your meals all week long. You have two options for veggie prep: You can chop and store them individually, or you can make what we like to call meal boxes. With a meal box (or bag), you can store all of the prepped vegetables for each meal of the week together. When it's time to cook, just pull out your meal box, and you're halfway to a cooked meal! For example, for the Spicy Tempeh Chili (page 174), your meal box would be the chopped onion, red and green bell peppers, and serrano pepper, chopped and ready to cook whenever you want to make your chili. Just make sure that whatever storage container you use is airtight.

Smoothies

Without a doubt, smoothies are the prep-ahead champions. We love to create smoothie bags, filled with all of the produce you need for the recipe, to store in the freezer. Then when it's smoothie time, you just pull out the bag, pop the frozen ingredients in the blender, and add whatever liquid and protein are called for in the recipe. This will save you a ton of cleanup and time, and will allow you to make delicious chilled smoothies without adding a lot of ice! That's what we like to call a win-win.

Post-Meal Prep (or, What to Do with Leftovers)

Leftovers are the curse of a cook who is cooking for one or two. With recipes that serve four, six, or even eight, we'll sometimes find ourselves drowning in storage containers filled with meals that we're sick of eating and that won't store for more than a couple of days. This leads to food fatigue (aka ordering delivery just to escape the monotony of a third day of stir-fry) or, even worse, massive food waste when we throw the untouched food away at the end of the week. The cycle of leftovers is real, but it doesn't have to take over your life. There are three steps to eliminating the tyranny of leftovers.

① PORTION | **The recipes in this book are a great first step—with only a few exceptions, we've created meals that are perfectly portioned to feed you, and maybe give you one extra meal.** But if there are other recipes you love and can't part with, try cutting them in half. It might take a little fourth-grade fraction math (the measurement guide on page 252 should help!), but simply halving the recipe will cut down on how much extra you'll have to eat.

② REMAKE | **The same ingredients do not need to make the same meal.** For example, imagine a mix of chicken, peppers, and onions—they could become fajitas, an Asian stir-fry, or a yummy Italian pasta dish. The same goes for your leftovers—they don't have to be the same flavors or even the same meal. Scramble your leftover dinner with eggs for a protein-rich breakfast. Add yesterday's roasted chicken and vegetables to some stock and make a hearty soup. Turn leftover fish into fish tacos. Think of your leftovers as super-prepped ingredients for another meal, and you'll be cooking and enjoying in no time.

③ FREEZE | **What if you love your meal, but you just don't want to eat it again in the next couple of days?** That's when your freezer becomes your best kitchen tool. Freeze your meal, making sure to label it with the name and date it was cooked, and enjoy it within the next few months. Inexpensive, individual aluminum containers (like the ones you get when you order takeout) are great for this because they can go straight from the freezer to the oven and are available cheaply at dollar stores. When we know there's a busy week coming up, we like to prepare in advance by stockpiling frozen leftovers. That way we can still eat homemade, even when we have literally no time to prepare a meal. Keep an eye out for the Freezer Friendly (TK) logo on recipes throughout this book—that tells you they're good to freeze and eat later!

Let's Get Cooking!

BREAKFAST

GOOD MORNING SUNSHINE! WE'LL BET BREAKFAST IS YOUR FAVORITE part of the day. Who doesn't love waking up an hour earlier than they need to, breaking out the cutting board, and dirtying 10 dishes before 7:00 a.m.?

Yeah, that is so not happening. We know breakfast is sometimes the hardest meal to cook, and the easiest meal to skip. Especially when you live by yourself, breakfast seems like an unnecessary burden when the snooze button on your phone is just so tempting. What could be the harm in skipping breakfast—saves you a few calories, right? Wrong. Skipping breakfast sets you up for a day of lower energy, midday cravings, and a slower metabolism. Plus one recent study found that working women who occasionally skipped breakfast had a 54 percent higher risk of eventually being diagnosed with type 2 diabetes.[1]

So we've convinced you to eat breakfast, but does that mean an extra-large bagel and shmear, or a big fruity muffin from the coffee shop? No! Drop the cheese Danish! Think about what your body is going through first thing in the morning. You've been fasting since dinner the night before, and your body is ready for its first shot of fuel for the day. What kind of fuel is a big carby breakfast, and how is that going to make you feel? How do you feel after a large bowl of spaghetti? It's delicious, but that big dose of carbohydrates is just setting you up for a big energy crash later on.

The bagel is out, the muffin is in the trash, and you're hungry . . . now what? The **Prep It Ahead** section in this chapter is there for you sleepyheads who are addicted to the snooze button and have mastered the skill of putting on lipstick while your sleep mask is still on. Just prep your breakfast the night before, and you can grab and go. But may we suggest taking 10 minutes to sit down, set the phone aside, and just enjoy your morning?

Once you're used to taking some time for breakfast in the morning, or if you're already someone who likes to be up for a while before leaving for work or the gym, take a look at the **Throw It Together** meals. These yummy recipes take very little time to put together (even less if you prepped your veggies on Sundays) and are a nice time to drink your coffee and mentally prepare for the day. Just make sure that if you don't have the time to completely wash your dishes, you at least rinse or soak them before leaving for work. Cleaning dried eggs off dishes is THE. WORST.

Then there's our favorite group of recipes, the **Take Your Time** breakfasts. These are for the days off work, weekends, work-from-home days, or any day when you have a little extra time and want to really start your day out right. Breakfast really is the most important meal of the day, and with these recipes it can also be the most delicious!

Bagel with Rosemary-Apricot "Jam"

VEGETARIAN

Making homemade jam is a simple and fun kitchen activity, and a great way to prep for your meals in advance since you can keep the jam in the refrigerator in an airtight container for up to 1 week.

Prep time: 5 minutes

Total time: 10 minutes

Makes 2 servings

---

6 dried apricots

1 teaspoon firmly packed brown sugar

¼ teaspoon chopped fresh rosemary

⅔ cup water

2 ounces cream cheese, divided

½ teaspoon grated orange zest

1 whole grain bagel, halved

1 tablespoon chopped pistachios

1. In a small saucepan, bring the apricots, brown sugar, rosemary, and water to a simmer over medium heat. Cook for 5 minutes, or until the apricots are soft.

2. Transfer the apricot mixture to a blender or food processor and puree until thick and slightly chunky. Add 1 ounce of the cream cheese and the orange zest and pulse until incorporated. Chill until ready to use.

3. Toast the bagel halves and spread with the remaining 1 ounce cream cheese. Spread the rosemary-apricot jam over the bagel halves and sprinkle with the pistachios.

Nutrition (per serving) • 235 calories, 6 g protein, 29 g carbohydrates, 4 g fiber, 10 g sugars, 12 g fat, 5.5 g saturated fat, 212 mg sodium

Oatmeal with Brown Sugar Pineapple Swirl

VEGETARIAN

Spice up the classic breakfast dish by adding yogurt, pumpkin seeds, and pineapple to your oatmeal. To prep ahead for the week, make a large batch of oatmeal at the beginning of the week, and keep 1-cup portions in airtight containers in the refrigerator for up to 1 week.

Prep time: 5 minutes

Total time: 10 minutes

Makes 1 serving

2 tablespoons finely chopped pineapple

2 teaspoons firmly packed brown sugar

½ cup rolled oats

1 cup water

2 tablespoons 2% plain Greek yogurt

1 tablespoon toasted pumpkin seeds

1. In a small bowl, combine the pineapple and brown sugar. Set aside.

2. In a small saucepan, combine the oats and water. Simmer over medium heat, stirring, for 4 minutes, or until soft.

3. Transfer the oatmeal to a bowl and stir in the yogurt. Swirl in the reserved pineapple mixture and top with the pumpkin seeds.

Nutrition (per serving) • 270 calories, 12 g protein, 42 g carbohydrates, 5 g fiber, 14 g sugars, 7 g fat, 1 g saturated fat, 39 mg sodium

DELICIOUS AND NUTRITIOUS

OATS | Our bones are, quite literally, the foundation for everything we do. Manganese is essential for strong bones; it increases their mineral density and helps build them. Manganese is also crucial for collagen development, which keeps your skin healthy and glowing. Oats are one of the best sources out there for manganese, so whether you get them in cookies or breakfast cereal, oats are helping make you beautiful from the inside out.

Crispy Garlic Fried Rice

VEGETARIAN

While it might seem like a nighttime treat, fried rice is a great breakfast dish with a healthy balance of protein, carbohydrates, and fiber. To make the rice extra crispy and cook time quick, precook the rice early in the week and add it to the pan cold. For a spicy kick, drizzle this dish with Sriracha before serving!

Prep time: 5 minutes

Total time: 15 minutes

Makes 2 servings

1 teaspoon + 1 tablespoon canola oil, divided

2 eggs, beaten

5 cloves garlic, minced

1½ cups cold cooked brown rice

2 teaspoons soy sauce

1 scallion, thinly sliced

1. In a medium nonstick skillet, heat 1 teaspoon of the oil over medium heat. Add the eggs and swirl to create an even layer. Cover and cook for 3 minutes, or until just set in the center. Transfer to a plate, roll up while still warm, and slice into ½"-thick strips. Set aside.

2. Wipe out the skillet. Add the remaining 1 tablespoon oil and the garlic and cook, stirring, over medium-low heat until slightly browned and crispy, 2 minutes. Remove the garlic from the skillet, leaving the oil. Set the garlic aside.

3. Add the rice to the skillet in an even layer. Cook for 30 seconds, or until the rice begins to crackle. Toss, spread in an even layer again, and cook for 30 seconds, or until the rice begins to crackle. Add the soy sauce, toss to coat, and cook, stirring, for 1 minute, or until the rice is warmed through.

4. Transfer the rice to 2 small bowls. Top each with half of the reserved crispy garlic, egg, and scallion.

Nutrition (per serving) • 333 calories, 11 g protein, 37 g carbohydrates, 3 g fiber, 1 g sugars, 15 g fat, 2.5 g saturated fat, 374 mg sodium

Sausage, Kale, and Apple Frittata

GLUTEN-FREE | FREEZER FRIENDLY

A frittata is basically a crust-free, easier-to-make quiche. And this one is even easier because it is prep-friendly for both the night before (chop the leek and kale in advance and store in the refrigerator) and the week or month before—the whole frittata, or leftover slices, will hold in the refrigerator wrapped in foil for up to 1 week or in the freezer for up to 1 month.

Prep time: 10 minutes

Total time: 30 minutes

Makes 4 servings

6 eggs

3 egg whites

¼ cup 1% milk

½ teaspoon kosher salt, divided

½ teaspoon ground black pepper, divided

2 teaspoons olive oil

1 small leek, white part only, rinsed and sliced into thin half-moons

3 kale leaves, stems removed, leaves chopped

4 links precooked turkey breakfast sausage, cut into ¼"-thick slices on a diagonal

½ crisp lightly sweet apple, such as Jazz, Ruby Frost, or Opal, cut into thin wedges

1. Preheat the oven to 450°F. In a bowl, whisk together the eggs, egg whites, milk, and ¼ teaspoon each of the salt and pepper. Set aside.

2. In a large ovenproof nonstick skillet, heat the oil over medium heat. Cook the leek, stirring, for 3 to 4 minutes, or until golden. Add the kale and the remaining ¼ teaspoon each salt and pepper and cook for 2 to 3 minutes, or until wilted. Add the sausage and cook for 2 minutes, or until heated through. Add the apple and cook for 1 to 2 minutes, or until heated through.

3. Pour in the reserved egg mixture and cook for 5 minutes, or until just barely set, swirling the pan and gently lifting the edges of the egg with a spatula to allow egg to flow underneath. Transfer the skillet to the oven and bake for 5 minutes, or until puffed, golden, and set.

4. Slice and serve or let cool completely before wrapping in foil.

Nutrition (per serving) • 252 calories, 16 g protein, 10 g carbohydrates, 1 g fiber, 4 g sugars, 16 g fat, 5 g saturated fat, 591 mg sodium

Blueberry, Flax, and Cardamom Muffins

VEGETARIAN | FREEZER FRIENDLY

Now this is the kind of muffin we love—low in calories and fat, high in protein and fiber. Plus, it has good-for-you ingredients like blueberries and flaxseeds. To prep ahead, make these at the beginning of the week and wrap in plastic wrap to store in the refrigerator for up to a week. You can also store them in the freezer for up to 6 months, for those random mornings when you didn't plan ahead and don't have time to cook.

Prep time: 5 minutes

Total time: 1 hour

Makes 6

1 cup all-purpose flour

¼ cup ground flaxseeds

Grated zest of ½ orange

¾ teaspoon baking powder

½ teaspoon ground cardamom

¼ teaspoon baking soda

Pinch of salt

1 egg

¼ cup honey

¼ cup fat-free plain kefir

¼ cup unsweetened applesauce

½ teaspoon vanilla extract

¾ cup frozen unsweetened blueberries

1. Preheat the oven to 350°F. Line 6 cups of a 12-cup muffin pan with paper liners.

2. In a medium bowl, combine the flour, flaxseeds, orange zest, baking powder, cardamom, baking soda, and salt.

3. In a separate bowl, combine the egg, honey, kefir, applesauce, and vanilla. Pour the wet ingredients into the dry and stir to combine. Fold in the blueberries and spoon the batter into the lined muffin cups. Bake for 25 minutes, or until a toothpick inserted in the center of a muffin comes out clean.

4. Let the muffins cool in the pan for 5 minutes, then remove to a rack to cool completely.

Nutrition (per serving) • 181 calories, 5 g protein, 34 g carbohydrates, 3 g fiber, 15 g sugars, 4 g fat, 0.5 g saturated fat, 165 mg sodium

Homemade Granola Four Ways

VEGAN

Whether it's for a snack or over yogurt for breakfast, granola has the possibility to be a healthy option. Unfortunately, it takes reading dozens of labels to locate a healthy bag in the grocery store. Save yourself calories and money by making one of these varieties—start with our base oat recipe, and add in fun flavors and ingredients. Once you get the hang of it, you can even experiment with making your own version!

Basic Granola

Prep time: 5 minutes

Total time: 30 minutes

Makes 8 servings

3 cups rolled oats

½ cup wheat germ

¼ cup ground flaxseeds

¼ teaspoon kosher salt

¼ cup maple syrup

¼ cup coconut oil

1. Preheat the oven to 350°F. Line a large rimmed baking sheet with parchment paper.

2. In a large bowl, combine the oats, wheat germ, flaxseeds, and salt.

3. In a small saucepan, combine the maple syrup and oil. Cook over medium-low heat until the oil melts.

4. Stir the maple mixture into the oat mixture until combined. Spread onto the baking sheet in an even layer and bake for 15 minutes, or until golden and crisp.

5. Cool completely and transfer to an airtight container. Store for up to 1 month.

Nutrition (per ½-cup serving) • 252 calories, 8 g protein, 32 g carbohydrates, 5 g fiber, 8 g sugars, 11 g fat, 6 g saturated fat, 63 mg sodium

Seeds and Spice Granola

Prep time: 5 minutes

Total time: 30 minutes

Makes 10 servings

Basic Granola recipe

$\frac{1}{2}$ cup raw pumpkin seeds

$\frac{1}{4}$ cup shelled sunflower seeds

2 tablespoons chia seeds

1 tablespoon sesame seeds

$2\frac{1}{4}$ teaspoons pumpkin pie spice

During step 2 of the Basic Granola recipe, add raw pumpkin seeds, sunflower seeds, chia seeds, sesame seeds, and pumpkin pie spice to the oat mixture.

Nutrition (per $\frac{1}{2}$-cup serving) • 284 calories, 9 g protein, 29 g carbohydrates, 6 g fiber, 6 g sugars, 15 g fat, 6 g saturated fat, 54 mg sodium

Chocolate, Coconut, and Banana Granola

Prep time: 5 minutes

Total time: 30 minutes

Makes 10 servings

Basic Granola recipe

3 tablespoons unsweetened cocoa powder

$\frac{1}{2}$ cup coarsely chopped unsweetened banana chips

$\frac{1}{4}$ cup toasted unsweetened coconut flakes

During step 3 of the Basic Granola recipe, add unsweetened cocoa powder to the oil and syrup mixture, and after the granola is baked in step 4, stir in $\frac{1}{2}$ cup coarsely chopped unsweetened banana chips and $\frac{1}{4}$ cup toasted unsweetened coconut flakes.

Nutrition (per $\frac{1}{2}$-cup serving) • 237 calories, 7 g protein, 29 g carbohydrates, 5 g fiber, 8 g sugars, 11 g fat, 6 g saturated fat, 51 mg sodium

Cherry, Almond, and Vanilla Granola

Prep time: 5 minutes

Total time: 30 minutes

Makes 10 servings

Basic Granola recipe

$\frac{3}{4}$ cup sliced almonds

4 teaspoons vanilla

$\frac{1}{2}$ cup dried cherries

During step 2 of the Basic Granola recipe, add sliced almonds to the oat mixture, then move to step 3 of the Basic Granola recipe and add vanilla extract to the oil and syrup mixture. After the granola is baked in step 4, mix in dried cherries.

Nutrition (per $\frac{1}{2}$-cup serving) • 268 calories, 8 g protein, 32 g carbohydrates, 7 g fiber, 9 g sugars, 12 g fat, 5 g saturated fat, 51 mg sodium

Chana Saag with Greek Yogurt

VEGETARIAN | FREEZER FRIENDLY

Change up your breakfast routine with Indian spices, lots of protein, and a quick grab-and-go dish that is anything but boring. Make the chana saag in advance, and eat it throughout the week for breakfast (or lunch, or dinner) or freeze for up to 3 months.

Prep time: 5 minutes

Total time: 15 minutes

Makes 4 servings

1 tablespoon canola oil

½ cup chopped onion

1 clove garlic, minced

1 teaspoon curry powder

1 teaspoon garam masala

1 can (14½ ounces) petite diced tomatoes

1 can (15 ounces) chickpeas, rinsed and drained

¼ teaspoon kosher salt

¼ teaspoon ground black pepper

5 ounces baby spinach

2 cups 2% plain Greek yogurt, divided

1. In a large nonstick skillet, heat the oil over medium-low heat. Cook the onion and garlic for 5 to 6 minutes, or until softened and translucent. Add the curry powder and garam masala and cook for 1 minute, or until fragrant.

2. Increase the heat to medium and add the tomatoes with their juices, the chickpeas, salt, and pepper and bring to a boil. Add the spinach and cook, stirring, for 2 to 3 minutes, or until wilted.

3. Place ½ cup yogurt in a bowl and top with one-quarter of the chana saag.

4. Cool the remaining chana saag and store in the refrigerator in an airtight container for up to 1 week or divide it into individual portions and freeze for up to 3 months. Reheat and serve each portion over ½ cup yogurt.

Nutrition (per serving) • 218 calories, 15 g protein, 25 g carbohydrates, 7 g fiber, 7 g sugars, 7 g fat, 2 g saturated fat, 645 mg sodium

Green Tea French Toast with Mandarin Orange Preserves

VEGETARIAN

Matcha, matcha, matcha . . . this green tea powder is as beloved for its beautiful color as it is for its health benefits (like metabolism boosts, detoxification, and antioxidants). By adding it into your French toast, you boost the nutrition of this morning treat, and you add a nice amount of caffeine without having to make a cup of tea!

Prep time: 5 minutes

Total time: 15 minutes

Makes 2 servings

½ teaspoon matcha (green tea) powder

½ cup fat-free milk, warmed

¼ teaspoon vanilla extract

¼ teaspoon ground cinnamon

⅛ teaspoon ground ginger

⅛ teaspoon ground cardamom

Pinch of ground cloves

Pinch of ground black pepper

1 egg

4 slices slightly stale whole wheat bread

2 tablespoons mandarin orange preserves

1. In a shallow bowl, combine the matcha powder and warm milk, whisking vigorously until the powder dissolves. Whisk in the vanilla, cinnamon, ginger, cardamom, cloves, and pepper. Add the egg and whisk until fully combined.

2. Heat a large skillet coated with cooking spray over medium heat. Dip 1 slice of the bread in the egg mixture, turn with a fork to dip the other side, and transfer to the skillet. Repeat with a second slice. Cook for 5 to 7 minutes, turning once, or until golden brown on both sides. Transfer to a plate and repeat with the remaining slices.

3. Meanwhile, in a small saucepan, heat the preserves over medium heat for 2 minutes, or until melted. Drizzle over the French toast and serve.

Nutrition (per serving) • 269 calories, 15 g protein, 42 g carbohydrates, 4 g fiber, 20 g sugars, 4 g fat, 1 g saturated fat, 316 mg sodium

Eggs with Crab and Tomato on Toast

Seafood and breakfast are a perfect pair—the low-fat protein provided by most seafood powers you through your morning and offsets the (healthy) fats in eggs. This simple breakfast toast comes together in a snap, but it's almost guaranteed to look so pretty you'll want to post a picture!

Prep time: 5 minutes

Total time: 10 minutes

Makes 1 serving

1 teaspoon olive oil

2 eggs

Pinch of kosher salt

Dash of hot sauce

2 ounces lump crabmeat

½ cup quartered cherry tomatoes

1 slice whole grain bread

1 tablespoon chopped parsley

1. In a small nonstick skillet, heat the oil over medium-low heat. In a small bowl, whisk together the eggs, salt, and hot sauce and add to the skillet. Cook, scrambling slowly using a silicone spatula or wooden spoon, for 2 minutes, or until large, soft curds begin to form.

2. Fold the crab and tomatoes into the eggs and cook for 2 minutes to just set, or until the eggs are cooked to your liking.

3. Meanwhile, toast the bread and cut in half. Transfer the egg mixture to the toast halves. Sprinkle with the parsley and more hot sauce, if desired.

Nutrition (per serving) • 415 calories, 34 g protein, 28 g carbohydrates, 5 g fiber, 6 g sugars, 17 g fat, 4 g saturated fat, 815 mg sodium

Goat Cheese and Mint Omelet

VEGETARIAN | ONE PAN

Omelets can be frustrating (and turn quickly into scrambled eggs) without the right dose of patience. Once you add your eggs to the hot pan and cover it with a lid, it's time to go hands off! Walk away from the stove, mash the goat cheese and mint, and wait (and wait) until the egg is set. It will happen faster than you think, and we promise you that if your pan is on medium heat, the bottom won't burn.

Prep time: 5 minutes

Total time: 10 minutes

Makes 1 serving

2 eggs

1 tablespoon finely chopped red onion

Pinch of kosher salt

Pinch of ground black pepper

1 ounce goat cheese

1 tablespoon finely chopped mint

1. In a small bowl, whisk together the eggs, onion, salt, and pepper. Coat a small nonstick skillet with cooking spray and warm over medium heat.

2. Pour the egg mixture into the skillet, cover, and cook for 1 minute, or until the egg is set.

3. Meanwhile, in a small bowl, mash together the goat cheese and mint.

4. Crumble the goat cheese mixture over half of the omelet. Fold the empty half over the filling and cook for 2 minutes, or until the filling is warmed through.

Nutrition (per serving) • 223 calories, 18 g protein, 2 g carbohydrates, 0 g fiber, 1 g sugars, 16 g fat, 7 g saturated fat, 393 mg sodium

Broiled Grapefruit

5 INGREDIENTS OR FEWER |VEGETARIAN

Broiling a grapefruit with a little bit of sugar smooths out its overly bitter flavor, and topping it with cashews adds a little crunch to make the texture of the dish more exciting. Save that other half of your grapefruit by wrapping it in plastic wrap and refrigerating, broiling it later in the week or using it for a Sunrise Citrus Smoothie (page 51).

Prep time: 5 minutes

Total time: 10 minutes

Makes 1 serving

½ **large ruby red grapefruit**

2 **teaspoons firmly packed brown sugar**

¼ **teaspoon ground cinnamon**

2 **tablespoons full-fat plain yogurt**

1 **tablespoon chopped roasted cashews**

1. Position a rack 4″ from the broiler element and heat the broiler to high.

2. Using a small paring knife, cut around each section of the grapefruit half to loosen the flesh and make it easier to eat. Set the grapefruit on a baking sheet and sprinkle with the brown sugar and cinnamon.

3. Broil for 3 minutes, or until the sugar melts and browns.

4. Top with the yogurt and cashews.

Nutrition (per serving) • 149 calories, 3 g protein, 27 g carbohydrates, 2 g fiber, 22 g sugars, 5 g fat, 1 g saturated fat, 62 mg sodium

DELICIOUS AND NUTRITIOUS

GRAPEFRUIT | There's a reason one of the most cited fad diets is the grapefruit diet. Multiple studies have confirmed that grapefruit are fat-burning superstars, and they help boost your metabolism. The antioxidants at work here are polyphenols, which can break down stored fat. Add that to the grapefruit's generous size and low calorie count, and you've got a great fruit for healthy eating.

Smoked Salmon and Egg Tartine

ONE PAN

In a simple dish like this, which is full of protein and healthy fats, great ingredients can make all the difference. Choose high-quality smoked salmon from sustainable brands, hearty multigrain bread, and fresh arugula for a delicious start to your day.

Prep time: 5 minutes

Total time: 10 minutes

Makes 1 serving

1 slice multigrain bread

1 egg, beaten

⅓ cup baby arugula

1 ounce smoked salmon

1 tablespoon crumbled goat cheese

Kosher salt and ground black pepper

1. Toast the bread.

2. Coat a small nonstick skillet with cooking spray and heat over medium heat. Cook the egg, stirring with a silicone spatula or wooden spoon, for 2 minutes, or until soft scrambled.

3. Place the baby arugula on the toast and top with the egg, salmon, and goat cheese. Season to taste with salt and pepper.

Nutrition (per serving) • 299 calories, 30 g protein, 16 g carbohydrates, 3 g fiber, 2 g sugars, 13 g fat, 4 g saturated fat, 409 mg sodium

Blueberry Muffin Breakfast Parfait

VEGETARIAN

You don't need to preheat the oven or pull out a baking pan to make this muffin—all you need is a mug and a microwave. Fresh blueberries add a lot of flavor, but you can substitute frozen blueberries that have been thawed when the fresh ones are out of season.

Prep time: 5 minutes

Total time: 10 minutes

Makes 1 serving

3 tablespoons almond flour

1 teaspoon ground flaxseeds

½ teaspoon baking powder

Pinch of ground cinnamon

Pinch of salt

1 egg

1 tablespoon unsweetened applesauce

1 tablespoon fat-free milk

4 tablespoons fresh blueberries, divided

½ cup 0% vanilla Greek yogurt

1. Lightly grease a large microwaveable mug or ramekin. In a small bowl, combine the flour, flaxseeds, baking powder, cinnamon, and salt. Mix in the egg, applesauce, and milk until fully incorporated. Stir in 2 tablespoons of the blueberries, and pour the mixture into the mug or ramekin.

2. Microwave on high power for 1 to 1½ minutes, or until a toothpick inserted in the center comes out clean. Cool briefly until cool enough to handle.

3. Crumble half the muffin into the bottom of a small jar, bowl, or parfait glass. Top with half the yogurt. Repeat layers with the remaining muffin and yogurt. Top with the remaining 2 tablespoons blueberries and enjoy.

Nutrition (per serving) • 320 calories, 23 g protein, 23 g carbohydrates, 4 g fiber, 16 g sugars, 17 g fat, 2 g saturated fat, 519 mg sodium

Steak and Eggs with Watermelon Chimichurri

GLUTEN-FREE

Watermelon is one of the few foods where we recommend buying it presliced in the produce section of your grocery store. Lugging home an entire watermelon, cutting off the rind, and slicing it all up for ¼ cup of ingredients? That's just not going to happen. But if you do see a small watermelon and are feeling up to the task, you can also use it for the Spicy Cool Mini Watermelon Skewers (page 77) or Spicy Watermelon Salad (page 138).

Prep time: 5 minutes

Total time: 15 minutes

Makes 1 serving

¼ cup chopped watermelon

2 tablespoons chopped parsley

1 tablespoon extra-virgin olive oil

2 teaspoons finely chopped jalapeño chile pepper

2 teaspoons lime juice

1 clove garlic, minced

Kosher salt and ground black pepper

3 ounces flank steak

1 egg

1. In a small bowl, mash the watermelon, parsley, oil, chile pepper, lime juice, garlic, and a pinch of salt and black pepper together until you have a chunky sauce.

2. Coat a small nonstick skillet with cooking spray and heat over medium heat. Season the steak with salt and black pepper and cook for 5 minutes, turning once, or until browned on both sides and just pink in the middle. Transfer to a cutting board and let rest.

3. Wipe out the skillet and coat with more cooking spray. Cook the egg sunny side up for 4 minutes, or until the white is set but the yolk is still runny.

4. Thinly slice the steak against the grain and top with the egg. Spoon the chimichurri over and enjoy.

Nutrition (per serving) • 350 calories, 25 g protein, 6 g carbohydrates, 1 g fiber, 3 g sugars, 24 g fat, 5 g saturated fat, 243 mg sodium

Peanut Butter Pancakes with Pomegranate Syrup

VEGETARIAN

There's no need to save pancakes for the weekend or think of them as an indulgence. These pancakes with pomegranate syrup mimic the flavors of a classic PB&J while delivering healthy fiber from the whole wheat flour and powerful antioxidants from the pomegranate juice.

Prep time: 5 minutes

Total time: 10 minutes

Makes 1 serving

¼ cup whole wheat flour

3 tablespoons almond milk

1½ teaspoons natural peanut butter

1 teaspoon baking powder

Pinch of kosher salt

¼ cup pomegranate juice

2 teaspoons honey

1. In a small bowl, combine the flour, milk, peanut butter, baking powder, and salt. Coat a nonstick skillet with cooking spray and heat over medium-low heat.

2. Pour the mixture into the skillet, forming 2 pancakes, and cook for 5 minutes, turning once, or until the bottoms are brown.

3. Meanwhile, in a small saucepan, combine the pomegranate juice and honey and bring to a boil. Cook for 5 minutes, or until syrupy.

4. Serve the pancakes with the syrup drizzled over the top.

Nutrition (per serving) • 243 calories, 6 g protein, 46 g carbohydrates, 4 g fiber, 22 g sugars, 5 g fat, 1 g saturated fat, 700 mg sodium

Butternut-Maple Amaranth Porridge

VEGETARIAN | GLUTEN-FREE | ONE PAN

Like quinoa, amaranth is a seed that mimics grains—and this porridge recipe turns it into a wholesome, warm breakfast cereal. Simmering it with butternut squash puree boosts the nutritional value and elevates this dish into a surprisingly healthy and delicious alternative to oatmeal.

Prep time: 5 minutes

Total time: 35 minutes

Makes 2 servings

1 cup 2% milk

½ cup amaranth

⅓ cup butternut squash puree (canned or frozen)

2 teaspoons maple syrup + more for drizzling

½ teaspoon ground cinnamon

¼ teaspoon ground nutmeg

Pinch of kosher salt

2 tablespoons chopped toasted hazelnuts

1. In a medium saucepan, combine the milk, amaranth, squash, maple syrup, cinnamon, nutmeg, and salt and bring to a boil. Reduce to a simmer and cook, covered, stirring occasionally, for 20 minutes, or until most of the liquid is absorbed.

2. Remove from the heat, stir, and let sit, covered, for 10 minutes, or until thickened.

3. Divide the porridge between 2 bowls. Top with the hazelnuts and a swirl of maple syrup.

Nutrition (per serving) • 328 calories, 12 g protein, 50 g carbohydrates, 5 g fiber, 15 g sugars, 10 g fat, 3 g saturated fat, 123 mg sodium

Portobello "Bacon" and Eggs

VEGETARIAN

Replace fatty, unhealthy bacon with our secret vegetable version. By tossing mushroom strips in soy sauce and sugar, then roasting until crispy, the mushrooms mimic the sweet and salty flavor of perfectly cured bacon. It won't trick your tastebuds, but it will satisfy any cravings for the flavor of bacon.

Prep time: 5 minutes

Total time: 50 minutes

Makes 1 serving

1 teaspoon olive oil

1 teaspoon reduced-sodium soy sauce or tamari

1 teaspoon firmly packed brown sugar

1 portobello mushroom cap, gilled and thinly sliced

2 eggs, beaten

Pinch of kosher salt

Pinch of ground black pepper

2 tablespoons part-skim ricotta cheese

$\frac{1}{2}$ teaspoon chopped fresh dill or chives

1. Preheat the oven to 350°F. Line a baking sheet with parchment paper.

2. In a small bowl, combine the oil, soy sauce or tamari, and brown sugar. Brush all over the mushroom slices and place on the baking sheet.

3. Bake the mushrooms for 45 minutes, turning once, or until crispy yet tender.

4. Meanwhile, warm a small skillet over medium heat. Cook the eggs, sprinkled with the salt and pepper, for 3 minutes, stirring, or until nearly set. Stir in the ricotta and dill or chives and cook for 1 minute, or until warmed through. Serve the "bacon" with the eggs.

Nutrition (per serving) • 265 calories, 19 g protein, 11 g carbohydrates, 1 g fiber, 7 g sugars, 17 g fat, 5 g saturated fat, 648 mg sodium

Egg Baked in Avocado

5 INGREDIENTS OR FEWER | GLUTEN-FREE | VEGETARIAN | ONE PAN

Set it and forget it with this simple baked meal. By the time you've put on your makeup and done your hair, just pull the avocado out of the oven and eat up! Wrap the remaining avocado half in plastic wrap, making sure to not leave any air between the avocado and the wrap, and store in the refrigerator. Use the half later in the week for another baked egg, or in our Amaranth Huevos Rancheros (page 47), Green Goddess Dip (page 71), Butternut Squash and Chard Mini Taco Bites (page 83), or Avocado Deviled Eggs (page 90).

Prep time: 2 minutes

Total time: 30 minutes

Makes 1 serving

½ avocado, halved and pitted

1 egg

2 tablespoons crumbled feta cheese

Dash of paprika

1. Preheat the oven to 425°F. Slice a sliver off the bottom round side of the avocado so it doesn't rock back and forth. Place on a baking sheet.

2. Scoop out about 1 tablespoon of flesh from the center of the avocado and crack the egg into the center.

3. Bake for 18 minutes, or until the egg is set. Sprinkle with the feta and paprika before eating.

Nutrition (per serving) • 260 calories, 12 g protein, 8 g carbohydrates, 5 g fiber, 2 g sugars, 21 g fat, 7 g saturated fat, 392 mg sodium

Poached Egg over Asparagus with Mustard Sauce

VEGETARIAN | GLUTEN-FREE

It might not come as a surprise that most brunch dishes are full of hidden calories, and one of the biggest perpetrators is yummy, creamy hollandaise sauce. This dish replaces the fatty sauce with our own low-fat, no-cook mustard version that you're sure to love.

Prep time: 5 minutes

Total time: 25 minutes

Makes 1 serving

4 spears asparagus, trimmed

1 teaspoon extra-virgin olive oil

Kosher salt and ground black pepper

1 teaspoon Dijon mustard

1 teaspoon low-fat mayonnaise

1 teaspoon champagne vinegar or white wine vinegar

¼ teaspoon sugar

2 cups water

1 egg

½ teaspoon grated lemon zest

1. Preheat the oven to 450°F. On a baking sheet, toss the asparagus with the oil and season with a pinch of salt and pepper. Bake for 10 minutes, or until tender and starting to brown.

2. Meanwhile, in a small bowl, combine the mustard, mayonnaise, vinegar, and sugar. Season to taste with salt and pepper. Set aside.

3. In a small saucepan over medium heat, bring the water to a simmer. Crack the egg into a small bowl. Swirl the water with a spoon and gently slide the egg into the saucepan. Poach for 3 to 4 minutes, or until the white is opaque but the yolk is still soft.

4. Set the asparagus on a warm plate and sprinkle with the lemon zest. Using a slotted spoon, transfer the egg on top of the asparagus. Drizzle with the reserved mustard sauce.

Nutrition (per serving) • 149 calories, 9 g protein, 8 g carbohydrates, 3 g fiber, 3 g sugars, 10 g fat, 2 g saturated fat, 357 mg sodium

DELICIOUS AND NUTRITIOUS

ASPARAGUS | Do you ever have days when you're feeling a little extra bloated, and you just know your body is carrying extra water? Well, we do! When we feel like that, we turn to asparagus, which contains high levels of asparagine, an amino acid that works as a natural diuretic.

Amaranth Huevos Rancheros

VEGETARIAN | GLUTEN-FREE

Replacing the fried tortillas in huevos rancheros with sautéed amaranth and corn ups the nutritional value of this recipe while maintaining the same flavors, while the radish, avocado, and salsa garnish makes this dish beautiful and even more nutritious.

Prep time: 5 minutes

Total time: 30 minutes

Makes 2 servings

½ **cup amaranth**

1 **tablespoon olive oil, divided**

½ **cup corn kernels**

¼ **teaspoon ground cumin**

¼ **cup loosely packed cilantro leaves**

2 **eggs**

Kosher salt and ground black pepper

2 **radishes, cut into matchsticks**

¼ **avocado, thinly sliced**

¼ **cup store-bought salsa**

1. Cook the amaranth according to package directions.

2. In a large nonstick skillet, heat 1 teaspoon of the oil over medium heat. Cook the prepared amaranth, corn, and cumin, stirring occasionally, for 3 minutes, or until the corn and amaranth are hot and the cumin is fragrant. Remove from the heat, stir in the cilantro, and spread the mixture evenly in 2 bowls.

3. Add the remaining 2 teaspoons oil to the skillet, increase the heat to medium high, and crack the eggs into the skillet. Cover and cook for 1 minute, or until set on the bottom. Carefully turn the eggs and cook for 1 to 2 minutes, or until the yolks are just set.

4. Place an egg in each bowl. Season to taste with salt and pepper. Garnish each serving with radish matchsticks, avocado slices, and salsa.

Nutrition (per serving) • 328 calories, 13 g protein, 34 g carbohydrates, 5 g fiber, 4 g sugars, 17 g fat, 3 g saturated fat, 387 mg sodium

SMOOTHIES

SMOOTHIES ARE SOME OF THE BEST COOKING-FOR-ONE RECIPES OUT there, and yet we still see smoothie recipes everywhere that serve two to four. What? We don't know about you, but smoothie parties aren't exactly a regular occurrence at our apartments. Smoothies are great because they're quick, healthy, and easy to enjoy on the go. They're also the perfect way to use leftover fruits and vegetables from the week's meals. What to do with half of an avocado or a few extra stalks of broccoli? Throw them in a smoothie!

Let's talk a little bit about smoothies and nutrition, because not all smoothies are made equally. In fact, the difference in nutrients between a fast-food smoothie and one you make at home can be significant. What a smoothie shouldn't be is a milkshake with a handful of kale thrown in. It can taste as good as a milkshake, but every single ingredient in your smoothie should provide you with health benefits.

The best smoothies are made up of the same core ingredient categories: fruit, vegetable, protein, and liquid. Sometimes the protein and the liquid are the same ingredient, or the liquid and the fruit. If your smoothie is a meal, and not a snack, make sure it provides you with at least 20 grams of protein to help you stay full and energetic. Smoothies are also a great way to sneak certain produce that you might have an aversion to (spinach?) into your diet without your tastebuds even realizing.

If you followed our meal prep guide on page 17, you already have smoothie bags ready to go in the freezer. This is the most prep you should do for a smoothie, and it will cut out a lot of the time they take to make. While smoothies are great on the go, you don't want to blend them in advance. Let most smoothies sit in the refrigerator, and you'll end up with a brown, separated mess that won't smell very appetizing. And while blending produce makes it easier for your body to absorb the nutrients, it also kick-starts the degrading process. So the longer your smoothie sits after you blend it, the fewer benefits you'll get from it.

Getting the perfect blend on your smoothie is all about layering. First, add the liquid ingredient (milk, yogurt, water, or juice); this will help the blender blades gain momentum. Then add lighter ingredients, like leafy greens, and top those with heavier ingredients such as frozen fruit or ice. The heavier ingredients push the lighter ones down into the blades, which helps you get a smoother, lighter end result.

If you're on the go, a good travel cup with a straw is all you need to enjoy your smoothie—we especially love the kind with milkshake-size straws for those extra-thick concoctions. But if you're staying home, don't limit your smoothie by throwing it in the nearest plastic cup. Grab a fun wine glass or cocktail glass (smoothie martini, anyone), or try making a smoothie bowl! To make a smoothie bowl you'll want to share on all of your social media accounts, just pour your smoothie into a soup bowl and top with a little bit of each ingredient you put in it. Then enjoy it like soup! There's no reason your smoothie can't be both nutritious and beautiful.

Berry Cobbler Smoothie

VEGAN | 5 OR FEWER INGREDIENTS | GLUTEN-FREE

This is a great smoothie to start your day—it is packed with protein and will keep you going until lunchtime. To prep it ahead, portion the berries in the freezer and combine the remaining ingredients in a jar in the fridge, where you can store it for up to 2 days.

Prep time: 5 minutes

Total time: 5 minutes

Makes 1 serving

1 cup frozen mixed berries

½ cup unsweetened almond or other nut milk

1 tablespoon almond or other nut butter

1 scoop vanilla protein powder

1 teaspoon ground cinnamon

In a blender, combine the berries, milk, nut butter, protein powder, and cinnamon. Blend for 1 minute, or until smooth.

Nutrition (per serving) • 362 calories, 39 g protein, 26 g carbohydrates, 7 g fiber, 14 g sugars, 14 g fat, 2.5 g saturated fat, 201 mg sodium

Sunrise Citrus Smoothie

VEGETARIAN | 5 INGREDIENTS OR FEWER | GLUTEN-FREE

With a bright, fresh flavor, this smoothie is the perfect wake-up-and-start-the-day breakfast! To prep it ahead, peel the orange and grapefruit, portion them into containers, and store in the refrigerator for up to 5 days so you can reach for them whenever the craving for this smoothie strikes. Or use the extra orange for the Orange-Cranberry Turkey Club Lettuce Wrap with Jicama (page 110).

Prep time: 10 minutes

Total time: 10 minutes

Makes 1 serving

½ **navel orange, segmented**

¼ **ruby red grapefruit, segmented**

½ **cup frozen pineapple chunks**

½ **cup 0% plain Greek yogurt**

1 **teaspoon vanilla extract**

In a blender, combine the orange, grapefruit, pineapple, yogurt, and vanilla. Blend for 1 minute, or until smooth.

Nutrition (per serving) • 189 calories, 13 g protein, 34 g carbohydrates, 4 g fiber, 24 g sugars, 1 g fat, 0 g saturated fat, 42 mg sodium

DELICIOUS AND NUTRITIOUS

ORANGES | Is there a time of year when you just *know* you're going to get sick? Rather than taking supplements, turn to everyone's favorite source of vitamin C: the trusty orange. The high amounts of vitamin C will boost your immune system to fight off colds and keep you healthy year-round.

Kickin' Green Smoothie

VEGETARIAN | GLUTEN-FREE

Though coconut water holds well in the refrigerator once opened, buy the smaller, 11-ounce cartons so there's less potential waste, or freeze leftovers in ice cube trays to add to your smoothies in place of regular ice. To prep this smoothie ahead, combine all of the ingredients except the banana in a jar or storage container and keep in the refrigerator for up to 1 day before blending. To make this recipe vegan, replace the Greek yogurt with protein powder and $\frac{1}{2}$ cup water.

Prep time: 5 minutes

Total time: 5 minutes

Makes 1 serving

$\frac{1}{4}$ **cup torn kale leaves or baby kale**

$\frac{1}{4}$ **cup baby spinach**

$\frac{1}{3}$-$\frac{1}{2}$ **cup coconut water**

$\frac{1}{2}$ **cup 0% plain Greek yogurt**

$\frac{1}{2}$ **medium banana**

2 or 3 ice cubes

In a blender, combine the kale, spinach, $\frac{1}{3}$ cup of the coconut water, the yogurt, banana, and ice. Blend for 1 minute, or until smooth, adding more coconut water if needed to reach desired consistency.

Nutrition (per serving) • 138 calories, 12 g protein, 24 g carbohydrates, 2 g fiber, 15 g sugars, 0 g fat, 0 g saturated fat, 74 mg sodium

Coffee-Mocha Smoothie

VEGETARIAN | GLUTEN-FREE

Replace your standard morning coffee with this deliciously energizing smoothie! To prep it ahead, make an extra portion of coffee in the morning and then refrigerate it (you can also add the milk to the coffee now to save a step later). Freeze your banana in advance to make your smoothie extra cold when you blend it.

Prep time: 5 minutes

Total time: 5 minutes

Makes 2 servings

⅔ **cup chilled brewed coffee**

1 frozen banana

1 tablespoon unsweetened cocoa powder

¼ **cup whole milk (or any milk)**

1 scoop whey protein powder

1 cup ice cubes

In a blender, combine the coffee, banana, cocoa, milk, protein powder, and ice. Blend for 1 minute, or until smooth.

Nutrition (per serving) • 133 calories, 11 g protein, 20 g carbohydrates, 2 g fiber, 11 g sugars, 2 g fat, 1 g saturated fat, 39 mg sodium

Gingered Winter Greens Smoothie

VEGETARIAN | GLUTEN-FREE

Fresh ginger is an excellent ingredient to keep in your kitchen: It is inexpensive, stores for a long time, and adds sharp, fresh flavor to smoothies. To prep this smoothie ahead, combine all of the ingredients except the ice in a jar and refrigerate. These ingredients will store in the refrigerator for up to 5 days, so you can make several portions at once.

Prep time: 5 minutes

Total time: 5 minutes

Makes 1 serving

1 cup coconut water

½ cup 0% plain Greek yogurt

1 kiwifruit, halved and peeled

1 large kale leaf, center rib removed

1 teaspoon chopped fresh ginger

½ teaspoon honey

Pinch of salt

1 cup ice cubes

In a blender, combine the coconut water, yogurt, kiwifruit, kale, ginger, honey, salt, and ice. Blend for 1 minute, or until smooth.

Nutrition (per serving) • 178 calories, 14 g protein, 31 g carbohydrates, 3 g fiber, 23 g sugars, 1 g fat, 0 g saturated fat, 250 mg sodium

---

Mango Oat Smoothie

VEGAN | 5 INGREDIENTS OR FEWER

Avoid a frustrating morning of peeling by cubing your mango in advance or buying frozen mango when fresh is out of season. Adding oats to your smoothie might seem unconventional, but you'll love how full the fiber makes you feel all morning.

Prep time: 5 minutes

Total time: 5 minutes

Makes 1 serving

1 cup almond milk (or other nondairy milk)

1 cup cubed fresh or frozen mango

½ cup ice cubes

¼ cup rolled oats

½ teaspoon ground cinnamon

In a blender, combine the milk, mango, ice, oats, and cinnamon. Blend for 1 minute, or until smooth.

Nutrition (per serving) • 222 calories, 6 g protein, 41 g carbohydrates, 6 g fiber, 23 g sugars, 5 g fat, 0 g saturated fat, 185 mg sodium

Peach Crisp Smoothie

VEGETARIAN

Try making a bowl out of this peach crisp smoothie, topping it with a sprinkle of oats, a few slices of banana, and a dab of Greek yogurt. Whether it's in a bowl or a glass, this smoothie will taste like you're having dessert for breakfast!

Prep time: 5 minutes

Total time: 5 minutes

Makes 2 servings

1 cup sliced frozen peaches

½ cup rolled oats

½ frozen banana

½ cup full-fat plain Greek yogurt

¼ cup whole milk (or any milk)

½ cup ice cubes

In a blender, combine the peaches, oats, banana, yogurt, milk, and ice. Blend for 1 minute, or until smooth.

Nutrition (per serving) • 217 calories, 11 g protein, 33 g carbohydrates, 4 g fiber, 15 g sugars, 5 g fat, 2.5 g saturated fat, 47 mg sodium

Maple Ricotta Cream

VEGETARIAN | GLUTEN-FREE

Ricotta isn't the first ingredient that comes to mind when we think of smoothies, but it makes this smoothie creamy and delicious and adds more protein than Greek yogurt (which you can swap in for the ricotta if you prefer). Use the other half of the pear for snacking or for the Pear-Ginger Smoothie (page 62) or Pear Panini with Ginger and Blue Cheese (page 105). Use the leftover ricotta in the Chocolate Citrus Ricotta Pot (page 209).

Prep time: 5 minutes

Total time: 5 minutes

Makes 1 serving

1 cup unsweetened almond milk

½ ripe pear

½ cup low-fat or part-skim ricotta cheese

1 tablespoon ground flaxseeds

2 teaspoons maple syrup

⅛ teaspoon ground cardamom or cinnamon

2 or 3 ice cubes

In a blender, combine the milk, pear, ricotta, flaxseeds, maple syrup, cardamom or cinnamon, and ice. Blend for 1 minute, or until smooth.

Nutrition (per serving) • 334 calories, 17 g protein, 46 g carbohydrates, 9 g fiber, 30 g sugars, 12 g fat, 4 g saturated fat, 486 mg sodium

Apple Spice Smoothie

VEGETARIAN | GLUTEN-FREE

Preserve the leftover half of your apple by sprinkling a little lemon juice on it and storing it in an airtight container after you make this smoothie. Later you can spread 1 tablespoon of almond butter on it for a 150-calorie afternoon snack. Freeze leftover coconut water in ice cube trays, or save it to use in the Spicy Thai Curry Soup (page 164).

Prep time: 5 minutes

Total time: 5 minutes

Makes 1 serving

½ **large apple, chopped**

½ **teaspoon ground cinnamon**

½ **cup full-fat plain Greek yogurt**

1 **teaspoon vanilla extract**

1 **tablespoon apple cider vinegar**

¼ **cup coconut water**

¾ **cup ice cubes**

In a blender, combine the apple, cinnamon, yogurt, vanilla, vinegar, coconut water, and ice. Blend for 1 minute, or until smooth.

Nutrition (per serving) • 187 calories, 11 g protein, 26 g carbohydrates, 4 g fiber, 18 g sugars, 5 g fat, 3 g saturated fat, 107 mg sodium

Cherry-Vanilla Smoothie

VEGETARIAN | 5 INGREDIENTS OR FEWER | GLUTEN-FREE

We won't blame you if you confuse this smoothie for a strawberry milkshake—it even looks like one! But instead of being full of fat and sugar, this smoothie is nearly fat-free and packs a meal's worth of protein. Now that's one sweet treat!

Prep time: 5 minutes

Total time: 5 minutes

Makes 1 serving

1¼ **cups 0% plain Greek yogurt**

1 cup unsweetened pitted frozen cherries (or fresh)

½ **cup ice water**

1 teaspoon vanilla extract

In a blender, combine the yogurt, cherries, water, and vanilla. Blend for 1 minute, or until smooth.

Nutrition (per serving) • 275 calories, 30 g protein, 35 g carbohydrates, 3 g fiber, 29 g sugars, 1 g fat, 0.5 g saturated fat, 106 mg sodium

PB&J Smoothie

VEGAN | GLUTEN-FREE | 5 INGREDIENTS OR FEWER

Turn your favorite childhood snack into your new favorite smoothie. Try freezing the grapes in advance to turn them into little fruit ice cubes!

Prep time: 5 minutes

Total time: 5 minutes

Makes 2 servings

1 cup unsweetened almond milk (or other milk)

½ **cup frozen raspberries**

½ **cup seedless red grapes**

2 tablespoons natural peanut butter

1 scoop protein powder

In a blender, combine the milk, raspberries, grapes, peanut butter, and protein powder. Blend for 1 minute, or until smooth.

Nutrition (per serving) • 218 calories, 16 g protein, 16 g carbohydrates, 3 g fiber, 9 g sugars, 11 g fat, 1.5 g saturated fat, 176 mg sodium

Peach-Chard Smoothie

VEGAN | GLUTEN-FREE | 5 INGREDIENTS OR FEWER

Make sure to buy canned coconut milk for this smoothie, not the kind from the carton. The rest of the coconut milk can be stored in a container (not the can) in the refrigerator and used in the Spiced Peanut Soup (page 158), Thai Chicken Sandwich (page 112), or Apple and Chicken Curry (page 171).

Prep time: 5 minutes

Total time: 5 minutes

Makes 1 serving

1 large leaf Swiss chard

1 ripe peach, pitted, peeled, and chopped, or 8 frozen peach slices

1 small orange, peeled, seeded, and chopped

½ cup well-stirred lite coconut milk

½ cup ice cubes (optional if using frozen peach slices)

In a blender, combine the chard, peach, orange, coconut milk, and ice. Blend for 1 minute, or until smooth.

Nutrition (per serving) • 231 calories, 5 g protein, 37 g carbohydrates, 6 g fiber, 27 g sugars, 9 g fat, 6 g saturated fat, 125 mg sodium

Sweet and Spicy Tropical Smoothie

VEGETARIAN | GLUTEN-FREE

Don't be scared of the ground red pepper (also known as cayenne pepper) in this recipe—it's balanced out by the sweetness of the pineapple and smoothness of the avocado. This is a great smoothie to make for a friend—it's portioned for 2 and perfect for an afternoon treat.

Prep time: 5 minutes

Total time: 5 minutes

Makes 2 servings

1 cup cubed frozen pineapple and/or mango

1 ripe avocado, halved, pitted, and peeled

2 pieces (1" each) fresh ginger, peeled

¼ teaspoon ground red pepper

2 tablespoons fresh lemon juice

1 scoop whey protein powder

½ cup coconut water

In a blender, combine the pineapple or mango, avocado, ginger, red pepper, lemon juice, protein powder, and coconut water. Blend for 1 minute, or until smooth.

Nutrition (per serving) • 280 calories, 11 g protein, 28 g carbohydrates, 9 g fiber, 14 g sugars, 16 g fat, 3 g saturated fat, 91 mg sodium

Pear-Ginger Smoothie

VEGAN | GLUTEN-FREE

Enjoy the sharpness of fresh ginger and cardamom in this light, snack-size smoothie. You can double the recipe for a larger, meal-size serving, or reserve the other half of the pear, wrapped in plastic wrap, for the Maple Ricotta Cream (page 57).

Prep time: 5 minutes

Total time: 5 minutes

Makes 1 serving

1 cup unsweetened almond milk (or vanilla almond milk)

1 cup baby spinach

$\frac{1}{2}$ pear, halved, cored, and chopped

1 teaspoon fresh lemon juice

$\frac{1}{2}$ teaspoon vanilla extract (omit if using vanilla almond milk)

$\frac{1}{2}$ teaspoon grated fresh ginger

$\frac{1}{8}$ teaspoon ground cardamom

In a blender, combine the milk, spinach, pear, lemon juice, vanilla (if using), ginger, and cardamom. Blend for 1 minute, or until smooth.

Nutrition (per serving) • 109 calories, 2 g protein, 18 g carbohydrates, 5 g fiber, 9 g sugars, 3 g fat, 0 g saturated fat, 211 mg sodium

Strawberry Patch Smoothie

VEGETARIAN

Strawberries and bananas are a classic flavor combination for a reason—they're delicious together! Make this smoothie when you're craving simple flavors with a big boost of protein, adding the flaxseeds in for extra protein and fiber.

Prep time: 5 minutes

Total time: 5 minutes

Makes 1 serving

1 cup frozen strawberries

½ cup 0% plain Greek yogurt

¼ cup rolled oats

½ banana

2–4 tablespoons water

1 tablespoon ground flaxseeds

In a blender, combine the strawberries, yogurt, oats, banana, 2 tablespoons of the water, and the flaxseeds. Blend for 1 minute, or until smooth, adding more water if needed to reach desired consistency.

Nutrition (per serving) • 294 calories, 18 g protein, 47 g carbohydrates, 9 g fiber, 18 g sugars, 5 g fat, 0.5 g saturated fat, 48 mg sodium

SNACKS

ACCORDING TO A USDA STUDY, WE AS AMERICAN WOMEN REALLY STINK AT making good snack choices. Women are eating two to four times more calories than we should through snacks, and even worse, they're "empty" calories (aka calories that provide no nutritional value).[1]

But we can fix that. Whether it's to get you through a tough workout or an even tougher meeting, a snack can be a little boost of flavor, nutrition, and energy that can make your day go from okay to great. But why should you take the time to make your own snack instead of just grabbing a bag of roasted nuts or a hummus and pretzels pack? Two reasons: calories and cost. The kohlrabi Veggie Chips Five Ways (page 84) cost 60 cents to make and have 40 calories. A bag of veggie chips from a vending machine is $2.25 and around 250 calories for an equivalent serving. So for a little more time, you can save money and calories, and give your body a much better treat.

For some Sunday fun, take a look at our **Prep It Ahead** recipes—you can make a batch of snacks for the week and pre-portion them out so all you have to do is grab and go. Portioning is key with snacks—sit down with a big bowl of popcorn or a plate of hummus, and it's easy to mindlessly consume way more than you planned. And speaking of hummus, avoid getting hummus fatigue by rotating carrots, celery, kale chips, peppers, and zucchini to make the same batch of dip taste like a brand-new snack each time.

The **Throw It Together** recipes can still be made on the spot or taken to work; you just want to keep the individual ingredients separate until it's time to eat—soggy crostini is definitely not appetizing. We all know the 3:00 p.m. slump that comes out of nowhere and makes us want to curl up under our desks with a nice blanket. That's exactly the time that a flavorful, protein-packed snack can come in to save the day.

So then the inevitable question: What exactly is a **Take Your Time** snack? Shouldn't a snack always be quick, something to grab out of the fridge and eat between meals? That's exactly the mind-set that leads us to eat empty, easy calories that don't actually help our bodies thrive throughout the day. So if you have some time on a Saturday afternoon or a lazy Sunday, take a little time for yourself and make a healthful, flavorful treat just for you or maybe for a friend who is coming over. A good TV show binge can be made even better with a snack that feels like it came from your favorite tapas place. It will taste better, and more importantly feel better, than a bag of chips.

Chocolate-Dipped Grapefruit

5 INGREDIENTS OR FEWER | VEGAN | GLUTEN-FREE

This gorgeous recipe truly can't be any easier. You can make 2 servings at once; just save the second serving in a parchment-lined airtight container and store for up to 3 days in the refrigerator. And don't skip the salt—it makes the chocolate extra delicious.

Prep time: 1 minute

Total time: 2 minutes

Makes 2 servings

1½ **ounces dark chocolate, chopped**

1 **grapefruit, peeled and segmented**

⅛ **teaspoon sea salt**

1. Place the chocolate in a microwaveable bowl. Microwave on high power in 10-second intervals until melted. Stir and let cool slightly.

2. Partially dip the grapefruit segments into the chocolate and set on a plate. Sprinkle with the salt.

Nutrition (per serving) • 158 calories, 2 g protein, 23 g carbohydrates, 3 g fiber, 19 g sugars, 7 g fat, 4 g saturated fat, 103 mg sodium

Black Bean Dip

VEGAN | FREEZER FRIENDLY | GLUTEN-FREE

Before you dive in with your carrot chips, divide this tasty dip into 6 portions and refrigerate the uneaten portions in airtight containers for up to 1 week, or freeze for up to 1 month. Serve with your favorite fresh veggies or baked chips.

Prep time: 5 minutes

Total time: 5 minutes

Makes 6 servings

1 can (15 ounces) low-sodium black beans, rinsed and drained

½ cup salsa

1 clove garlic, minced

½ teaspoon ground cumin

¼ cup chopped cilantro

1 teaspoon fresh lime juice

⅛ teaspoon kosher salt

In a food processor, combine the beans, salsa, garlic, and cumin. Pulse until well combined. If the mixture seems too thick, loosen it with a little water. Transfer to a bowl and stir in the cilantro, lime juice, and salt.

Nutrition (per serving) • 46 calories, 3 g protein, 9 g carbohydrates, 3 g fiber, 1 g sugars, 0 g fat, 0 g saturated fat, 238 mg sodium

Roasted Cherry Tomatoes

VEGETARIAN | GLUTEN-FREE | 5 INGREDIENTS OR FEWER

An overnight stay in the oven is what makes these tomatoes really special. Once you try them, they will become your ultimate prep-ahead snack; they're also tasty on sandwiches or in salads. Store roasted tomatoes in an airtight container in the refrigerator for up to 3 days.

Prep time: 5 minutes

Total time: 5 minutes plus overnight rest in the oven

Makes 2 servings

2 teaspoons olive oil

2 teaspoons honey (optional)

1 pint cherry tomatoes, halved

¼ teaspoon kosher salt

1. Preheat the oven to 450°F. Line a baking sheet with a silicone baking liner or coat with cooking spray.

2. In a medium bowl, whisk together the oil and honey (if using) until well mixed. Add the tomatoes and toss until coated.

3. Spread on the baking sheet and sprinkle with the salt.

4. Put the baking sheet in the oven and immediately turn off the oven. Leave the tomatoes in the oven overnight without opening the door. The tomatoes will be both crispy and chewy.

Nutrition (per serving) • 67 calories, 1 g protein, 6 g carbohydrates, 2 g fiber, 4 g sugars, 5 g fat, 1 g saturated fat, 204 mg sodium

Baba Ghanoush

VEGAN | GLUTEN-FREE

Eggplants come in all shapes and sizes, so be sure to select one with a shallow, round scar on the bottom—it has fewer seeds and is less bitter. If you don't have enough time to make the whole recipe, prepare the eggplant through step 1 and refrigerate until you're ready to proceed with step 2. The finished dip can be refrigerated in an airtight container for up to 1 week, so it's ready whenever you are with carrot sticks, cucumber coins, or pita wedges.

Prep time: 5 minutes

Total time: 30 minutes

Makes 2 servings

1 medium eggplant

1 teaspoon olive oil

1½ tablespoons lemon juice

1½ tablespoons tahini

1 clove garlic, minced

½ teaspoon kosher salt

5 basil leaves

1. Preheat the oven to 450°F. Halve the eggplant lengthwise, rub with the oil, and place cut side down on a baking sheet. Roast for 20 to 25 minutes, or until the skin has collapsed and the flesh is very tender. Let cool until you can handle it easily.

2. Remove the peel and transfer the flesh to a food processor. Add the lemon juice, tahini, garlic, and salt and process until smooth. Pulse in the basil leaves.

Nutrition (per serving) • 115 calories, 4 g protein, 14 g carbohydrates, 5 g fiber, 6 g sugars, 6 g fat, 1 g saturated fat, 401 mg sodium

Pumpkin Seed Clusters

VEGAN | GLUTEN-FREE | 5 INGREDIENTS OR FEWER

Don't relegate pumpkin seeds to the fall after pumpkin picking—they're delicious (and nutritious) all year long. To prep your snack in advance, make the clusters and store in an airtight container for up to 1 week.

Prep time: 1 minute

Total time: 25 minutes

Makes 2 servings

¼ **cup pumpkin seeds**

2 tablespoons dried cranberries

1 teaspoon maple syrup

¼ **teaspoon garam masala**

Pinch of kosher salt

1. Preheat the oven to 300°F. Coat a baking sheet with cooking spray.

2. In a small bowl, combine the pumpkin seeds, cranberries, maple syrup, garam masala, and salt. Dollop 4 spoonfuls onto the baking sheet. Bake for 20 minutes, or until the seeds are golden. Cool before eating.

Nutrition (per serving) • 159 calories, 5 g protein, 11 g carbohydrates, 1 g fiber, 7 g sugars, 11 g fat, 2 g saturated fat, 77 mg sodium

Green Goddess Dip

ONE PAN | VEGETARIAN | GLUTEN-FREE

The bright green color is only part of what's to love about this dip. It's also low in calories and carbs, and full of healthy fats from the yogurt, egg, and avocado. Make in advance and store for up to a week in the refrigerator, and serve with crudités or tortilla chips.

Prep time: 5 minutes

Total time: 5 minutes

Makes 2 servings

¼ cup 0% plain Greek yogurt

½ avocado

1 hard-cooked egg

3 tablespoons fresh flat-leaf parsley leaves

3 tablespoons basil leaves

1 scallion, chopped

1 small clove garlic, minced

1 teaspoon fresh lime juice

⅛ teaspoon ground red pepper

⅛ teaspoon kosher salt

In a food processor or blender, combine the yogurt, avocado, egg, parsley, basil, scallion, garlic, lime juice, red pepper, and salt. Process until smooth.

Nutrition (per serving) • 121 calories, 7 g protein, 6 g carbohydrates, 3 g fiber, 2 g sugars, 8 g fat, 1.5 g saturated fat, 169 mg sodium

Beet and Dill Hummus

VEGAN | GLUTEN-FREE

Boiling beets doesn't add too much time to your cooking process, but if you're really in a hurry, the refrigerated case in the produce section usually has cooked beets available. The prepared hummus will keep in an airtight container in the refrigerator for up to 1 week.

Prep time: 5 minutes

Total time: 20 minutes

Makes 4 servings

4 small beets, peeled and chopped

1 can (15 ounces) chickpeas, rinsed and drained

⅓ cup chopped fresh dill

¼ cup fresh orange juice

3 tablespoons tahini

3 cloves garlic, smashed

¼ teaspoon kosher salt

1. Place the beets in a medium saucepan and cover with water. Bring to a boil and cook for 15 minutes, or until soft. Drain.

2. In a food processor, combine the beets, chickpeas, dill, orange juice, tahini, garlic, and salt. Process for 2 minutes, or until smooth. Chill until ready to serve.

Nutrition (per serving) • 169 calories, 6 g protein, 22 g carbohydrates, 5 g fiber, 8 g sugars, 7 g fat, 1 g saturated fat, 370 mg sodium

DELICIOUS AND NUTRITIOUS

BEETS | How long can you make it in spin class before you start faking those clicks? Well, according to one study, the nitrates in beets might help you last longer and end the class with lower blood pressure. In fact, the cyclists in the study went 16 percent longer after regularly eating beets, compared with their placebo counterparts, and had lower blood pressure when they completed their workout.

Honey Black Pepper Snack Mix

GLUTEN-FREE | VEGETARIAN

This tasty snack mix is a little sweet, a little salty, and has enough protein to keep you going through your day. Plus, it's ready in a snap and is special enough (are those blueberries?!) to make all of your coworkers jealous.

Prep time: 1 minute

Total time: 10 minutes

Makes 1 serving

¼ **cup almonds**

1½ **teaspoons honey**

½ **teaspoon extra-virgin olive oil**

½ **teaspoon ground black pepper**

Pinch of kosher salt

1 **tablespoon dried blueberries**

1. Preheat the oven to 450°F. Line a baking sheet with foil.

2. In a small bowl, toss the almonds with the honey, oil, pepper, and salt. Spread on the baking sheet and roast for 6 minutes, or until deep amber in color. Transfer to a bowl and toss with the blueberries.

Nutrition (per serving) • 295 calories, 8 g protein, 23 g carbohydrates, 6 g fiber, 13 g sugars, 20 g fat, 1.5 g saturated fat, 149 mg sodium

Pistachio-Parsley Pesto Crostini

VEGETARIAN

The secret to this pesto is that we've replaced much of the olive oil with orange juice and Greek yogurt. This makes it a little creamy, a little sweet, and a lot lower in fat and calories. We call that a win-win-win!

Prep time: 1 minute

Total time: 5 minutes

Makes 2 servings

2 tablespoons roasted pistachios

²/₃ cup fresh flat-leaf parsley leaves

½ small shallot, coarsely chopped

1 tablespoon extra-virgin olive oil

1 teaspoon fresh orange juice

1 tablespoon full-fat plain Greek yogurt

Pinch of kosher salt

Pinch of ground black pepper

4 thin slices baguette

1. In a food processor, combine the pistachios, parsley, and shallot. Pulse until finely chopped. With the processor running, drizzle in the oil and orange juice. Transfer to a bowl and stir in the yogurt, salt, and pepper.

2. To serve, toast the baguette slices under a broiler or in a toaster oven and spread with the pesto.

Nutrition (per serving) • 203 calories, 6 g protein, 23 g carbohydrates, 2 g fiber, 3 g sugars, 11 g fat, 1.5 g saturated fat, 301 mg sodium

Blackberry-Corn Salsa

ONE PAN | VEGAN | GLUTEN-FREE

Who says salsa has to have tomatoes? Make a bowl of summer for yourself with fresh berries and corn (try cutting it off the ear for extra flavor!). You can keep the salsa in the refrigerator for up to a week after preparing.

Prep time: 5 minutes

Total time: 5 minutes

Makes 4 servings

1¼ cups (6 ounces) blackberries, halved, divided

⅓ cup fresh or frozen and thawed corn

1 tablespoon chopped white onion

1 tablespoon chopped cilantro

2 teaspoons fresh lime juice

1 teaspoon chopped serrano pepper

1 teaspoon olive oil

Pinch of kosher salt

Pinch of ground black pepper

In a small bowl, lightly mash ¼ cup of the blackberries with a fork. Stir in the remaining blackberries, corn, onion, cilantro, lime juice, serrano pepper, oil, salt, and black pepper. Taste and adjust seasoning. Refrigerate until ready to use.

Nutrition (per serving) • 41 calories, 1 g protein, 7 g carbohydrates, 2 g fiber, 3 g sugars, 1.5 g fat, 0 g saturated fat, 33 mg sodium

Ricotta, Lemon, and Basil Stuffed Cherry Tomatoes

ONE PAN | GLUTEN-FREE | VEGETARIAN

For an elevated snack that comes together quickly, make these light stuffed tomatoes. Be sure to prepare them wherever and whenever you want to eat them, since they're most delicious right after stuffing.

Prep time: 5 minutes

Total time: 5 minutes

Makes 1 serving

---

4 cherry tomatoes, halved

¼ teaspoon kosher salt, divided

2 tablespoons ricotta cheese

1 tablespoon chopped basil

½ teaspoon grated lemon zest

⅛ teaspoon ground black pepper

1 teaspoon extra-virgin olive oil

1. Hollow out the insides of the cherry tomato halves with a spoon and sprinkle with a pinch of the salt.

2. In a small bowl, mix together the cheese, basil, lemon zest, pepper, and the remaining salt. Spoon the ricotta mixture into the tomato halves, drizzle with the oil, and enjoy.

Nutrition (per serving) • 99 calories, 4 g protein, 5 g carbohydrates, 1 g fiber, 2 g sugars, 7 g fat, 2 g saturated fat, 522 mg sodium

Spicy Cool Mini Watermelon Skewers

GLUTEN-FREE | VEGETARIAN

Simple bamboo skewers work perfectly for this plate-free snack; you can usually find them in the kitchen supply section of your grocery store. Store the extra dressing in the refrigerator for up to 1 week, and use on more skewers or as salad dressing.

Prep time: 10 minutes

Total time: 10 minutes

Makes 1 serving

2 tablespoons fresh lime juice

1 teaspoon honey

1 clove garlic

½ jalapeño chile pepper, seeded

Pinch of kosher salt

¼ cup extra-virgin olive oil

4 cubes (1″) watermelon

4 cucumber half-moons (½″ thick)

4 cherry tomatoes

1. In a blender, combine the lime juice, honey, garlic, jalapeño pepper, and salt to make the dressing. Blend until smooth. With the blender running, stream in the oil.

2. On two 6″ skewers, alternate the cubes of watermelon with the cucumber half-moons and tomatoes. Drizzle with 1½ tablespoons of the vinaigrette.

Nutrition (per serving) • 181 calories, 2 g protein, 14 g carbohydrates, 2 g fiber, 10 g sugars, 14 g fat, 2 g saturated fat, 33 mg sodium

Pineapple Ham Tostada

ONE PAN | GLUTEN-FREE | 5 INGREDIENTS OR FEWER

The sweet pineapple and salty ham combine in this recipe for a savory treat that's a lot lighter than Hawaiian pizza.

Prep time: 5 minutes

Total time: 5 minutes

Makes 1 serving

1 corn tortilla (6" diameter)

2 thin slices deli ham

¼ cup thinly sliced pineapple

2 tablespoons shredded Cheddar cheese

Preheat the oven to 400°F. Toast the tortilla for 3 minutes, or until crisp. Top the tortilla with the ham and pineapple, and sprinkle with the cheese. Return to the oven and toast for 2 minutes, or until the cheese has melted.

Nutrition (per serving) • 173 calories, 10 g protein, 20 g carbohydrates, 2 g fiber, 6 g sugars, 7 g fat, 4 g saturated fat, 253 mg sodium

Cantaloupe with Feta and Walnuts

VEGETARIAN | ONE PAN | GLUTEN-FREE | 5 INGREDIENTS OR FEWER

Reserve the extra cantaloupe from this simple, yet delicious, recipe for snacking or for Minty Cantaloupe Salad (page 214).

Prep time: 5 minutes

Total time: 5 minutes

Makes 1 serving

¼ small cantaloupe, rind removed, cut into 1" cubes

2 tablespoons crumbled feta cheese

6 chopped walnuts

⅛ teaspoon ground cinnamon

In a small bowl, combine the cantaloupe, cheese, walnuts, and cinnamon. Mix well.

Nutrition (per serving) • 230 calories, 8 g protein, 16 g carbohydrates, 3 g fiber, 12 g sugars, 17 g fat, 5.5 g saturated fat, 339 mg sodium

Caramelized Leek Dip with Asparagus

GLUTEN-FREE | VEGETARIAN

Think of this as the fancier version of sour cream and onion dip (no football game required). Instead of chips, lightly boiled asparagus makes an excellent dip delivery tool.

Prep time: 2 minutes

Total time: 15 minutes

Makes 1 serving

1 teaspoon olive oil

1 medium leek, sliced

1 clove garlic, minced

Pinch of kosher salt

Pinch of ground black pepper

4 spears asparagus, trimmed

2 tablespoons reduced-fat sour cream

1 tablespoon shredded Gruyère cheese

1. In a small skillet, heat the oil over medium heat. Cook the leek, garlic, salt, and pepper for 10 minutes, or until very soft and beginning to brown. Remove from the heat.

2. Meanwhile, in a small saucepan, bring ½″ of water to a simmer. Cook the asparagus spears for 1 minute, or until tender-crisp.

3. Stir the sour cream and cheese into the leeks. Serve warm, with the asparagus spears.

Nutrition (per serving) • 180 calories, 6 g protein, 18 g carbohydrates, 3 g fiber, 5 g sugars, 11 g fat, 4.5 g saturated fat, 360 mg sodium

Mashed Pea Tartine

VEGETARIAN

Fresh spring peas are nothing like their canned cousins. Small and crisp, they need only a couple of minutes at a boil to mash perfectly. The green of the peas and the pink of the radish make a colorful topping for hearty, whole grain bread.

Prep time: 2 minutes

Total time: 10 minutes

Makes 1 serving

¼ cup vegetable broth

½ cup shelled or frozen peas

1 teaspoon fresh lemon juice

Pinch of kosher salt

Pinch of ground black pepper

1 slice whole grain bread

1 radish, thinly sliced

½ teaspoon extra-virgin olive oil

1 teaspoon shaved Parmesan cheese

1. In a small saucepan, bring the broth to a boil. Add the peas and cook for 2 minutes, or until heated through. Remove from the heat and mash with a fork until chunky. Season with the lemon juice, salt, and pepper.

2. Meanwhile, toast the bread.

3. Spread the pea mixture on top of the toast and top with the radish slices. Drizzle the oil over top and sprinkle with the cheese.

Nutrition (per serving) • 155 calories, 8 g protein, 22 g carbohydrates, 5 g fiber, 5 g sugars, 4 g fat, 1 g saturated fat, 366 mg sodium

Strawberry-Avocado Scallion Salsa

ONE PAN | VEGAN | GLUTEN-FREE

For a pretty presentation, serve this salsa with blue corn tortilla chips. Wrap the other half of the avocado tightly in plastic wrap without leaving any air between the wrap and the avocado and save it for Green Goddess Dip (page 71) or Butternut Squash and Chard Mini Taco Bites (page 83).

Prep time: 5 minutes

Total time: 10 minutes

Makes 2 servings

½ **pound strawberries, chopped**

½ **avocado, chopped**

3 scallions, thinly sliced

1½ **tablespoons fresh orange juice**

1 tablespoon finely chopped cilantro

1 small clove garlic, minced

⅛ **teaspoon sea salt**

In a medium bowl, gently combine the strawberries, avocado, scallions, orange juice, cilantro, garlic, and salt. Allow the flavors to meld for 5 minutes before serving.

Nutrition (per serving) • 104 calories, 2 g protein, 14 g carbohydrates, 5 g fiber, 7 g sugars, 6 g fat, 1 g saturated fat, 106 mg sodium

DELICIOUS AND NUTRITIOUS

AVOCADO | Healthy fats, lots of nutrients, and (yum) guacamole! You might think you know everything there is to know about avocados, but did you know that they're an amazing source of potassium? Like, even better than bananas? They are! Most of us don't get enough potassium in our diets, which is unfortunate because potassium is an important mineral. Increased potassium intake is known to reduce blood pressure, which is the major risk factor for heart attacks, kidney failure, and strokes.

Steamed Broccoli with Miso Peanut Butter Dip

VEGETARIAN

Adding the miso peanut butter dip to your broccoli gives this snack extra protein and healthy fats, and makes simple cooked broccoli feel like a special treat. Just don't overcook your broccoli; keep it nice and crisp to complement the smooth peanut butter.

Prep time: 10 minutes

Total time: 15 minutes

Makes 1 serving

1 cup broccoli florets

1 teaspoon white miso paste

2 teaspoons hot water

1 tablespoon peanut butter

1 teaspoon rice vinegar

1 teaspoon honey

1. Place the broccoli in a microwaveable dish with 1 tablespoon of water. Cover and microwave on high power for 2 minutes, or until bright green and tender-crisp.

2. Meanwhile, in a small bowl, mix the miso with the hot water until smooth. Mix in the peanut butter, vinegar, and honey until smooth and combined. Serve with the warm broccoli.

Nutrition (per serving) • 152 calories, 6 g protein, 15 g carbohydrates, 3 g fiber, 8 g sugars, 8 g fat, 1 g saturated fat, 236 mg sodium

DELICIOUS AND NUTRITIOUS

BROCCOLI | High in fiber, low in calories, and full of great nutrients like folate, potassium, and vitamin C—what's not to love about broccoli? Roast, steam, or eat it raw; just don't boil it—that will zap about 90 percent of the nutrients out by the time it's done cooking!

Butternut Squash and Chard Mini Taco Bites

VEGETARIAN

To prep these mini taco bites in advance, bake all of the ingredients at once and use later. Store baked wontons in an airtight container at room temperature for up to 1 week and the squash-chard mixture in an airtight container in the refrigerator for up to 1 week. When you're ready to eat, reheat individual servings in the microwave on high for about 1 minute.

Prep time: 5 minutes

Total time: 40 minutes

Makes 4 servings

2 cups peeled and cubed butternut squash (½" pieces)

1 medium shallot, chopped (about ½ cup)

4 leaves Swiss chard, sliced in half lengthwise and cut into ½" pieces

1 tablespoon olive oil

2 teaspoons chili powder

½ teaspoon sea salt

8 wonton wrappers

½ avocado, sliced

½ cup salsa

3 tablespoons low-fat sour cream or plain yogurt

¼ cup cilantro leaves

1. Preheat the oven to 400°F. Coat a baking sheet with cooking spray.

2. In a bowl, toss together the squash, shallot, chard, oil, chili powder, and salt. Spread evenly on the baking sheet. Bake, stirring halfway through, for 30 minutes, or until the squash is fork-tender and the chard is toasted and crispy.

3. Coat the underside of a muffin pan with cooking spray. Lightly coat both sides of the wonton wrappers with cooking spray and set between the inverted muffin cups to look like a small taco shell. Do not overlap.

4. Bake the wonton wrappers for 5 minutes, or until golden and crispy. Remove the wontons from the muffin pan and fill with the squash-chard mixture. Top with the avocado, salsa, sour cream or yogurt, and a sprinkle of cilantro.

Nutrition (per serving) • 191 calories, 5 g protein, 29 g carbohydrates, 4 g fiber, 4 g sugars, 8 g fat, 2 g saturated fat, 631 mg sodium

Veggie Chips
Five Ways

ONE PAN | VEGAN | 5 INGREDIENTS OR FEWER | GLUTEN-FREE

Choice is the name of the game with our veggie chips—just pick whichever vegetable is in season, on sale, or available at your local market. Try out our different seasoning blends, some of which you can make at home, and some that can be found in the specialty foods section of the grocery store.

PREP THE VEGGIES:

CELERIAC: 1 medium celeriac, peeled and thinly sliced ¹⁄₁₆″ thick

YUCCA: ½ medium yucca, peeled and thinly sliced ¹⁄₁₆″ thick

JICAMA: 1 medium jicama, peeled and thinly sliced ¹⁄₁₆″ thick

KOHLRABI: 2 medium kohlrabi, peeled and thinly sliced ¹⁄₁₆″ thick, lay the slices on paper towels, sprinkle with salt, and let sit for 15 minutes

Salted Veggie Chips

Prep time: 5 minutes

Total time: 25 minutes

Makes 1 serving

Choice of veggie

¼–½ teaspoon kosher salt

1. Preheat the oven to 375°F and coat 2 baking sheets with cooking spray.

2. Blot dry, then proceed and lay the slices in a single layer on the baking sheets, coat with cooking spray, and sprinkle with the salt to taste and desired seasonings.

3. Bake, rotating the sheets and swapping positions halfway through, until the edges begin to brown and dry out, 8 to 10 minutes for yucca, 15 to 20 minutes for the others. To test crispiness, let a chip cool on the counter for 30 seconds and taste. Let cool for 10 minutes before serving. Store the cooled chips in an airtight container at room temperature for up to 1 week.

Nutrition (per serving) •
Celeriac: 195 calories, 7 g protein, 42 g carbohydrates, 8 g fiber, 7 g sugars, 2 g fat, 0.5 g saturated fat, 847 mg sodium
Yucca: 331 calories, 3 g protein, 78 g carbohydrates, 4 g fiber, 3 g sugars, 1 g fat, 0 g saturated fat, 422 mg sodium
Jicama: 255 calories, 5 g protein, 58 g carbohydrates, 32 g fiber, 12 g sugars, 1 g fat, 0 g saturated fat, 420 mg sodium
Kohlrabi: 40 calories, 2 g protein, 8 g carbohydrates, 5 g fiber, 3 g sugars, 1 g fat, 0 g saturated fat, 420 mg sodium

Garlic Veggie Chips

Salted Veggie Chips Recipe

¾ teaspoon garlic powder

¾ teaspoon ground cumin

⅛ teaspoon crushed red-pepper flakes (or more to taste)

Before baking, mix garlic powder, cumin, and red-pepper flakes and sprinkle the mixture over the veggies.

Nutrition (per serving in addition to veggie): 14 calories, 1 g protein, 2 g carbohydrates, 1 g fiber, 0 g sugars, 0 g fat, 0 g saturated fat, 4 mg sodium

Vinegar Veggie Chips

Salted Veggie Chips Recipe

1½ tablespoons white wine vinegar

¼ teaspoon ground black pepper

Before baking, mix white wine vinegar and ground black pepper and sprinkle the mixture over the veggies.

Nutrition (per serving in addition to veggie): 2 calories, 0 g protein, 0 g carbohydrates, 0 g fiber, 0 g sugars, 0 g fat, 0 g saturated fat, 0 mg sodium

Ras el Hanout Veggie Chips

Salted Veggie Chips Recipe

1 teaspoon ras el hanout

To incorporate this Moroccan spice mixture with a whole lot of flavor, sprinkle ras el hanout over veggies before baking.

Nutrition (per serving in addition to veggie): 3 calories, 0 g protein, 0 g carbohydrates, 0 g fiber, 0 g sugars, 0 g fat, 0 g saturated fat, 7 mg sodium

Za'atar Veggie Chips

Salted Veggie Chips Recipe

1 teaspoon za'atar

Sprinkle this Middle Eastern spice mixture with a bright, herbal, nutty flavor over veggies before baking.

Nutrition (per serving in addition to veggie): 3 calories, 0 g protein, 0 g carbohydrates, 0 g fiber, 0 g sugars, 0 g fat, 0 g saturated fat, 7 mg sodium

Quick Fridge Pickles Three Ways

VEGAN | ONE PAN | GLUTEN-FREE

Pickles can be so much more than cucumbers—carrots, celery, cauliflower, green beans and more—can all be pickled in a vinegar mixture in the refrigerator and stored for up to 3 weeks. Then they're ready to go as a quick, crunchy snack.

TO PREP THE VEGGIES:

CARROTS: 2 medium carrots, cut into 2" lengths (for the thicker parts, quarter them lengthwise, and for the thinner parts, cut them in half lengthwise)

CELERY: 4 medium ribs, trimmed, peeled, halved lengthwise (quartering the bottoms if too large), and cut into 2" to 3" lengths

CAULIFLOWER: 2 cups fresh 1" florets

GREEN BEANS: ⅓ pound green beans, washed, trimmed, and halved crosswise

Mustard Coriander Chili Pickled Veggies

Prep time: 5 minutes

Total time: 15 minutes

active time + cooling

Makes 2 servings

Choice of veggie

½ cup distilled white vinegar

½ cup water

1 tablespoon maple syrup

2 teaspoons sea salt

½ teaspoon mustard seeds

½ teaspoon coriander seeds

¼ teaspoon crushed red-pepper flakes (or 1 or 2 dried chile peppers)

1. Place veggies in a clean 1-quart glass jar.

2. In a small saucepan, stir together the vinegar, water, maple syrup, salt, mustard seeds, coriander seeds, and red-pepper flakes (or chile peppers). Bring to a gentle simmer over medium-high heat, stirring to dissolve the salt.

3. Pour the hot mixture into the jar with the veggies. Cool to room temperature, uncovered. Cover and refrigerate for 12 to 24 hours before eating. Store in the refrigerator for up to 3 weeks.

Dill-Fennel-Black Pepper Pickled Veggies

Prep time: 5 minutes

Total time: 15 minutes

active time + cooling

Makes 2 servings

Choice of veggie

½ **cup distilled white vinegar**

½ **cup water**

1 tablespoon maple syrup

2 teaspoons sea salt

½ **teaspoon black peppercorns**

½ **teaspoon fennel seeds**

½ **teaspoon dill seeds**

1. Place veggies in a clean 1-quart glass jar.

2. In a small saucepan, stir together the vinegar, water, maple syrup, salt, black peppercorns, fennel seeds, and dill seeds. Bring to a gentle simmer over medium-high heat, stirring to dissolve the salt.

3. Pour the hot mixture into the jar with the veggies. Cool to room temperature, uncovered. Cover and refrigerate for 12 to 24 hours before eating. Store in the refrigerator for up to 3 weeks.

Turmeric-Cumin Pickled Veggies

Prep time: 5 minutes

Total time: 15 minutes

active time + cooling

Makes 2 servings

Choice of veggie

½ **cup distilled white vinegar**

½ **cup water**

1 tablespoon maple syrup

2 teaspoons sea salt

½ **teaspoon cumin seeds**

¼ **teaspoon celery seeds**

¼ **teaspoon ground turmeric**

1. Place veggies in a clean 1-quart glass jar.

2. In a small saucepan, stir together the vinegar, water, maple syrup, salt, cumin seeds, celery seeds, and ground turmeric. Bring to a gentle simmer over medium-high heat, stirring to dissolve the salt.

3. Pour the hot mixture into the jar with the veggies. Cool to room temperature, uncovered. Cover and refrigerate for 12 to 24 hours before eating. Store in the refrigerator for up to 3 weeks.

Nutrition (per serving)
Carrots with brine absorption: 35 calories, 1 g protein, 9 g carbohydrates, 2 g fiber, 6 g sugars, 0 g fat, 0 g saturated fat, 674 mg sodium
Celery with brine absorption: 23 calories, 1 g protein, 5 g carbohydrates, 1 g fiber, 4 g sugars, 0 g fat, 0 g saturated fat, 696 mg sodium
Cauliflower with brine absorption: 37 calories, 2 g protein, 8 g carbohydrates, 2 g fiber, 5 g sugars, 0 g fat, 0 g saturated fat, 664 mg sodium
Green beans with brine absorption: 31 calories, 1 g protein, 7 g carbohydrates, 2 g fiber, 5 g sugars, 0 g fat, 0 g saturated fat, 636 mg sodium

Tamari-Almond Cauliflower Bites

VEGAN | GLUTEN-FREE

You can bake these cauliflower bites in advance, then allow them to cool completely before storing in an airtight container in the refrigerator for up to 1 week. Enjoy them at room temperature or reheat in the microwave on high for about 1 minute.

Prep time: 5 minutes

Total time: 25 minutes

Makes 2 servings

1 tablespoon almond butter

1 tablespoon tamari

2 teaspoons coconut oil or olive oil

2 teaspoons rice vinegar

1 teaspoon oat flour or gluten-free flour

1 teaspoon water

2½ cups cauliflower florets (about ½ medium head), broken into bite-size pieces

1 scallion, thinly sliced

1. Preheat the oven to 450°F. Coat a baking sheet with cooking spray.

2. In a large bowl, whisk together the almond butter, tamari, oil, vinegar, flour, and water until smooth. Add the cauliflower florets and toss until well coated.

3. Spread out on the baking sheet and bake, stirring halfway through, for 20 minutes, or until tender. Sprinkle with the scallion before serving.

Nutrition (per serving) • 132 calories, 6 g protein, 9 g carbohydrates, 4 g fiber, 3 g sugars, 9 g fat, 4 g saturated fat, 511 mg sodium

Baked Rosemary Apple and Manchego on Crackers

ONE PAN | VEGETARIAN

Taking the time to bake the apple with rosemary and apple cider transforms it from a boring fruit into a sweet and caramelized flavor nugget. Add a little savory manchego cheese on top, and your kitchen will start to feel like your favorite tapas bar.

Prep time: 5 minutes

Total time: 20 minutes

Makes 2 servings

1 apple (such as Braeburn or Jonathan), halved, cored, and cut into 8 pieces

1 teaspoon fresh rosemary leaves

1 tablespoon unsweetened apple cider

Pinch of kosher salt

8 shredded-wheat crackers, such as Triscuits

1 ounce manchego cheese, cut into 8 pieces

1. Preheat the oven to 400°F. On a baking sheet, toss the apple with the rosemary and apple cider, and sprinkle with the salt. Bake, stirring once, for 15 minutes, or until the apple is soft and golden. Cool slightly.

2. To serve, top each cracker with a slice of manchego and a piece of baked apple.

Nutrition (per serving) • 196 calories, 6 g protein, 26 g carbohydrates, 4 g fiber, 10 g sugars, 9 g fat, 4 g saturated fat, 315 mg sodium

Avocado Deviled Eggs

VEGETARIAN | ONE PAN | GLUTEN-FREE

Adding avocado to deviled eggs ups the protein, healthy fat, and flavor value of this classic snack. Wrap the rest of the avocado tightly in plastic wrap and use it for Spiced Sweet Potato Fries with Creamy Avocado Dip (page 91), Black Bean and Brussels Sprouts Burritos (page 98), or SLT Sammy (page 103).

Prep time: 5 minutes

Total time: 5 minutes

Makes 2 servings

2 hard-cooked eggs

¼ avocado

1 tablespoon mayonnaise

½ teaspoon fresh lemon juice

¼ teaspoon Dijon mustard

⅛ teaspoon onion powder

⅛ teaspoon garlic powder

⅛ teaspoon ground cumin

1. Halve the eggs lengthwise and remove the yolks to a small bowl. Set the whites aside.

2. To the yolks, add the avocado, mayonnaise, lemon juice, mustard, onion powder, garlic powder, and cumin. Gently smash and stir until well blended and smooth. Spoon into the reserved egg whites and serve.

Nutrition (per serving) • 167 calories, 7 g protein, 3 g carbohydrates, 2 g fiber, 1 g sugars, 14 g fat, 3 g saturated fat, 123 mg sodium

Spiced Sweet Potato Fries with Creamy Avocado Dip

VEGAN | GLUTEN-FREE

How do we make this avocado dip so creamy without any dairy? The silken tofu and avocado combine to create the creamy, thick texture usually found only in dairy-based dips. Wrap the remaining avocado tightly in plastic wrap and save it for another tasty dip, like our Green Goddess Dip (page 71).

Prep time: 10 minutes

Total time: 30 minutes

Makes 2 servings

1 sweet potato, cut lengthwise into wedges

2 teaspoons extra-virgin olive oil

1 teaspoon Cajun seasoning, divided

⅛ teaspoon hot Hungarian paprika

½ avocado

¼ cup (2.5 ounces) silken tofu

1 tablespoon fresh lime juice

⅛ teaspoon kosher salt

1. Preheat the oven to 450°F. Place the sweet potato on a baking sheet and drizzle with the oil. Toss to coat. Sprinkle with ½ teaspoon of the Cajun seasoning and the paprika. Bake for 15 minutes, or until the wedges are soft inside with a crisp crust.

2. Meanwhile, in a small bowl, stir together the avocado, tofu, lime juice, the remaining ½ teaspoon Cajun seasoning, and salt until smooth. Serve the avocado dip with the fries.

Nutrition (per serving) • 196 calories, 4 g protein, 18 g carbohydrates, 5 g fiber, 3 g sugars, 13 g fat, 2 g saturated fat, 455 mg sodium

WRAPS & SANDWICHES

THE TWO-MARTINI LUNCHES OF *MAD MEN* ENDED DECADES AGO, BUT sometimes it feels like eating lunch without a screen in front of your face is a luxury nowadays as most people end up eating quickly, barely thinking about what they're actually putting in their body, and yet spending $10 to $15 for a sad chopped salad. There's so much wrong with the average lunch, we don't even know where to begin.

So let's start with the basics—the same sort of lunch that your mom made you when you were 7 is still the best simple, tasty, and filling option. Sandwiches are a classic for a reason, and—even though fear of bread makes them seem unhealthy—they're actually the perfect delivery system for a balanced meal of protein, vegetables, and healthy carbohydrates. Sandwiches transport well, don't require a microwave, and don't even demand utensils or a plate if your office kitchen is lacking options.

Getting into the habit of packing a lunch starts with the right tools. You don't need a lunch box, but good storage containers help a lunch get to the office without getting crushed. If your workplace doesn't have a refrigerator (or has coworkers who like to snag food), an insulated lunch bag is a great option to transport your lunch and assorted snacks for the day. There are lots of cute options these days, so you won't look like a second grader on your way to school.

Before you start building your sandwich or rolling your wrap, a quick word on bread. The carb you choose can make all of the difference in both the flavor and nutrition of your meal. Instead of choosing from the bread aisle at the grocery store, go to the bakery—that's where the fresh, whole grain options can be found. You know what's even better than sliced bread—unsliced bread! As for tortillas or wraps, read the label before picking your package. There can be a major difference in calories and carbohydrates between tortillas that look nearly identical.

Most importantly, try to really enjoy your lunch—take your time to taste and savor it. It might not be an hour, and it might not involve cocktails, but your lunch break can still be a nice time to enjoy delicious food you made for yourself, and maybe even bond with coworkers. The time you saved by making your meal in advance, instead of standing in line for a salad or waiting for the microwave to be free for your frozen meal, can be spent going for a quick walk around the block or chatting with a new work friend. And try to avoid eating your lunch in front of a screen—the mindless Internet scrolling can wait until later, and so can your emails.

Tuna Tacos

GLUTEN-FREE

Prep these tacos ahead by making the tuna mixture and the cabbage slaw and storing them separately in the refrigerator for up to 3 days. If you're really short on time, buy pre-shredded coleslaw mix, which usually contains grated carrots.

Prep time: 5 minutes

Total time: 10 minutes

Makes 1 serving

1 can (5 ounces) albacore tuna, drained

2 tablespoons fresh lime juice

2 tablespoons finely chopped red onion

1 tablespoon chopped cilantro, plus additional for garnish

1½ teaspoons extra-virgin olive oil

Pinch of kosher salt

Pinch of ground black pepper

½ cup shredded red cabbage

¼ cup grated carrots

1–2 tablespoons finely chopped pickled jalapeño chile peppers and some of their juice

2 corn tortillas (6″ diameter)

1. In a bowl, mix the tuna, lime juice, onion, cilantro, oil, salt, and black pepper.

2. In a separate bowl, combine the cabbage, carrots, and jalapeño peppers with their juice.

3. Warm the tortillas according to package directions. Top with the tuna mixture, red cabbage slaw, and more chopped cilantro.

Nutrition (per serving) • 391 calories, 30 g protein, 32 g carbohydrates, 5 g fiber, 4 g sugars, 16 g fat, 3 g saturated fat, 793 mg sodium

Kale Quesadillas

ARIAN | GLUTEN-FREE | ONE PAN | PACK FOR LUNCH

which replace tortillas with kale, are a prep-ahead dream—
d, so you can make them the night before and then take them
ve some cook time, prep your vegetables in advance and store
h, onion, and garlic together in a container in the refrigerator.
e vegetables through step 1, cool, and refrigerate until ready to
Warm the vegetables back up before proceeding with step 2.

s

1 teaspoon olive oil

1 cup cubed butternut squash, pumpkin, or sweet potato

3 tablespoons finely chopped onion

2 cloves garlic, minced

4 leaves kale

½ cup shredded part-skim mozzarella cheese

1 tablespoon pico de gallo or prepared salsa

1. In a nonstick skillet, warm the oil over medium heat. Cook the onion, garlic, and your choice of squash, pumpkin, or sweet potato, for 8 minutes, or until softened. Mash lightly.

2. On a work surface, layer 1 kale leaf, 2 tablespoons of the cheese, half the vegetable mixture, 2 tablespoons more cheese, and another kale leaf. Repeat with the remaining ingredients.

3. Wipe out the skillet and return to medium heat. Carefully transfer 1 quesadilla to the skillet and cook for 2 to 4 minutes, turning once, or until the cheese is melted. Repeat with the second quesadilla. Serve with the pico de gallo or salsa.

Nutrition (per serving) • 273 calories, 19 g protein, 21 g carbohydrates, 3 g fiber, 6 g sugars, 14 g fat, 6.5 g saturated fat, 492 mg sodium

Smoked Salmon Grilled Cheese

VEGETARIAN | ONE PAN | PACK FOR LUNCH

This sandwich comes together quickly and can store for up to a day in the refrigerator before eating (no need to reheat it!). Use extra radishes in the Chimichurri Tofu Sandwich (page 113), Thai Beef Salad with Mint (page 134), or Jicama Orange Salad with Scallion and Radish (page 132). Use extra goat cheese in the Beets with Goat Cheese and Chermoula (page 143), Goat Cheese and Sesame Tartine (page 104), or Apple Galette with Chèvre and Tahini-Honey Drizzle (page 220).

Prep time: 5 minutes

Total time: 10 minutes

Makes 1 serving

1½ teaspoons grainy or Dijon mustard

2 slices rye bread

2 ounces smoked salmon

½ cup arugula

1 radish, thinly sliced

1 ounce soft goat cheese or cream cheese, softened

1. Coat a small skillet with cooking spray and set it over medium heat.

2. Spread the mustard on 1 slice of the bread. Top with the salmon, arugula, and radish. Spread the cheese on the remaining bread slice and place on top of the radish, cheese side down; squish slightly.

3. Place the sandwich in the skillet. Cook for 4 minutes, turning once, or until toasted.

Nutrition (per serving) • 447 calories, 45 g protein, 33 g carbohydrates, 4 g fiber, 3 g sugars, 15 g fat, 6 g saturated fat, 703 mg sodium

Orange Beef Sandwich

ONE PAN | PACK FOR LUNCH

To prep this sandwich ahead, peel and cut the orange, slice the precooked beet—which you should be able to find in the produce section of your supermarket—and dress the greens. Refrigerate, separately, for up to 2 days. Snack on the remaining orange, or use it in the Sunrise Citrus Smoothie (page 51). Use blue cheese in Pear Panini with Ginger and Blue Cheese (page 105) or as a savory accent to Ginger-Poached Pear with Pomegranate (page 218).

Prep time: 5 minutes

Total time: 10 minutes

Makes 1 serving

1 tablespoon prepared horseradish

2 slices firm whole grain bread

2 ounces sliced roast beef

$\frac{1}{2}$ ounce blue or gorgonzola cheese

$\frac{1}{2}$ small orange, peeled and cut into segments

1 small cooked beet, sliced

$\frac{1}{2}$ cup baby kale or baby spinach

$\frac{1}{2}$ teaspoon extra-virgin olive oil

$\frac{1}{2}$ teaspoon balsamic vinegar

Pinch of kosher salt

1. Spread the horseradish on 1 slice of the bread. Top with the roast beef, cheese, orange, and beet.

2. In a small bowl, toss the baby kale or spinach with the oil, vinegar, and salt. Top the beet with the greens and the second slice of bread.

Nutrition (per serving) • 332 calories, 23 g protein, 36 g carbohydrates, 7 g fiber, 13 g sugars, 11 g fat, 4 g saturated fat, 972 mg sodium

Black Bean and Brussels Sprouts Burritos

VEGETARIAN | PACK FOR LUNCH

This burrito is great to prep in advance. Roast the Brussels sprouts in step 1, make the beans in step 2, and prepare the rice. Store each separately in the fridge and pick up the recipe at step 3 later. You can rewarm the separate ingredients or eat the burrito cold (it's delicious!). Transfer leftover enchilada sauce to a freezer-safe container and store in the freezer until you're ready to make these again.

Prep time: 10 minutes

Total time: 35 minutes

Makes 2 servings

¼ pound Brussels sprouts, trimmed and halved (quartered if large)

2 teaspoons olive oil, divided

¼ yellow onion, sliced

½ small clove garlic, minced

¾ cup canned low-sodium black beans, rinsed and drained

¼ cup canned red or green enchilada sauce

2 tablespoons water

¼ teaspoon ground cumin

Pinch of kosher salt

Pinch of crushed red-pepper flakes or ground black pepper

1 tablespoon finely chopped cilantro

½ cup prepared brown rice, warmed

2 multigrain wraps (8″ diameter)

¼ avocado, diced

1 tablespoon crumbled Cotija cheese

Hot sauce (optional)

1. Preheat the oven to 425°F. On a small baking sheet, toss the sprouts with 1 teaspoon of the oil and roast for 15 to 20 minutes, or until tender and browned. Set aside.

2. Meanwhile, in a medium skillet, heat the remaining 1 teaspoon oil over medium heat. Cook the onion and garlic for 5 minutes, or until the onion begins to soften. Add the beans, enchilada sauce, water, cumin, salt, and red-pepper flakes or black pepper and bring to a simmer. Reduce the heat and cook, stirring often, for 10 to 15 minutes, or until the onion is soft and the mixture thickens.

3. Stir the cilantro into the rice and divide between the wraps. Top the rice with the bean mixture, Brussels sprouts, avocado, cheese, and hot sauce (if desired). Roll up the burritos, tucking in the sides as you go.

Nutrition (per serving) • 446 calories, 16 g protein, 57 g carbohydrates, 16 g fiber, 4 g sugars, 18 g fat, 6 g saturated fat, 763 mg sodium

DELICIOUS AND NUTRITIOUS

BEANS | There are more bean varieties out there than Kardashians, but whether you're eating mung beans or chickpeas, the nutrition is the same: Beans are an excellent plant source of protein, fiber, and a long list of nutrients. But as with most great things, moderation is key—beans are high in calories and carbohydrates.

Buffalo Chicken Sandwich

ONE PAN | PACK FOR LUNCH

This is a great sandwich for using leftover roasted chicken, or even grocery store rotisserie chicken in a pinch. To prep in advance, mix the shredded chicken with the hot sauce and blue cheese dressing and slice the onion ahead of time. Then your sandwich will be ready to make when you are ready to eat. Swap out the whole wheat roll for a large, hearty piece of lettuce and turn it into a tasty, spicy lettuce wrap.

Prep time: 5 minutes

Total time: 10 minutes

Makes 1 serving

3 ounces cooked chicken breast (no skin), shredded

1 tablespoon hot sauce

1 tablespoon blue cheese dressing

1 whole wheat roll, split

1 thin slice red onion

1 leaf Boston lettuce

In a bowl, mix together the chicken, hot sauce, and blue cheese dressing. Pile on the bottom half of the roll and top with the onion and lettuce. Cover with the top half of the roll.

Nutrition (per serving) • 294 calories, 29 g protein, 17 g carbohydrates, 3 g fiber, 4 g sugars, 12 g fat, 2.5 g saturated fat, 870 mg sodium

Fried Egg Sandwich

VEGETARIAN | ONE PAN

Who says eggs are just for breakfast? Eggs are a perfect protein source filled with healthy fats, and they cook up a lot faster than most other proteins. So go ahead and have breakfast for lunch, or dinner!

Prep time: 5 minutes

Total time: 10 minutes

Makes 1 serving

1½ teaspoons olive oil, divided

2 cups baby spinach

Sea or kosher salt

1 egg

Ground black pepper

1 slice whole grain bread

1 thick slice tomato

1 ounce fresh mozzarella cheese, sliced

Hot sauce or spicy ketchup (optional)

1. In a medium skillet, heat ½ teaspoon of the oil over medium heat. Cook the spinach and a pinch of salt, covered, for 2 minutes, or until the spinach wilts. Transfer to a plate. Wipe out the skillet and place it over medium-high heat.

2. Heat the remaining 1 teaspoon oil in the skillet. Crack in the egg and sprinkle with a pinch of salt and a grind of fresh black pepper. Cook for 1 minute, cover, and cook for 1 to 3 minutes, or until the white is set to your liking.

3. Meanwhile, toast the bread. Layer the spinach, tomato, mozzarella, and egg on the toast. Drizzle with hot sauce or spicy ketchup, if desired.

Nutrition (per serving) • 306 calories, 16 g protein, 18 g carbohydrates, 5 g fiber, 3 g sugars, 19 g fat, 7 g saturated fat, 532 mg sodium

Spicy Crab Melt

ONE PAN

This is one tasty melt fresh out of the oven—so don't try to make it travel. Quickly throw it together under the broiler in your oven (or toaster oven) and enjoy as soon as it's ready!

Prep time: 5 minutes

Total time: 10 minutes

Makes 1 serving

1 slice whole grain bread

2 ounces lump crabmeat (about ⅓ cup)

1 tablespoon chopped red onion

1 teaspoon chopped fresh basil

1 teaspoon hot sauce

1 teaspoon olive oil

2 tablespoons shredded 2% Cheddar cheese

½ cup arugula

½ teaspoon fresh lemon juice

1. Position a rack 6" from the broiler element and heat the broiler. Toast the bread under the broiler or in a toaster.

2. In a bowl, stir together the crab, onion, basil, hot sauce, and oil. Place the toast on a small baking sheet. Pile the crab mixture on the toast, top with the cheese, and broil for 2 to 3 minutes, or until the cheese is bubbly.

3. Toss the arugula with the lemon juice and serve on the side.

Nutrition (per serving) • 204 calories, 18 g protein, 13 g carbohydrates, 2 g fiber, 2 g sugars, 9 g fat, 3 g saturated fat, 567 mg sodium

SLT Sammy

ONE PAN | PACK FOR LUNCH

Replacing bacon with salmon in our SLT adds healthy fat to this sandwich—and eliminates the need to clean up greasy bacon splatter! Rub the cut portion of the remaining avocado with lemon juice, wrap tightly in plastic wrap, and refrigerate. Use it in the Black Bean and Brussels Sprouts Burritos (page 98), Roasted Veggie Sandwich (page 114), or Amaranth Huevos Rancheros (page 47). Reserve leftover salmon for the Smoked Salmon and Egg Tartine (page 39).

Prep time: 5 minutes

Total time: 10 minutes

Makes 1 serving

1 slice pre-packaged (not a bakery loaf) sourdough bread

¼ avocado

1½ tablespoons 0% plain Greek yogurt

1½ teaspoons fresh dill, chopped

1 teaspoon fresh lemon juice

½ clove garlic, minced

Pinch of kosher salt

1 leaf butter lettuce

1 thick slice tomato

2 ounces Nova smoked salmon

1. Toast the bread.

2. In a small bowl, with a fork, smash together the avocado, yogurt, dill, lemon juice, garlic, and salt. Slather on the toast.

3. Top with the lettuce, tomato, and smoked salmon.

Nutrition (per serving) • 398 calories, 43 g protein, 30 g carbohydrates, 4 g fiber, 3 g sugars, 13 g fat, 2.5 g saturated fat, 380 mg sodium

Goat Cheese and Sesame Tartine

ONE PAN | PACK FOR LUNCH | 5 INGREDIENTS OR FEWER

This sandwich reminds us of the simple, fresh lunches you might see French women buying at the local café. This recipe calls for herbed (not plain) goat cheese, which you can substitute in place of plain in the Smoked Salmon Grilled Cheese (page 96), Beets with Goat Cheese and Chermoula (page 143), or Goat Cheese and Mint Omelet (page 37).

Prep time: 5 minutes

Total time: 10 minutes

Makes 1 serving

---

1 piece (4" long) sesame baguette or whole wheat baguette

1 teaspoon toasted sesame oil

1 slice (½ ounce) prosciutto, torn

2 tablespoons thinly sliced roasted red peppers

1 tablespoon herbed (or plain) goat cheese, crumbled

1. Position a rack in the top third of the oven and heat the broiler.

2. Slice the baguette in half lengthwise. Brush the cut sides with the oil. Top with the prosciutto, peppers, and cheese. Place on a baking sheet and broil for 2 minutes, or until the bread begins to char.

Nutrition (per serving) • 242 calories, 12 g protein, 28 g carbohydrates, 2 g fiber, 1 g sugars, 10 g fat, 3 g saturated fat, 773 mg sodium

Pear Panini with Ginger and Blue Cheese

VEGETARIAN | 5 INGREDIENTS OR FEWER

Panini presses take up way too much space; try our simple trick instead to get the same pressed sandwich deliciousness. Use the leftover pear in the Maple Ricotta Cream (page 57) or Pear-Ginger Smoothie (page 62).

Prep time: 5 minutes

Total time: 10 minutes

Makes 1 serving

½ teaspoon grated fresh ginger

2 slices whole wheat or whole grain sourdough bread (½" thick)

2 tablespoons (1 ounce) crumbled blue cheese, divided

¼ red pear, sliced lengthwise

¼ cup baby arugula, kale, or spinach

1. Rub the ginger across 1 side of each slice of bread. Sprinkle 1 tablespoon of the blue cheese on 1 slice. Top the cheese with the pear, greens, and remaining 1 tablespoon cheese. Set the remaining slice of bread on top.

2. Coat a grill pan or skillet with cooking spray and heat over medium-high heat. Place the sandwich in the pan, cover with parchment paper, and set a large skillet on top to press. Cook for 4 minutes, turning once, or until grill marks form on both sides and the cheese melts.

Nutrition (per serving) • 312 calories, 12 g protein, 38 g carbohydrates, 5 g fiber, 9 g sugars, 11 g fat, 5.5 g saturated fat, 698 mg sodium

Peach and Arugula Grilled Cheese

VEGETARIAN | 5 INGREDIENTS OR FEWER | ONE PAN

Peaches might not be a typical sandwich ingredient, but they're certainly a tasty one! If you want to make 1 serving of this grilled cheese, just have the extra peach half as a snack or store it for up to 3 days in the refrigerator in an airtight container.

Prep time: 5 minutes

Total time: 10 minutes

Makes 2 servings

4 slices multigrain bread

2 ounces good Cheddar cheese, grated

1 peach, halved, pitted, and sliced

1 cup baby arugula

¼ teaspoon kosher salt

1. Arrange 2 slices of the bread on a clean work surface. Divide the cheese, peach, and arugula between the bread slices. Season with the salt. Top with the remaining bread.

2. Lightly coat a large nonstick skillet with cooking spray and heat over medium heat. Cook the sandwiches for 4 to 8 minutes, turning once, or until the bread is golden and the cheese is melted. Slice in half, if desired, and serve.

Nutrition (per serving) • 306 calories, 16 g protein, 36 g carbohydrates, 9 g fiber, 12 g sugars, 12 g fat, 6 g saturated fat, 688 mg sodium

Grilled Chocolate Banana Sandwich

VEGAN | 5 INGREDIENTS OR FEWER | ONE PAN

Sometimes you just need a sweet treat, and this treat also has enough protein and fiber to serve as a whole meal. Enjoy this sandwich warm from the skillet, and feel like a kid sneaking dessert before dinner.

Prep time: 5 minutes

Total time: 10 minutes

Makes 2 servings

2 tablespoons almond butter (or any nut butter)

4 slices whole grain bread

1 ounce dark chocolate, chopped

1 small banana, sliced

Pinch of kosher salt

1. Spread the almond butter on 2 slices of the bread and top with equal amounts of the chocolate and banana. Sprinkle with the salt. Top with the remaining bread slices and press down to compress.

2. Coat a large skillet with cooking spray and heat over medium heat. Cook the sandwiches for 4 minutes, turning once, or until the bread is golden brown and the chocolate has melted.

Nutrition (per serving) • 357 calories, 11 g protein, 46 g carbohydrates, 8 g fiber, 17 g sugars, 16 g fat, 4 g saturated fat, 297 mg sodium

Collard Turkey Wraps

GLUTEN-FREE | PACK FOR LUNCH

Collard leaves are a perfect substitute for wheat wraps because they're large and hearty, so they won't break when you roll them around your turkey. If you're feeling adventurous, try replacing any wrap in this book with collard leaves.

Prep time: 5 minutes

Total time: 15 minutes

Makes 2 servings

1 small carrot, grated

¼ cup apricot all-fruit spread

¼ teaspoon curry powder

¼ teaspoon kosher salt

4 large collard leaves

4 ounces turkey lunchmeat

½ cup sliced roasted red peppers

½ cup sprouts

1. In a small bowl, combine the carrot, apricot spread, curry powder, and salt.

2. Cut off the firm white stalks from the collard leaves. With a sharp knife, fillet off the thickest parts of the remaining stalks that run down the leaves.

3. Place 2 collard leaves head to foot (stalks at opposite ends) and partially overlap the leaves. Spread half of the carrot-apricot mixture along the bottom third of the leaves. Top with half each of the turkey, roasted peppers, and sprouts. Tightly roll the leaves, beginning from the bottom and tucking in the sides as you go. Cut in half on a bias, securing each half with a wooden pick. Repeat with the remaining ingredients.

Nutrition (per serving) • 164 calories, 13 g protein, 28 g carbohydrates, 2 g fiber, 17 g sugars, 1 g fat, 0 g saturated fat, 981 mg sodium

Hawaiian Pizza Sandwich

PACK FOR LUNCH

A small (8-ounce) can of pineapple rings works great in this recipe, but fresh pineapple will taste great on this sandwich, too.

Prep time: 5 minutes

Total time: 15 minutes

Makes 2 servings

---

2 slices Canadian bacon

¼ cup mayonnaise

2 oil-packed sun-dried tomatoes, finely chopped

1 small clove garlic, minced

2 slices whole grain bread

2 slices part-skim mozzarella, Swiss cheese, or provolone

2 thinly sliced pineapple rings

1 cup arugula

1 teaspoon extra-virgin olive oil

1 teaspoon red wine vinegar

Pinch of salt

1. In a small skillet, cook the Canadian bacon over medium-high heat for 5 to 6 minutes, turning once, or until browned on both sides.

2. Meanwhile, in a small bowl, combine the mayonnaise, sun-dried tomatoes, and garlic.

3. Spread 1 tablespoon of the tomato-mayo sauce on 1 side of each of the bread slices and top with 1 slice hot Canadian bacon, 1 slice cheese, and 1 pineapple ring.

4. In a separate small bowl, toss the arugula with the oil, vinegar, and salt. Top each pineapple ring with half the arugula. Reserve any extra tomato-mayo mixture in the fridge for another sandwich.

Nutrition (per serving) • 445 calories, 17 g protein, 18 g carbohydrates, 3 g fiber, 5 g sugars, 34 g fat, 7 g saturated fat, 773 mg sodium

Orange-Cranberry Turkey Club Lettuce Wrap with Jicama

GLUTEN-FREE | PACK FOR LUNCH

The lettuce wraps save calories and carbs, but you can replace them with an 8-inch whole wheat tortilla if you prefer—just add a cup of baby kale or lettuce to the wrap to add in healthy greens. Save the remaining half orange for the Sunrise Citrus Smoothie (page 51) and the remaining half avocado for the Black Bean and Brussels Sprouts Burritos (page 98), SLT Sammy (page 103), or Spicy Tempeh Chili (page 174).

Prep time: 5 minutes

Total time: 15 minutes

Makes 2 servings

1 orange

½ avocado

2 large lettuce leaves (iceberg, romaine, or red leaf)

2 ounces deli turkey

2 ounces thinly sliced jicama

1 slice cooked bacon, crumbled

½ tomato, cored, halved, and sliced

2 tablespoons dried cranberries

1. Peel the orange and segment it over a bowl, squeezing the juice from the membranes. Remove the segments with a fork or slotted spoon, and reserve half of them for another use (see headnote).

2. In the bowl with the orange juice, smash the avocado with a fork.

3. Lay out the lettuce leaves on a work surface and spread each with half of the avocado mixture. Set half the turkey, jicama, bacon, tomato, orange segments not reserved for another use, and cranberries on each. Roll up like a burrito, tucking in the sides as you go. Cut through the middle, if desired, securing each half with a wooden pick.

Nutrition (per serving) • 168 calories, 8 g protein, 20 g carbohydrates, 5 g fiber, 11 g sugars, 8 g fat, 2 g saturated fat, 319 mg sodium

Baja Apple Salsa Burrito

If your grocery store doesn't have cod, any light, flaky white fish will work well on the grill; if you need help, the person at the fish counter at the grocery store can point you in the right direction. Use the other half of the jicama for the Orange-Cranberry Turkey Club Lettuce Wrap with Jicama (page 110) or Jicama Orange Salad with Scallion and Radish (page 132). Think about doubling up this recipe the next time you have guests—it's the perfect party platter!

Prep time: 10 minutes

Total time: 25 minutes

Makes 2 servings

1 ear fresh corn, shucked and silks removed

½ sweet crisp apple, such as Honeycrisp, Braeburn, or Fuji, quartered and cored

¼ medium red onion

½ small jicama, peeled and cubed (about ½ cup)

1½ tablespoons fresh lime juice

1½ teaspoons chopped cilantro leaves

¼ teaspoon kosher salt, divided

⅛ teaspoon ground black pepper, divided

½ teaspoon olive oil

⅛ teaspoon chili powder

½ pound cod loin (or similar white flaky fish), cut into 2 pieces

2 whole grain tortillas (10″ diameter)

1. Heat a grill or grill pan to medium heat. Brush and oil the grates. Grill the corn, apple, and onion for 7 minutes, or until charred and tender. When they're cool enough to handle, cut the corn kernels from the cob and chop the apple and onion. Transfer everything to a medium bowl. Stir in the jicama, lime juice, and cilantro. Season with half the salt and pepper. Set aside to let the flavors meld.

2. In a small bowl, stir together the oil and chili powder. Spread over the fish, and sprinkle with the remaining salt and pepper. Grill the fish, turning once, for 6 minutes, or until it flakes easily.

3. Divide the fish between the tortillas, top with the apple salsa, and roll up, folding in the sides as you go.

Nutrition (per serving) • 365 calories, 30 g protein, 56 g carbohydrates, 10 g fiber, 9 g sugars, 6 g fat, 0.5 g saturated fat, 754 mg sodium

Thai Chicken Sandwich

PACK FOR LUNCH

This sandwich creates its own accompanying snack—use the leftover carrot, cucumber, and scallion to dip into Beet and Dill Hummus (page 72) or Baba Ghanoush (page 69).

Prep time: 15 minutes

Total time: 25 minutes

Makes 2 servings

¼ **cup unsalted roasted peanuts**

2 tablespoons well-stirred lite coconut milk

1 teaspoon less-sodium soy sauce

1 teaspoon honey

1 teaspoon rice vinegar

1 teaspoon hot sauce or Sriracha

¼ **teaspoon peeled, finely chopped fresh ginger**

½ **cup chopped cucumber**

½ **small carrot, grated**

½ **scallion, thinly sliced**

1 tablespoon chopped fresh mint

Squeeze of lime juice

½ **teaspoon toasted sesame oil**

Pinch of kosher salt

4 slices whole grain bread or 2 whole wheat pitas

1 cup shredded cooked chicken

1. In a blender or food processor, combine the peanuts, coconut milk, soy sauce, honey, vinegar, hot sauce, and ginger. Blend or process into a slightly chunky mixture. Set aside.

2. In a small bowl, toss together the cucumber, carrot, scallion, mint, lime juice, oil, and salt.

3. Spread 1 tablespoon of the reserved peanut mixture on 1 side of each of the bread slices. Top 2 of the slices with an equal amount of the chicken and the cucumber mixture. Top with the remaining bread slice, peanut sauce–side down. (If using pitas, open them, divide the chicken and the cucumber mixture between them, and drizzle with the peanut mixture.)

Nutrition (per serving) • 412 calories, 34 g protein, 34 g carbohydrates, 6 g fiber, 9 g sugars, 16 g fat, 3.5 g saturated fat, 477 mg sodium

Chimichurri Tofu Sandwich

VEGAN

If you've ever had bland tofu, it's either because it wasn't properly pressed to get all of the excess water out or wasn't properly seasoned so don't skip step one. Use any extra radishes in the Smoked Salmon Grilled Cheese (page 96) or Thai Beef Salad with Mint (page 134). If you have extra tofu, use it for the Udon Soup with Broccoli, Tofu, and Ginger (page 156).

Prep time: 5 minutes

Total time: 1 hour 45 minutes

Makes 2 servings

8 ounces regular firm tofu

⅓ cup fresh cilantro

⅓ cup fresh flat-leaf parsley

3 tablespoons extra-virgin olive oil

1 clove garlic

2 teaspoons fresh oregano or 1 teaspoon dried

2 teaspoons red wine vinegar

½ teaspoon kosher salt

⅛ teaspoon ground black pepper

⅛ teaspoon crushed red-pepper flakes

2 whole wheat rolls, split

1 cup baby arugula

1 radish, cut into matchsticks

1. Line a plate with several sheets of paper towel. Place the tofu on it, set another sheet of paper towel and a plate on top, and add a weight such as a skillet or soup can on top of the plate. Set aside for 20 to 30 minutes.

2. Meanwhile, in a food processor, combine the cilantro, parsley, oil, garlic, oregano, vinegar, salt, black pepper, and red-pepper flakes. Pulse until the chimichurri is emulsified. (Alternatively, finely chop the cilantro, parsley, garlic, and oregano and shake vigorously in a sealed jar with the oil, vinegar, salt, black pepper, and red-pepper flakes. Either way it's made, the chimichurri can be stored in an airtight container in the refrigerator for up to 1 week.)

3. Transfer the chimichurri to a large bowl. Cut the tofu crosswise into 4 planks and add to the bowl, tossing to coat. Marinate for 1 hour at room temperature.

4. Heat a nonstick skillet over medium heat. Without brushing off the marinade, sear the tofu for 4 minutes, turning once, or until golden brown all over.

5. Meanwhile, toast the rolls in a toaster oven or under the broiler and top each bottom half with half the arugula. Top each with 2 pieces of the tofu and half the radish. Spread the leftover chimichurri over the top buns, top the sandwiches, and cut in half.

Nutrition (per serving) • 368 calories, 13 g protein, 18 g carbohydrates, 3 g fiber, 3 g sugars, 27 g fat, 3.5 g saturated fat, 637 mg sodium

Roasted Veggie Sandwich

VEGETARIAN | PACK FOR LUNCH

Feel free to swap in other vegetables that you happen to have on hand for the roasted vegetable mix. You can use the leftover avocado for the Black Bean Burrito Salad (page 135), Green Goddess Dip (page 71), Butternut Squash and Chard Mini Taco Bites (page 83), or Egg Baked in Avocado (page 45). Replace the yogurt with 2 teaspoons of olive oil to make this recipe vegan.

Prep time: 10 minutes

Total time: 40 minutes

Makes 2 servings

1 small zucchini, cut lengthwise into 4 slices

2 portobello mushrooms, stems removed

1 small yellow bell pepper, quartered

1 tablespoon + 1 teaspoon olive oil, divided

Kosher salt

¼ teaspoon ground black pepper

¼ avocado

1 tablespoon low-fat plain yogurt (regular or Greek)

½ chipotle chile pepper in adobo sauce, finely chopped

2 teaspoons fresh lime juice, divided

1 cup baby kale or baby spinach

4 slices firm whole grain bread

1. Preheat the oven to 400°F. On a baking sheet, toss the zucchini, mushrooms, and bell pepper with 1 tablespoon of the oil. Sprinkle with ½ teaspoon salt and the black pepper. Roast for 25 minutes, turning the vegetables once, or until tender and brown in spots. Remove the vegetables as they finish cooking.

2. Meanwhile, in a small bowl with a fork, smash together the avocado, yogurt, chile pepper, 1 teaspoon of the lime juice, and a pinch of salt.

3. Toss the baby kale or spinach with the remaining 1 teaspoon oil, remaining 1 teaspoon lime juice, and a pinch of salt.

4. Spread the avocado mixture on each slice of bread. Top 2 of the slices with the roasted vegetables, greens, and remaining bread, avocado side down.

Nutrition (per serving) • 301 calories, 11 g protein, 34 g carbohydrates, 8 g fiber, 9 g sugars, 15 g fat, 2 g saturated fat, 851 mg sodium

SALADS

SALADS MIGHT HAVE ONE OF THE WORST REPUTATIONS OF ANY TYPE OF meal—they're either a flavorless diet food or shockingly unhealthy fast-food option: colorless, tasteless lettuce with sparse toppings and a fatty dressing. It's time to change how you think about salads, and embrace this perfect meal option for one.

Let's start with the base—there are so many more options than iceberg lettuce. Consider kale, spinach, arugula, spring mixes, or even no greens at all (see chicken, tuna, and egg salad options); you're only limited by your grocery store. Most of the recipes in this section are ripe for substitution. Don't like kale? Switch in spinach, or even a grain like bulgur or quinoa. Make salads work for you, and have fun improvising and replacing.

Because there's so little cooking or manipulating happening to the ingredients, it's best to make salads with in-season ingredients. Bad tomatoes or out-of-season cucumbers can make the whole thing taste off, but fresh, crispy asparagus in-season can make a salad the best meal of the day.

Most of our salads are quick to throw together, so here they're divided up more by what can be made ahead and transported without losing flavor. Our **Prep It Ahead** recipes can even be made the night before and packed for lunch. For the **Throw It Together** recipes, you'll want to prep the ingredients but wait to combine them. And the **Take Your Time** salads are best prepared and eaten on the spot, and are great for weekend lunches or weeknight dinners.

One of our favorite ways to transport our lunch salads is in a Mason jar. You can turn most of these recipes into Mason jar salads: Just layer the ingredients, and when you're ready to eat, you'll pour the salad out of the Mason jar and onto a plate. Voilà! Instant salad. Just make sure you layer the salad, starting from the bottom of the jar, in this order: salad dressing, grain and/or protein, toppings (vegetables, fruit, seeds, and nuts), and finally your leafy greens. This Instagram-worthy presentation is sure to make your followers jealous!

Bulgur Salad with Cucumber and Tomatoes

VEGETARIAN | ONE PAN | PACK FOR LUNCH

If you follow our prep-ahead guide and cook a batch of grains at the beginning of the week, then the rest of this salad will come together in about 5 minutes. As a bonus, this salad only gets better as it sits, so you can store it in an airtight container in the refrigerator for up to 5 days and enjoy it all week.

Prep time: 5 minutes

Total time: 30 minutes

Makes 2 servings

½ cup bulgur wheat

1 small shallot, minced (about 3 tablespoons)

1½ tablespoons extra-virgin olive oil

2 teaspoons fresh lemon juice

Kosher salt and ground black pepper

1 cup sun-gold cherry tomatoes, halved

1 cup chopped cucumber

¼ cup fresh flat-leaf parsley leaves, chopped

2 tablespoons shelled pistachios, chopped

¼ cup crumbled reduced-fat feta cheese

1. Prepare the bulgur according to package directions. Fluff and set aside.

2. In a large bowl, combine the shallot, oil, and lemon juice. Whisk well and season to taste with salt and pepper.

3. Add the cooked bulgur, tomatoes, cucumber, and parsley and toss to combine. Divide evenly between 2 bowls and top with the pistachios and cheese.

Nutrition (per serving) • 359 calories, 13 g protein, 40 g carbohydrates, 9 g fiber, 6 g sugars, 18 g fat, 4.5 g saturated fat, 508 mg sodium

Walnut Slaw with Cilantro

VEGAN | GLUTEN-FREE | PACK FOR LUNCH

Packaged coleslaw mix saves you a lot of time for this recipe. Once it's prepared, you can store this slaw in an airtight container in the refrigerator for up to 3 days. Save the other half of the apple for snacking or for the Light and Lemony Chicken Salad (page 119).

Prep time: 10 minutes

Total time: 10 minutes

Makes 2 servings

⅓ cup walnuts, chopped

2 tablespoons fresh lime juice

1 tablespoon safflower or olive oil

½ teaspoon Dijon mustard

4 cups (about 5 ounces) store-bought coleslaw mix

½ apple, cut into matchsticks

½ cup cilantro, chopped

Kosher salt and ground black pepper

1. In a medium skillet, toast the walnuts over medium heat for 5 minutes, or until fragrant. Set aside.

2. In a large bowl, whisk together the lime juice, oil, and mustard. Add the coleslaw mix, apple, and cilantro, and toss with the dressing to coat. Season to taste with salt and pepper. Enjoy right away, or refrigerate for 1 hour for the flavors to meld, if desired. Sprinkle with the reserved walnuts before serving.

Nutrition (per serving) • 220 calories, 4 g protein, 15 g carbohydrates, 4 g fiber, 8 g sugars, 18 g fat, 1.5 g saturated fat, 199 mg sodium

Light and Lemony Chicken Salad

GLUTEN-FREE | ONE PAN | PACK FOR LUNCH

You can use chicken that you roasted in advance, pieces of rotisserie chicken, or even grilled chicken from the deli section of the grocery store in this salad. To prep the ingredients, cut your grapes, celery, and shallot ahead of time and store them in the refrigerator.

Prep time: 10 minutes

Total time: 10 minutes

Makes 2 servings

1 grilled chicken breast, chopped

½ cup grapes, halved

½ small apple, chopped

⅓ cup 0% plain Greek yogurt

¼ cup pistachios, chopped

1 small rib celery, sliced

1 small shallot, finely chopped

1½ tablespoons fresh lemon juice

¼ teaspoon kosher salt

¼ teaspoon ground black pepper

Salad greens, for serving

Mint leaves, for serving

Lemon wedges, for serving

In a medium bowl, toss the chicken with the grapes, apple, yogurt, pistachios, celery, shallot, lemon juice, salt, and pepper. Serve over salad greens topped with mint leaves and lemon wedges.

Nutrition (per serving) • 243 calories, 21 g protein, 22 g carbohydrates, 4 g fiber, 14 g sugars, 9 g fat, 1.5 g saturated fat, 376 mg sodium

Greek Salad–Tabbouleh Mash Up

VEGETARIAN | ONE PAN | PACK FOR LUNCH

This salad combines two lunch favorites in one tasty bowl, and you can make it up to a day in advance and store in the refrigerator. To prep ahead, prepare the bulgur earlier in the week and chop the veggies and keep them in an airtight container.

Prep time: 10 minutes

Total time: 25 minutes

Makes 2 servings

⅓ cup bulgur wheat

2 tablespoons red wine vinegar

1 tablespoon extra-virgin olive oil

2 tablespoons chopped fresh mint + leaves for serving

2 tablespoons chopped fresh flat-leaf parsley

1 tablespoon chopped fresh oregano

½ cup cherry tomatoes, halved

½ cup chopped cucumber

½ cup chopped red bell pepper

½ cup canned no-salt-added chickpeas, rinsed and drained

¼ cup chopped red onion

2 tablespoons chopped pitted kalamata olives

2 tablespoons crumbled feta cheese

Ground black pepper

1. Prepare the bulgur according to package directions. Set aside to cool. When cooled, fluff with a fork and stir in the vinegar, oil, mint, parsley, and oregano.

2. To serve, divide the bulgur between 2 bowls and top each with the tomatoes, cucumber, bell pepper, chickpeas, onion, olives, and cheese. Garnish with mint leaves and season with black pepper.

Nutrition (per serving) • 339 calories, 10 g protein, 39 g carbohydrates, 9 g fiber, 5 g sugars, 16 g fat, 4 g saturated fat, 512 mg sodium

Five Fast Dressings and Vinaigrettes

Strawberry Balsamic Dressing

VEGAN | GLUTEN-FREE

We love the texture of strawberry seeds in a thick dressing, but if you prefer a smoother texture, you can press this dressing through a fine-mesh sieve before storing it in the refrigerator in an airtight container for up to 1 week.

Prep time: 5 minutes

Total time: 5 minutes

Makes 10 servings

(1¼ cups)

6 ounces strawberries, halved (1 cup)

¼ cup white balsamic vinegar

¼ cup water

¼ cup olive oil

3 scallions, chopped

1 tablespoon mint leaves, chopped

1 teaspoon Dijon mustard

¼ teaspoon salt

¼ teaspoon ground black pepper

In a blender, combine the strawberries, vinegar, water, oil, scallions, mint, mustard, salt, and pepper. Process until smooth.

Nutrition (per 2-tablespoon serving) • 61 calories, 0 g protein, 3 g carbohydrates, 0 g fiber, 2 g sugars, 6 g fat, 1 g saturated fat, 54 mg sodium

Ginger Vinaigrette

VEGAN | GLUTEN-FREE

Fresh ginger makes this vinaigrette sharp and flavorful, and reminiscent of our favorite sushi-spot salad dressing.

Prep time: 5 minutes

Total time: 5 minutes

Makes 4 servings (½ cup)

1 tablespoon low-sodium soy sauce

1½ teaspoons red wine vinegar

½ teaspoon toasted sesame oil

1 teaspoon peeled and grated fresh ginger

1 teaspoon honey or agave nectar

1 small clove garlic, smashed

½ teaspoon Dijon mustard

½ cup canola oil

Salt and ground black pepper

In a blender, combine the soy sauce, vinegar, sesame oil, ginger, honey or agave, garlic, and mustard. Blend until smooth. With the motor running, slowly add the canola oil until emulsified. Season with salt and pepper.

Nutrition (per 2-tablespoon serving) • 120 calories, 0 g protein, 2 g carbohydrates, 0 g fiber, 1 g sugars, 13 g fat, 1 g saturated fat, 139 mg sodium

Miso Dressing

VEGAN | GLUTEN-FREE

You can find miso paste in the Asian aisle of your grocery store, and once you add it to your kitchen arsenal, we promise you'll find yourself using it all the time.

Prep time: 5 minutes

Total time: 5 minutes

Makes 4 servings (½ cup)

2 tablespoons warm water

1 tablespoon sweet white miso paste

1 tablespoon low-sodium tamari or soy sauce

1 tablespoon rice vinegar

1 tablespoon mirin

½ teaspoon crushed red-pepper flakes (optional)

¼ teaspoon toasted sesame oil

1 piece (1") fresh ginger, peeled and finely chopped

1 small clove garlic, minced

¼ cup grapeseed oil

In a blender, combine the water, miso, tamari or soy sauce, vinegar, mirin, red-pepper flakes (if using), sesame oil, ginger, and garlic. Blend until smooth. With the motor running, drizzle in the grapeseed oil and blend until smooth and emulsified.

Nutrition (per 2-tablespoon serving) • 115 calories, 1 g protein, 4 g carbohydrates, 0 g fiber, 2 g sugars, 11 g fat, 1 g saturated fat, 297 mg sodium

Buttermilk Dressing

VEGETARIAN | GLUTEN-FREE

Low-fat buttermilk allows this creamy dressing to be lower in calories and fat than other creamy sauces. Store this dressing in the refrigerator for up to 1 week.

Prep time: 5 minutes

Total time: 5 minutes

Makes 4 servings (½ cup)

2 small cloves garlic

½ teaspoon kosher salt

½ cup low-fat buttermilk

4 teaspoons fresh lemon juice or white wine vinegar

2 teaspoons honey mustard

½ teaspoon ground black pepper

1. On a cutting board, mince the garlic. Sprinkle with the salt and continue to mince, using the side of the knife to further smash the garlic to form a paste.

2. In a bowl, whisk together the buttermilk, lemon juice or vinegar, salty garlic, mustard, and pepper.

Nutrition (per 2-tablespoon serving) • 19 calories, 1 g protein, 3 g carbohydrates, 0 g fiber, 2 g sugars, 0 g fat, 0 g saturated fat, 298 mg sodium

Maple Vinaigrette

VEGAN | GLUTEN-FREE

Instead of honey, using maple syrup in this dressing makes it vegan! It also has an amazing refrigerator shelf life of up to 1 month, so you won't risk wasting it if your week gets busy.

Prep time: 5 minutes

Total time: 5 minutes

Makes 8 servings (about 1 cup)

¼ cup apple cider vinegar

3 tablespoons pure maple syrup

1½ teaspoons Dijon mustard

1 teaspoon finely chopped shallot

¼ teaspoon finely chopped rosemary

Kosher salt and ground black pepper

¾ cup pure olive oil

In a 1-quart jar, combine the vinegar, maple syrup, mustard, shallot, rosemary, and a pinch of salt and pepper. Cover well with the lid and shake until combined. Add the oil and shake vigorously until emulsified. Season to taste with additional salt and pepper.

Nutrition (per 2-tablespoon serving) • 144 calories, 0 g protein, 6 g carbohydrates, 0 g fiber, 5 g sugars, 14 g fat, 2 g saturated fat, 53 mg sodium

Waldorf Chicken Salad Cups

ONE PAN | GLUTEN-FREE | PACK FOR LUNCH

These salad cups make a great lunch; just make the salad in advance and pack it separately from the lettuce leaves, pecans, and tarragon leaves. Put it all together when you're ready to eat, and enjoy the envy of your coworkers. To help your celery keep longer in the refrigerator, remove it from the bag and wrap it in foil.

Prep time: 10 minutes

Total time: 15 minutes

Makes 2 servings

2 tablespoons 0% plain Greek yogurt

1½ tablespoons fresh lemon juice

2 teaspoons extra-virgin olive oil

2 teaspoons chopped fresh tarragon + leaves for serving

1½ teaspoons Dijon mustard

¼ teaspoon kosher salt

¼ teaspoon ground black pepper

1 cup (about 5 ounces) chopped cooked chicken breast

½ cup chopped celery

½ cup chopped apple

½ cup halved grapes

¼ cup chopped red onion

6 butter lettuce leaves

¼ cup chopped toasted pecans

1. In a medium bowl, whisk together the yogurt, lemon juice, oil, tarragon, mustard, salt, and pepper. Fold in the chicken, celery, apple, grapes, and onion.

2. Divide the lettuce between 2 plates and top with the chicken mixture. Top with the pecans and extra tarragon leaves.

Nutrition (per serving) • 327 calories, 26 g protein, 19 g carbohydrates, 3 g fiber, 12 g sugars, 17 g fat, 2.5 g saturated fat, 411 mg sodium

Asparagus, Tuna, and Chickpea Salad

GLUTEN-FREE | ONE PAN | PACK FOR LUNCH

Don't skip the radishes in this recipe; they add an extra crunch to the salad and make it even more delicious. Look for thin, early-spring asparagus so that you can easily eat it raw.

Prep time: 10 minutes

Total time: 10 minutes

Makes 2 servings

1 bag (5 ounces) mixed greens

1 cup canned chickpeas, rinsed and drained

½ bunch asparagus, trimmed and very thinly sliced on a diagonal

1 can (5 ounces) water-packed tuna, drained

½ teaspoon chopped fresh thyme

2 tablespoons extra-virgin olive oil

3 tablespoons fresh lemon juice (from 1 lemon)

Kosher salt and ground black pepper

2 radishes, cut into matchsticks

In a large bowl, combine the greens, chickpeas, asparagus, tuna, and thyme. Drizzle with the oil and lemon juice, and toss to coat. Season to taste with salt and pepper. Divide between 2 plates and top with the radishes.

Nutrition (per serving) • 401 calories, 30 g protein, 29 g carbohydrates, 9 g fiber, 6 g sugars, 19 g fat, 3 g saturated fat, 497 mg sodium

Fennel, Carrot, and Tarragon Salad

VEGAN | GLUTEN-FREE

Shaving your fennel and carrots with a peeler turns them into beautiful vegetable ribbons, but it also slices them so thinly that you don't have to cook them, saving lots of prep work and time.

Prep time: 10 minutes

Total time: 15 minutes

Makes 2 servings

1 tablespoon pine nuts

2 tablespoons canola oil

1 tablespoon fresh orange juice

1 tablespoon finely chopped shallot

1 tablespoon finely chopped fresh tarragon

1 teaspoon Dijon mustard

Kosher salt and ground black pepper

4 cups chopped romaine lettuce

1 bulb fennel, halved, cored, and shaved with a peeler

4 small carrots, shaved with a peeler

¼ red onion, very thinly sliced

1. In a small skillet, toast the pine nuts over medium heat for 5 minutes, or just until they take on color. Remove from the skillet and set aside.

2. Meanwhile, in a pint-size jar, combine the oil, orange juice, shallot, tarragon, and mustard. Cover and shake until blended. Season to taste with salt and pepper.

3. In a bowl, combine the romaine, fennel, carrots, and onion. Add enough dressing to coat, and toss to combine. Arrange on 2 plates, top with the reserved pine nuts, and serve with any remaining dressing.

Nutrition (per serving) • 262 calories, 5 g protein, 25 g carbohydrates, 9 g fiber, 8 g sugars, 18 g fat, 1.5 g saturated fat, 344 mg sodium

Crab Bruschetta Panzanella

Panzanella is an Italian salad that replaces lettuce with crusty toasted bread—sign us up! This recipe mimics the flavors of bruschetta and adds lump crabmeat for an extra boost of protein.

Prep time: 5 minutes

Total time: 10 minutes

Makes 1 serving

2 slices whole grain bread

1 clove garlic, halved

1 cup arugula leaves

¾ cup cherry tomatoes, halved

1 small cucumber, peeled, seeded, and chopped

¼ small red onion, sliced

2 tablespoons chopped fresh basil

3 ounces lump crabmeat

1 tablespoon olive oil

1 tablespoon lemon juice

Kosher salt and ground black pepper

1. Toast the slices of bread and rub with half of the clove of garlic. Cut the toast into cubes and add to a bowl with the arugula, tomatoes, cucumber, onion, basil, and crab.

2. Finely chop the remaining half clove of garlic. In a small bowl, whisk together the chopped garlic, oil, lemon juice, and a pinch of salt and pepper. Pour over the salad and toss to coat.

Nutrition (per serving) • 385 calories, 23 g protein, 44 g carbohydrates, 15 g fiber, 9 g sugars, 16 g fat, 2 g saturated fat, 731 mg sodium

Spinach and Egg Salad

VEGETARIAN | GLUTEN-FREE | ONE PAN | PACK FOR LUNCH

Keeping hard-cooked eggs in the refrigerator during the week is a smart way to have protein ready to go—and it makes putting this salad together a snap.

Prep time: 5 minutes

Total time: 5 minutes

Makes 1 serving

2 cups baby spinach

½ cup cherry tomatoes, halved

½ cup sliced yellow bell pepper

2 tablespoons sliced almonds

1 tablespoon red wine vinegar

1 hard-cooked egg

Kosher salt and ground black pepper

In a bowl, combine the spinach, tomatoes, bell pepper, almonds, and vinegar. Using the fine holes of a box grater, grate the egg over top. Season to taste with salt and black pepper.

Nutrition (per serving) • 197 calories, 11 g protein, 15 g carbohydrates, 6 g fiber, 5 g sugars, 11 g fat, 2 g saturated fat, 146 mg sodium

Ultimate Tuna Salad

GLUTEN-FREE | PACK FOR LUNCH

You'll fall in love with the beautiful colors of this salad before you even taste it, but, trust us, you'll love it even more once you taste it! Don't skip the flax and sesame seeds—they add protein and nutrients to the salad.

Prep time: 5 minutes

Total time: 10 minutes

Makes 2 servings

---

1 cup broccoli florets

1 tablespoon water

1 can (15 ounces) no-salt-added navy beans, rinsed and drained

1 cup cherry tomatoes, halved

1 can (5 ounces) chunk light tuna packed in water, drained

½ cup chopped roasted red pepper

⅓ cup chopped carrot

1 tablespoon extra-virgin olive oil

2 teaspoons balsamic vinegar

1 teaspoon flaxseeds

1 teaspoon sesame seeds

Kosher salt and ground black pepper

1 cup baby spinach

1 cup torn red leaf lettuce

2 tablespoons shredded Cheddar cheese

1. Place the broccoli in a microwaveable dish with the water. Cover and cook on high power for 2 minutes, or until bright green and tender-crisp.

2. In a large bowl, toss together the beans, tomatoes, broccoli, tuna, roasted red pepper, carrot, oil, vinegar, flaxseeds, sesame seeds, and a pinch of salt and black pepper.

3. Combine the spinach and lettuce and divide between 2 plates. Top with the tuna mixture and sprinkle with the cheese.

Nutrition (per serving) • 343 calories, 25 g protein, 35 g carbohydrates, 13 g fiber, 6 g sugars, 12 g fat, 3 g saturated fat, 459 mg sodium

Harvest Chicken Salad

GLUTEN-FREE | PACK FOR LUNCH

We replace mayonnaise with plain yogurt in this recipe to reduce fat and add protein and tanginess. You can save the other half of the pear for snacking, or wrap it in plastic wrap to use in the Pear-Ginger Smoothie (page 62) or Pear Panini with Ginger and Blue Cheese (page 105).

Prep time: 5 minutes

Total time: 10 minutes

Makes 1 serving

2 tablespoons sliced almonds

¼ cup fat-free plain yogurt

1½ teaspoons country Dijon or Dijon mustard

Kosher salt and ground black pepper

1 cup chopped cooked chicken breast

1 cup baby spinach, chopped

½ pear, chopped

1 rib celery, thinly sliced on a diagonal

2 tablespoons raisins or dried cranberries

1. In a skillet, toast the almonds over medium heat for 5 minutes, or until they're just taking on color. Set aside.

2. Meanwhile, in a small bowl, combine the yogurt, mustard, a pinch of salt and pepper, and a splash of water to loosen.

3. In a medium bowl, combine the chicken, spinach, pear, celery, raisins or cranberries, and reserved almonds. Drizzle the dressing over the salad and toss to coat.

Nutrition (per serving) • 451 calories, 50 g protein, 41 g carbohydrates, 7 g fiber, 24 g sugars, 11 g fat, 2 g saturated fat, 511 mg sodium

Shepherd's Salad

VEGETARIAN | GLUTEN-FREE | PACK FOR LUNCH

Use both green and red peppers in this salad to add flavor and color. You can use the leftover bell peppers in the Roasted Veggie Sandwich (page 114) or Spicy Tempeh Chili (page 174).

Prep time: 15 minutes

Total time: 15 minutes

Makes 2 servings

---

5 teaspoons olive oil

2 teaspoons apple cider vinegar

2 teaspoons lemon juice

¼ teaspoon kosher salt

⅛ teaspoon ground black pepper

1 plum tomato, seeded and chopped

½ cucumber, seeded and chopped

½ red bell pepper, seeded and chopped

½ green bell pepper, seeded and chopped

¼ cup chopped red onion

6 black olives (such as kalamata), pitted and halved

2 tablespoons chopped fresh flat-leaf parsley

1 tablespoon chopped fresh mint

1 tablespoon chopped fresh dill

¼ cup crumbled feta cheese

1. In a small bowl, whisk together the oil, vinegar, lemon juice, salt, and black pepper.

2. In a large bowl, combine the tomato, cucumber, peppers, onion, olives, parsley, mint, and dill. Pour the dressing over the salad, toss gently, and sprinkle with the cheese.

Nutrition (per serving) • 246 calories, 6 g protein, 11 g carbohydrates, 2 g fiber, 6 g sugars, 21 g fat, 6 g saturated fat, 797 mg sodium

Jicama Orange Salad with Scallion and Radish

VEGETARIAN | GLUTEN-FREE

This is a salad you'll want to post on social media—take the time to artfully arrange your oranges, and feel like a chef as you gently top them with the colorful vegetables. Your followers (and tastebuds) will thank you!

Prep time: 10 minutes

Total time: 15 minutes

Makes 2 servings

2 tablespoons fresh lime juice

2 teaspoons extra-virgin olive oil

2 teaspoons honey

½ pound jicama, peeled and cut into matchsticks

2 scallions, thinly sliced

4 radishes, thinly sliced

2 oranges

1. In a medium bowl, whisk together the lime juice, oil, and honey. Add the jicama, scallions, and radishes and toss to coat. Set aside.

2. Slice off the top and bottom of an orange. Set the orange, flat side down, on a cutting board and remove the peel by running a paring knife from top to bottom, taking the white pith along with the peel. Slice the peeled orange into 3 or 4 rounds, then arrange the orange slices on a plate. Repeat with the other orange. Loosely pile the veggie mixture in the center of the oranges, and drizzle any collected juice over, if desired.

Nutrition (per serving) • 185 calories, 3 g protein, 36 g carbohydrates, 9 g fiber, 20 g sugars, 5 g fat, 1 g saturated fat, 12 mg sodium

Shaved Asparagus and Lamb Salad

GLUTEN-FREE

Don't be worried about cooking lamb—it's as simple as any other meat; just make sure you don't overcook it and that you rest it before slicing.

Prep time: 5 minutes

Total time: 15 minutes

Makes 1 serving

2 lamb chop lollipops (about 3 ounces)

Kosher salt and ground black pepper

2 teaspoons olive oil

1 teaspoon red wine vinegar

¼ teaspoon chopped fresh rosemary

2 cups mixed greens

2 spears asparagus, trimmed

¼ cup orange sections

1. Remove the bones from the lamb chops and season with salt and pepper. In a small skillet coated with cooking spray, sear the lamb over medium-high heat for 5 to 8 minutes, turning once, or until browned and a thermometer inserted in the center registers 145°F for medium-rare. Rest for 5 minutes before thinly slicing.

2. Meanwhile, in a small bowl, whisk together the oil, vinegar, rosemary, and a pinch of salt and pepper.

3. Add the greens to a medium bowl. Using a vegetable peeler, shave the asparagus over the greens. Add the dressing and toss to coat. Transfer to a plate. Arrange the lamb and orange sections on top.

Nutrition (per serving) • 260 calories, 21 g protein, 12 g carbohydrates, 4 g fiber, 6 g sugars, 15 g fat, 3.5 g saturated fat, 379 mg sodium

Thai Beef Salad with Mint

GLUTEN-FREE

The fish sauce and lime juice dressing on this salad adds the Thai flavors that complement the beef and mint. While cooking beef on the stove might make this feel like dinner, don't hesitate to cook this low-calorie salad up for a light lunch.

Prep time: 5 minutes

Total time: 15 minutes

Makes 2 servings

1 boneless beef strip steak (1½" thick), about 10 ounces

Kosher salt and ground black pepper

2 tablespoons fresh lime juice

1 tablespoon fish sauce

1 cup thinly sliced radishes

¼ cup sliced red onion

½ medium cucumber, unpeeled, thinly sliced

¼ cup fresh mint leaves, chopped

10 large basil leaves, chopped

4 cups chopped romaine lettuce hearts (about 2 hearts)

1. Preheat a grill or a lightly oiled skillet over medium-high heat. Season the steak on both sides with salt and pepper. Grill or pan-fry the steak for 8 to 10 minutes, turning once, or until a thermometer inserted in the center registers 145°F for medium-rare. Set aside and keep warm.

2. Meanwhile, in a large bowl, whisk together the lime juice and fish sauce. Reserve 1 tablespoon of this mixture. Add the radishes, onion, cucumber, mint, basil, and romaine to the bowl and toss well. Arrange the salad on a serving platter.

3. Thinly slice the steak crosswise against the grain and toss with the reserved dressing. Arrange on top of the salad and serve immediately.

Nutrition (per serving) • 313 calories, 41 g protein, 11 g carbohydrates, 4 g fiber, 4 g sugars, 12 g fat, 4.5 g saturated fat, 983 mg sodium

Black Bean Burrito Salad

VEGAN | GLUTEN-FREE | PACK FOR LUNCH

Do you ever order a burrito just to open it up and eat it with a fork? Skip the wasted tortilla and get straight to the point with this yummy recipe. Precook your rice to eliminate some prep time. Rub the flesh of the remaining avocado with lime juice, wrap in plastic wrap, and refrigerate. Use in the Roasted Veggie Sandwich (page 114) or Amaranth Huevos Rancheros (page 47).

Prep time: 5 minutes

Total time: 15 minutes

Makes 2 servings

1 cup canned black beans, rinsed and drained

½ teaspoon garlic salt

1 teaspoon water

½ roasted red pepper, seeded

1 tablespoon olive oil

1 teaspoon fresh lime juice

½ teaspoon agave nectar or honey

Dash of hot-pepper sauce (optional)

Kosher salt and ground black pepper

1 cup cooked brown rice, warmed

½ avocado, chopped

1 small ripe tomato, chopped

½ small red onion, thinly sliced

4 pickled jalapeño chile pepper slices

Cilantro leaves, for garnish

1. In a small saucepan, combine the beans, garlic salt, and water. Cook over medium heat for 5 minutes, or until warmed through.

2. Meanwhile, in a blender, combine the roasted red pepper, oil, lime juice, agave or honey, and hot sauce (if using). Puree until smooth, loosening with a splash of water, if needed, to make a pourable consistency. Season to taste with salt and black pepper.

3. Divide the beans, rice, avocado, tomato, onion, and jalapeño pepper between 2 wide, shallow bowls. Drizzle with the roasted red pepper sauce, top with cilantro leaves, and serve.

Nutrition (per serving) • 378 calories, 11 g protein, 52 g carbohydrates, 14 g fiber, 3 g sugars, 15 g fat, 2.5 g saturated fat, 950 mg sodium

Tuna with Snap Peas and Watermelon Radish

GLUTEN-FREE | ONE PAN | PACK FOR LUNCH

Don't be dismayed at the 45-minute wait time for this salad; you're working for only 5 minutes to put it together, so you can do something else while you wait for it to chill. We love the crisp, sprightly taste and starchy texture of sugar snap peas, but if they aren't available, you can substitute green beans.

Prep time: 5 minutes

Total time: 45 minutes

Makes 2 servings

1 jar (6.7 ounces) oil-packed tuna fillets, drained

¼ pound sugar snap peas, cut into thirds

1 watermelon radish or 3 regular radishes, halved and thinly sliced

1 teaspoon toasted sesame seeds

¼ cup Ginger Vinaigrette (page 122)

2 tablespoons fresh mint leaves, coarsely chopped

Kosher salt and freshly ground black pepper

In a medium bowl, stir together the tuna, snap peas, radishes, and sesame seeds. Add the vinaigrette, mint, a pinch of salt, and a few grinds of pepper. Toss well to combine. Chill for 30 minutes to 1 hour to allow the flavors to come together.

Nutrition (per serving) • 435 calories, 24 g protein, 8 g carbohydrates, 2 g fiber, 4 g sugars, 35 g fat, 4 g saturated fat, 631 mg sodium

Potato Leek Salad

VEGAN | GLUTEN-FREE | PACK FOR LUNCH

What makes this potato salad really special is roasting, instead of boiling, the potatoes. Roasting adds more flavor and texture, keeping it from moving into the mushy, almost mashed, potatoes territory.

Prep time: 5 minutes

Total time: 30 minutes

Makes 2 servings

1 small leek, white and light green parts only, coarsely chopped

6 teaspoons olive oil, divided

½ pound baby gold potatoes, quartered

Kosher salt and ground black pepper

1 tablespoon white wine vinegar

½ teaspoon Dijon mustard

2 cups (2 ounces) baby arugula

½ cup shredded radicchio

1. Preheat the oven to 375°F. In a bowl, toss the leek with 1 teaspoon of the oil and arrange on one-half of a baking sheet. Toss the potatoes with 2 teaspoons of the oil and a pinch of salt and pepper and arrange on the other half of the baking sheet. Roast for 20 minutes, or until the leek is caramelized and the potatoes are tender. Cool briefly.

2. In a food processor or blender, puree the leek with the remaining 3 teaspoons oil, the vinegar, and mustard. Season to taste with salt and pepper.

3. To serve, toss the potatoes with 1 tablespoon leek dressing. In a medium bowl, toss the arugula and radicchio with the remaining dressing. Divide the greens between 2 plates and top with the potatoes.

Nutrition (per serving) • 226 calories, 3 g protein, 24 g carbohydrates, 3 g fiber, 3 g sugars, 14 g fat, 2 g saturated fat, 211 mg sodium

Spicy Watermelon Salad

VEGETARIAN | GLUTEN-FREE

Pickling the jalapeño and onion in vinegar before adding them to this salad takes away some of the heat and bitterness and allows them to offset the sweetness of the watermelon and tomato. Make this salad in the middle of the summer when all of the ingredients are at their peak.

Prep time: 15 minutes

Total time: 30 minutes

Makes 2 servings

¼ **cup sliced red onion**

¼ **to ½ jalapeño chile pepper, seeded and sliced**

½ **cup white vinegar**

4 cups peeled, cubed seedless watermelon

4 small heirloom tomatoes (such as Campari), halved or quartered

¼ **teaspoon kosher salt**

¼ **teaspoon ground black pepper**

¼ **teaspoon ground cumin**

2 tablespoons crumbled Cotija or feta cheese

1 tablespoon pumpkin seeds (pepitas)

1 tablespoon cilantro leaves

Lime wedges, for serving

1. In a small bowl, combine the onion, jalapeño pepper, and vinegar. Set aside for 15 to 20 minutes.

2. Arrange the watermelon and tomatoes on a plate. Drain the onion and jalapeño, reserving 1 tablespoon of the vinegar. Add the onion and jalapeño to the watermelon and tomatoes.

3. In a small bowl, stir together the reserved vinegar, salt, black pepper, and cumin. Sprinkle over the watermelon mixture and top with the cheese, pumpkin seeds, and cilantro. Serve with lime wedges.

Nutrition (per serving) • 210 calories, 11 g protein, 32 g carbohydrates, 4 g fiber, 24 g sugars (19 g from the watermelon), 7 g fat, 3.5 g saturated fat, 509 mg sodium

Bacon, Egg, and Asparagus Brunch Salad

GLUTEN-FREE

Poached eggs require a little trick to make perfectly: swirling the water before you drop them in. Make sure you get a nice little whirlpool going in your pot, then drop the egg in the center of the swirl to get a perfect poach without losing too much white.

Prep time: 10 minutes

Total time: 40 minutes

Makes 2 servings

2 slices bacon, chopped

1 small shallot, chopped

2 tablespoons sherry vinegar or red wine vinegar

2 teaspoons olive oil

1 tablespoon chopped fresh parsley leaves

2 teaspoons chopped fresh thyme leaves

1 teaspoon Dijon mustard

Kosher salt and ground black pepper

½ pound asparagus, trimmed

2 eggs

4 cups (4 ounces) baby arugula

1 tablespoon grated Parmesan cheese

1. In a medium skillet, cook the bacon over medium-high heat for 8 minutes, or until crisp. With a slotted spoon, transfer to a paper towel–lined plate and set aside.

2. Remove and discard all but 1 tablespoon of the bacon fat from the skillet, reduce the heat to medium, and add the shallot. Cook for 4 minutes, or until tender. Add the vinegar, scraping up the browned bits with a wooden spoon. Remove the skillet from the heat and stir in the oil, herbs, mustard, and a pinch of salt and pepper. Set aside.

3. Bring a medium saucepan of water to a simmer over medium-high heat. Reduce the heat to low, add the asparagus, and cook for 2 minutes, or until tender-crisp. Remove from the water and set aside.

4. Return the water to a low simmer, swirl the water, and drop 1 egg into the middle. Cook the egg for 4 minutes, or until the white is set but the yolk is runny. Remove with a slotted spoon and transfer to a plate. Repeat with the remaining egg.

5. In a bowl, toss the arugula with 2 tablespoons of the dressing and divide between 2 plates. Top each with asparagus, an egg, and bacon. Drizzle with the remaining warm dressing and top with the grated cheese.

Nutrition (per serving) • 272 calories, 14 g protein, 10 g carbohydrates, 4 g fiber, 4 g sugars, 20 g fat, 6.5 g saturated fat, 812 mg sodium

Spinach Salad with Pomegranate, Lentils, and Pistachios

VEGAN | GLUTEN-FREE | PACK FOR LUNCH

The sweet and salty of pomegranates and pistachios make the flavors of this salad really special. If you cook your lentils in advance, it comes together in no time. You can substitute brown lentils, if desired.

Prep time: 10 minutes

Total time: 40 minutes

Makes 2 servings

1 tablespoon extra-virgin olive oil

1 small shallot, finely chopped

1 small hot red chile pepper, such as a Fresno, finely chopped

$\frac{1}{2}$ teaspoon ground cumin

$\frac{1}{4}$ teaspoon ground coriander

$\frac{1}{4}$ teaspoon ground cinnamon

$\frac{1}{4}$ teaspoon kosher salt

$\frac{1}{2}$ cup French green (le Puy) lentils, picked through, rinsed, and drained

$1\frac{1}{2}$ cups water

3 cups (3 ounces) baby spinach

$\frac{1}{4}$ cup pomegranate seeds

$\frac{1}{4}$ cup chopped fresh cilantro

$\frac{1}{4}$ cup chopped fresh flat-leaf parsley

$\frac{1}{4}$ cup chopped pistachios

1 tablespoon fresh lemon juice

1 teaspoon finely grated lemon zest

Ground black pepper

1. In a medium saucepan, heat the oil over medium heat until shimmering. Cook the shallot and chile pepper, stirring, for 8 minutes, or until the shallot is translucent. Add the cumin, coriander, cinnamon, and salt and stir for 1 minute, or until fragrant. Add the lentils and water and bring to a boil. Cover and reduce the heat to a simmer. Cook, stirring occasionally, for 30 minutes, or until the lentils are completely tender and the liquid has been absorbed.

2. In a large bowl, toss the lentils with the spinach, pomegranate seeds, cilantro, parsley, pistachios, lemon juice and zest, and black pepper to taste.

Nutrition (per serving) • 376 calories, 17 g protein, 46 g carbohydrates, 12 g fiber, 6 g sugars, 14 g fat, 2 g saturated fat, 322 mg sodium

Spicy Baby Potato Salad

VEGETARIAN | GLUTEN-FREE | PACK FOR LUNCH

Fresh green beans are very important for this recipe; canned or frozen won't have the same crunch and will go soggy under the weight of the mayonnaise and potatoes.

Prep time: 5 minutes

Total time: 40 minutes

Makes 1 serving

4 ounces baby potatoes

¼ cup chopped green beans

1 tablespoon mayonnaise

1 teaspoon chopped jalapeño chile pepper

1 teaspoon fresh lime juice

Kosher salt and ground black pepper

1 hard-cooked egg, quartered

1 teaspoon chopped fresh flat-leaf parsley

1. Place the potatoes in a medium saucepan and add enough water to cover. Bring to a boil over medium-high heat and cook for 10 minutes, or until tender. Drain, cool, and cut them in half.

2. In a bowl, mix the potatoes with the green beans, mayonnaise, jalapeño pepper, and lime juice. Season with salt and black pepper. Top with the egg and sprinkle with the parsley.

Nutrition (per serving) • 261 calories, 9 g protein, 21 g carbohydrates, 3 g fiber, 3 g sugars, 16 g fat, 3 g saturated fat, 463 mg sodium

Portobello Salad

VEGAN | GLUTEN-FREE

This salad roasts for a long time but takes very little active work. Just make sure you enjoy it while the mushrooms are still warm and have their caramelized crunch.

Prep time: 5 minutes

Total time: 30 minutes

Makes 2 servings
---

2 portobello mushroom caps, gilled and cut into 1" pieces

2 teaspoons extra-virgin olive oil

Kosher salt and ground black pepper

2 cups shredded kale leaves

2 cups baby spinach

½ cup mung bean sprouts

1 small raw red beet, peeled and cut into ½" cubes

¼ cup torn basil leaves

¼ cup Miso Dressing (page 143)

1½ tablespoons roasted sunflower seeds

1. Preheat the oven to 450°F. On a baking sheet, toss the mushrooms with the oil, a pinch of salt, and a few grinds of pepper. Spread out evenly in a single layer and roast for 10 minutes, or until they start to caramelize. Stir and continue to roast for 10 minutes, or until all sides are well caramelized.

2. In a large bowl, combine the kale, spinach, bean sprouts, beet, basil, and roasted mushrooms. Toss with the dressing and top with the sunflower seeds. Serve while the mushrooms are still warm.

Nutrition (per serving) • 314 calories, 9 g protein, 23 g carbohydrates, 6 g fiber, 8 g sugars, 23 g fat, 2.5 g saturated fat, 522 mg sodium

Beets with Goat Cheese and Chermoula

VEGETARIAN | GLUTEN-FREE

Chermoula is a marinade or sauce used in many Mediterranean countries including Algeria, Morocco, and Tunisia. There are a lot of regional variations—you can include or substitute onion, black pepper, saffron, or ground chile pepper in your version. It can be made up to 2 days ahead and stored in the refrigerator. Bring to room temperature before using.

Prep time: 10 minutes

Total time: 40 minutes

Makes 2 servings

4 medium beets, trimmed

1 ounce goat cheese, crumbled

CHERMOULA

½ cup fresh cilantro leaves

½ cup fresh flat-leaf parsley leaves

2 tablespoons fresh lemon juice

2 small cloves garlic, minced

1 teaspoon ground cumin

½ teaspoon smoked paprika

¼ teaspoon kosher salt

⅛ teaspoon chili powder (optional)

2 tablespoons extra-virgin olive oil

1. Preheat the oven to 400°F. Wrap the beets in a piece of foil and place on a baking sheet. Roast for 30 to 40 minutes, or until the beets are tender enough to be pierced with a fork. When they're cool enough to handle, remove the skins and slice the beets into ¼"-thick rounds. Arrange the beet slices on a large serving platter.

2. **To make the chermoula:** In a food processor, combine the cilantro, parsley, lemon juice, garlic, cumin, paprika, salt, and chili powder (if using). Pulse until the herbs are just coarsely chopped and the ingredients are combined. Transfer to a bowl and stir in the oil.

3. To serve, dollop the chermoula over the beets, and scatter the goat cheese on top.

Nutrition (per serving) • 267 calories, 7 g protein, 19 g carbohydrates, 6 g fiber, 12 g sugars, 19 g fat, 5 g saturated fat, 504 mg sodium

Kale Salad with Wild Rice, Grilled Chicken, and Apples

GLUTEN-FREE

Precook your grains and chicken to save time on this recipe. Save the apple by sprinkling it with lemon juice and wrapping it in plastic wrap, and use leftover wild rice for Salmon Cakes with Horseradish Sauce (page 175).

Prep time: 5 minutes

Total time: 25 minutes

Makes 1 serving

1 boneless, skinless chicken breast (about 3 ounces)

Kosher salt and ground black pepper

1 tablespoon chopped walnuts

1 tablespoon apple cider vinegar

2 teaspoons olive oil

½ teaspoon Dijon mustard

½ teaspoon honey

2 cups chopped kale

⅓ cup cooked wild rice

½ apple, thinly sliced

½ cup thinly sliced white button mushrooms

1. Preheat a grill or grill pan to medium-high heat and oil the grates. Season the chicken breast with salt and pepper and grill for 8 minutes, turning once, or until a thermometer inserted in the thickest part registers 165°F. Set aside.

2. Meanwhile, in a dry skillet, toast the walnuts over medium heat for 5 minutes, or until fragrant.

3. In a bowl, stir together the vinegar, oil, mustard, honey, and a pinch of salt and pepper. Add the kale, wild rice, apple, and mushrooms and toss to coat. Slice the chicken and place on top of the salad along with the walnuts.

Nutrition (per serving) • 398 calories, 24 g protein, 35 g carbohydrates, 5 g fiber, 14 g sugars, 20 g fat, 2.5 g saturated fat, 465 mg sodium

DELICIOUS AND NUTRITIOUS

KALE | This gorgeous green is the darling of the food world for many reasons, but we love it for one in particular—how it protects our baby blues. With the amount of time we spend looking at computer screens (guilty!) and phone screens (double guilty!), our eyes need all the protection they can get, and kale is the best source out there of lutein. Lutein protects and maintains healthy cells in our eyes—so you could say kale helps you *look* your best (sorry, we had to!).

SOUPS

WE'RE NOT SURE WHY SO MANY PEOPLE FEAR MAKING SOUP AT HOME—it's simple to make, healthy, and super easy to freeze and store for later. In fact, soup is one of the best ways to add a ton of vegetables to your diet in a single meal. And the best part is that soup is nearly foolproof—it's pretty hard to overcook, undercook, burn, or really ruin soup. Plus, the ingredients are so flexible and easy to substitute. Soup is great for both the adventurous and newbie cooks among us.

To start your soup, it's important to have a good base. Store-bought broth (especially low-sodium varieties) works well, or bouillon cubes if you're short on space. But making stock at home is literally as easy as boiling a pot of water, and it freezes perfectly until you're ready to use it—so why not try it? Simple, delicious stock can be made from ingredients you were just going to throw away! As we outlined on page 8, save extra scraps of vegetables and chicken bones in a storage bag in your freezer, until you have a few cups' worth of ingredients (stock is really flexible and can be made from many different ingredients—you don't even need chicken bones). Put all of your ingredients in a large stockpot and fill the pot with water until it covers them completely. If you have a fresh onion, carrots, or some garlic, throw those in the pot as well. Bring the pot to a boil over medium-high heat, then skim the foam from the top and reduce the heat to low. Cook for 2 hours. Strain the stock through a colander, pressing the ingredients to extract their flavors. Refrigerate the stock overnight, then skim off and discard any solidified fat from the top.[1] Now you can freeze your stock and use it whenever you need it!

For an easy lunch, choose one of our **Prep It Ahead** soups to take to work. With a good thermos, you can even heat it up before you leave and eat it hot at your desk. Or try our soup-in-a-jar recipes and make your own instant soup (just add water!). Our **Throw It Together** recipes are perfect easy weeknight meals, and a few of them are even cold soups that taste great after a long, hot summer day. You can cook them up quickly, and they come together even faster if you prepped your vegetables in advance. And if you feel like unlocking your inner Julia Child, our **Take Your Time** soups simmer on the stove, make your kitchen smell heavenly, and are Instagram-worthy—we promise.

Soup is a perfect leftover—a lot of soup recipes are even better the next day! Store soup in your refrigerator for up to 5 days. For freezing, portion your soup into resealable plastic freezer bags once it has cooled down, then place the bags on a plate in the freezer until they're frozen solid. Your flat soup pouches will store easily in your freezer until you're ready to eat them. To thaw soup, just move the freezer bag to the fridge for 24 hours, and it will be ready to heat and eat.

Chicken and Asparagus Soup

ONE PAN | PACK FOR LUNCH

To remove asparagus stems, you can chop them off, or you can use our favorite trick—bend the stalk about one-third up from the base until you feel resistance and snap off the bottom. Then use the stems in step 1 to give your broth extra flavor. To prep this soup ahead, cut the asparagus and radishes ahead of time, keeping the radish in a small bowl of water to retain its color and texture, and store both in the refrigerator. You can also prep the asparagus stock ahead of time, through step 1, and just return it to a simmer before proceeding with step 2.

Prep time: 10 minutes

Total time: 40 minutes

Makes 2 servings

2 cups low-sodium chicken broth

½ bunch asparagus, woody stems removed and reserved, tops chopped

¾ cup canned white beans (such as cannellini), rinsed and drained

½ cup shredded cooked chicken breast

¼ cup ditalini or elbow macaroni

⅛ teaspoon kosher salt

⅛ teaspoon ground black pepper

2 radishes, cut into matchsticks

2 tablespoons grated Parmesan cheese

2 lemon wedges

1. In a medium saucepan, combine the broth with the asparagus stems. Bring to a boil, reduce the heat, and simmer for 15 minutes. Remove and discard the stems, and bring the broth back to a simmer.

2. Add the chopped asparagus, beans, chicken, pasta, salt, and pepper and cook for 12 minutes, or until the asparagus is tender and the pasta is al dente. Ladle into bowls and top with the radishes, cheese, and a squeeze of lemon.

Nutrition (per serving) • 252 calories, 25 g protein, 30 g carbohydrates, 6 g fiber, 3 g sugars, 4 g fat, 1.5 g saturated fat, 600 mg sodium

French Lentil and Fennel Soup

ONE PAN | GLUTEN-FREE | PACK FOR LUNCH

When choosing tomato paste, look for the variety that comes in a tube (instead of a can) because it will last a lot longer in your refrigerator once opened. And if you can't find green lentils, you can substitute brown. To prep this soup ahead, chop all the vegetables, but wait to chop the tarragon until you cook the soup. Looking to use up that extra fennel? You can double the recipe for this soup, use it for Cod with Fennel and Pineapple Salsa (page 179), or add a bit extra to Fennel, Carrot, and Tarragon Salad (page 126).

Prep time: 10 minutes

Total time: 45 minutes

Makes 2 servings

1 tablespoon olive oil

½ small bulb fennel, chopped

¼ yellow onion, chopped

2 small carrots (not baby carrots), chopped

1 clove garlic, sliced

1½ teaspoons tomato paste

2 cups low-sodium chicken broth

¾ cup canned diced tomatoes with their juice

¼ cup French green (le Puy) lentils, picked through, rinsed, and drained

½ teaspoon kosher salt

¼ teaspoon ground black pepper

1 tablespoon finely chopped fresh tarragon leaves

Grated Parmesan cheese (optional)

1. In a medium saucepan, heat the oil over medium heat. Cook the fennel, onion, carrots, and garlic for 8 to 10 minutes, or until softened.

2. Add the tomato paste and cook for 1 minute, or until slightly darkened.

3. Add the broth, tomatoes and juice, lentils, salt, and pepper and bring to a boil. Lower the heat to maintain a bare simmer and cook for 25 minutes, or until the lentils are tender. Remove from the heat and stir in the tarragon. Serve with cheese, if desired.

Nutrition (per serving) • 226 calories, 10 g protein, 31 g carbohydrates, 8 g fiber, 8 g sugars, 7 g fat, 1 g saturated fat, 874 mg sodium

Minted Pea Soup

PACK FOR LUNCH

This fresh spring soup is just as delicious chilled as it is hot, so it's a great lunch option for those without a microwave (or where the microwave is always occupied). To prep this soup ahead, chop the vegetables, but wait to chop the mint until you cook the soup. You can also chill it after making it, through step 1, and enjoy the soup cold.

Prep time: 5 minutes

Total time: 25 minutes

Makes 2 servings

1 tablespoon unsalted butter

½ yellow onion, chopped

1 clove garlic, halved

1 pound fresh or frozen peas

2 cups low-sodium chicken broth

¼ teaspoon kosher salt

⅛ teaspoon ground black pepper

1 tablespoon finely chopped fresh mint

2 slices baguette, cut ½" thick

2 tablespoons crumbled feta cheese

1. In a medium saucepan, melt the butter over medium heat. Cook the onion for 10 minutes, or until softened. Mince half the clove of garlic and add it to the saucepan, along with the peas, broth, salt, and pepper. Bring to a boil, reduce the heat, and simmer for 5 minutes, or until the peas are tender. Transfer to a blender and puree until smooth. Return the soup to the saucepan, stir in the mint, and keep warm over low heat.

2. Toast the baguette slices, and rub each while hot with the remaining half clove of garlic. Ladle the soup into 2 bowls, top with the cheese, and serve with the garlicky baguette.

Nutrition (per serving) • 324 calories, 18 g protein, 45 g carbohydrates, 11 g fiber, 13 g sugars, 9 g fat, 5 g saturated fat, 768 mg sodium

Lentil Hot Pot

VEGETARIAN | ONE PAN | PACK FOR LUNCH | GLUTEN-FREE

Jarred artichokes are a great buy because they store for a while in the refrigerator. But if you're short on space, try this trick: Just buy exactly as many artichoke hearts as you need from the grocery store salad bar. To prep this dish ahead, cook the lentils according to step 1; return to a simmer and heat through before proceeding with step 2. Use extra goat cheese in Beets with Goat Cheese and Chermoula (page 143), Smoked Salmon Grilled Cheese (page 96), or Goat Cheese and Sesame Tartine (page 104).

Prep time: 5 minutes

Total time: 40 minutes

Makes 2 servings

1½ cups low-sodium vegetable broth

½ cup brown lentils, picked through, rinsed, and drained

4 canned artichoke hearts in water, quartered

3 cups baby spinach

1 ounce goat cheese, crumbled

1½ teaspoons toasted sesame oil, plus more to drizzle (optional)

⅛–¼ teaspoon crushed red-pepper flakes

1. In a large skillet, bring the broth to a boil. Stir in the lentils, cover, and reduce the heat to medium-low. Simmer for 25 minutes, or until the lentils are soft.

2. Stir in the artichoke hearts, spinach, cheese, oil, and red-pepper flakes. Cover and simmer for 2 to 3 minutes, or until the spinach wilts. Divide between 2 bowls and serve with an additional drizzle of oil on top, if desired.

Nutrition (per serving) • 282 calories, 17 g protein, 38 g carbohydrates, 17 g fiber, 2 g sugars, 7 g fat, 2.5 g saturated fat, 388 mg sodium

Pasta e Fagioli in a Jar

VEGAN | ONE PAN | PACK FOR LUNCH

Marinara sauce, when mixed with boiling water, becomes a delicious broth for our take on this Italian soup. If you set aside a bit of extra pasta next time you make it, this soup in a jar will come together in a snap.

Prep time: 5 minutes

Total time: 10 minutes

Makes 1 serving

½ **cup marinara sauce**

½ **cup frozen peas and carrots**

⅓ **cup canned cannellini beans, rinsed and drained**

½ **cup ditalini pasta, prepared according to package directions**

1 tablespoon fresh basil leaves

1 cup boiling water

1. In a 1-quart jar or container with a lid, layer the ingredients in the following order: marinara sauce, peas and carrots, beans, cooked pasta, and basil. Cap the jar and refrigerate until ready to eat.

2. To serve, pour the boiling water into the jar, stir (or cap and gently shake), and enjoy.

Nutrition (per serving) • 366 calories, 17 g protein, 70 g carbohydrates, 10 g fiber, 11 g sugars, 3 g fat, 0.5 g saturated fat, 845 mg sodium

Chicken Noodle Soup in a Jar

ONE PAN | PACK FOR LUNCH

Layering the ingredients in your jar isn't just for good looks—it keeps the ingredients stored properly so they cook up perfectly with boiling water. Slice your remaining half carrot and half celery rib into sticks for snacking with dip later in the day.

Prep time: 5 minutes

Total time: 15 minutes

Makes 1 serving

1 low-sodium chicken bouillon cube

½ carrot, finely chopped

½ rib celery, finely chopped

½ cup shredded cooked chicken

2 ounces egg noodles, prepared according to package directions (about ½ cup cooked)

1 tablespoon fresh dill

1 cup boiling water

1. Crush the bouillon cube with the back of a spoon and transfer to a 1-quart jar or container with a lid. Layer the ingredients in the following order: carrot, celery, chicken, cooked noodles, and dill. Cap the jar and refrigerate until ready to eat.

2. To serve, pour the boiling water into the jar, stir (or cap and gently shake) to dissolve the bouillon, and let stand for 5 minutes. Stir (or shake) again and enjoy.

Nutrition (per serving) • 253 calories, 26 g protein, 25 g carbohydrates, 2 g fiber, 3 g sugars, 5 g fat, 1 g saturated fat, 615 mg sodium

SAUSAGE, KALE, AND APPLE
FRITTATA | PAGE 30

HOMEMADE GRANOLA | PAGE 32

SMOKED SALMON AND EGG TARTINE
PAGE 39

PEANUT BUTTER PANCAKES WITH POMEGRANATE SYRUP
PAGE 42

EGG BAKED IN AVOCADO | PAGE 45

KICKIN' GREEN SMOOTHIE | PAGE 52

STRAWBERRY PATCH SMOOTHIE | PAGE 63

CHOCOLATE-DIPPED GRAPEFRUIT | PAGE 66

PISTACHIO-PARSLEY PESTO CROSTINI | PAGE 74

STRAWBERRY-AVOCADO SCALLION SALSA
PAGE 81

SPICED SWEET POTATO FRIES WITH
CREAMY AVOCADO DIP | PAGE 91

SUMMER GARDEN SOUP IN A JAR
PAGE 154

RASPBERRY GAZPACHO | PAGE 157

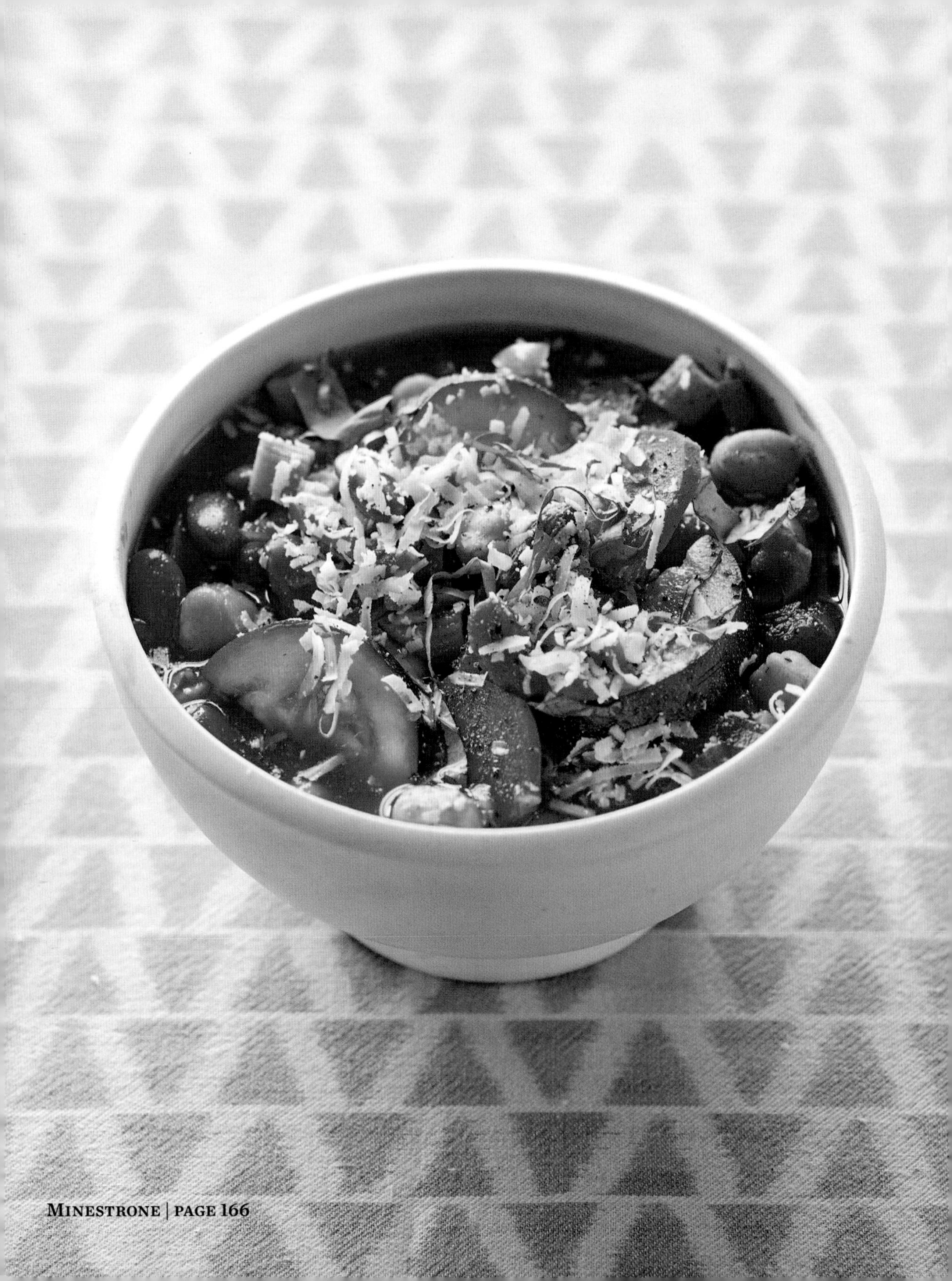

MINESTRONE | PAGE 166

BEETS WITH GOAT CHEESE AND
CHERMOULA | PAGE 143

CRAB BRUSCHETTA PANZANELLA | PAGE 127

Ramen in a Jar

VEGETARIAN | ONE PAN | PACK FOR LUNCH

Why throw away the ramen flavor packet and replace it with a bouillon cube? Because those packets are full of sodium, preservatives, and calories that you don't need. This version will be more flavorful and nutritious. You can save prep time by buying pre-cooked eggs from the grocery store salad bar. Use the rest of the scallions in Spicy Thai Curry Soup (page 164), Hearty Miso Soup (page 160), Strawberry Balsamic Dressing (page 121), Jicama Orange Salad with Scallion and Radish (page 132), or Thai Chicken Sandwich (page 112).

Prep time: 10 minutes

Total time: 15 minutes

Makes 1 serving

1 low-sodium chicken or vegetable bouillon cube

½ cup fresh or frozen shelled edamame

½ cup thinly sliced carrot

½ scallion, sliced

1 hard-cooked egg, sliced

½ package (1.5 ounces) ramen noodles, cooked according to package directions (discard flavoring packet)

1 cup boiling water

1. Crush the bouillon cube with the back of a spoon and transfer to a 1-quart jar or container with a lid. Layer the ingredients in the following order: edamame, carrot, scallion, egg, and cooked noodles. Cap the jar and refrigerate until ready to eat.

2. To serve, pour the boiling water into the jar, stir (or cap and gently shake) to dissolve the bouillon, and let stand for 5 minutes. Stir (or shake) again and enjoy.

Nutrition (per serving) • 307 calories, 17 g protein, 41 g carbohydrates, 8 g fiber, 6 g sugars, 9 g fat, 1.5 g saturated fat, 781 mg sodium

Summer Garden Soup in a Jar

VEGAN | ONE PAN | PACK FOR LUNCH

If you're missing 1 or 2 of the vegetables in this recipe, feel free to experiment with substitutions! Just make sure you replicate the portion size, and chop into equal-size pieces so the veggies cook evenly. Slice the second half of your zucchini into sticks for afternoon snacking.

Prep time: 5 minutes

Total time: 10 minutes

Makes 1 serving

1 low-sodium chicken or vegetable bouillon cube

½ cup chopped zucchini

½ cup cherry tomatoes, halved

⅓ cup canned kidney beans, rinsed and drained

¼ cup fresh or frozen corn

¼ cup quartered fresh or frozen cut green beans

1 tablespoon chopped fresh herbs (such as basil, thyme, parsley)

1 cup boiling water

1. Crush the bouillon cube with the back of a spoon and transfer to a 1-quart jar or container with a lid. Layer the ingredients in the following order: zucchini, tomatoes, beans, corn, green beans, and herbs. Cap the jar and refrigerate until ready to eat.

2. To serve, pour the boiling water into the jar, stir (or cap and gently shake) to dissolve the bouillon, and let stand for 5 minutes. Stir (or shake) again and enjoy.

Nutrition (per serving) • 176 calories, 10 g protein, 34 g carbohydrates, 11 g fiber, 8 g sugars, 1 g fat, 0 g saturated fat, 526 mg sodium

Black Bean Soup with Mango

VEGAN | PACK FOR LUNCH | GLUTEN-FREE

If you're taking this soup in for lunch, pack the mango separately so you can reheat the soup, then top with the cold mango for a chilled sweet treat on top of your soup. Use the rest of the mango in the Mango Oat Smoothie (page 55).

Prep time: 5 minutes

Total time: 15 minutes

Makes 2 servings

2 teaspoons olive oil

¼ cup chopped onion

1 can (15 ounces) black beans, rinsed and drained

1 cup low-sodium vegetable or chicken broth

1 teaspoon ground cumin

1 teaspoon garlic powder

1 teaspoon fresh lime juice

¼ cup chopped mango

1. In a medium saucepan, heat the oil over medium heat. Cook the onion for 4 minutes, or until translucent. Add half of the beans and the broth. Bring to a simmer.

2. Transfer the soup to a blender and puree until smooth. Return the soup to the saucepan with the remaining beans, the cumin, garlic powder, and lime juice and simmer for 5 minutes to meld the flavors. Divide between 2 bowls and top each with 2 tablespoons of the mango.

Nutrition (per serving) • 186 calories, 8 g protein, 29 g carbohydrates, 9 g fiber, 5 g sugars, 5 g fat, 0.5 g saturated fat, 563 mg sodium

Udon Soup with Broccoli, Tofu, and Ginger

VEGAN | ONE PAN | PACK FOR LUNCH

Udon noodles are a fun way to mix up soup fatigue—they're thick and hearty, easy to grab with chopsticks, and extra fun to slurp. If you buy a 14- or 16-ounce block of tofu, reserve 8 ounces (in water) for the Chimichurri Tofu Sandwich (page 113).

Prep time: 5 minutes

Total time: 10 minutes

Makes 1 serving

2 ounces dry udon noodles

1 cup low-sodium vegetable broth

2 teaspoons white (shiro) miso

½ cup chopped broccoli

½ cup cubed firm tofu

1 teaspoon finely chopped fresh ginger

1. Prepare the noodles according to package directions and drain.

2. In a saucepan, bring the broth to a simmer over medium-high heat. Reduce the heat to medium and add the miso, stirring until dissolved. Add the broccoli, tofu, and ginger. Cook for 1 to 2 minutes, or until the broccoli is tender. Stir in the noodles to heat through.

Nutrition (per serving) • 330 calories, 17 g protein, 51 g carbohydrates, 6 g fiber, 5 g sugars, 5 g fat, 0.5 g saturated fat, 554 mg sodium

Raspberry Gazpacho

VEGAN | ONE PAN | PACK FOR LUNCH

Why use two types of peppers? Fresh heat from the jalapeño and a sweet-tart flavor from the Peppadews offer a balanced gazpacho with depth of flavor. Before buying a jar of Peppadews, check your grocery store's salad or olive bar to see if you can buy just a few. Use the remaining cucumber in the Thai Chicken Sandwich (page 112), Crab Bruschetta Panzanella (page 127), or Bulgur Salad with Cucumber and Tomatoes (page 117).

Prep time: 10 minutes

Total time: 15 minutes

Makes 2 servings

1 package (6 ounces) raspberries (about 1 cup), plus more for garnish (optional)

1 medium tomato, seeded

½ seedless cucumber, peeled and chopped, plus more for garnish (optional)

½ jalapeño chile pepper, seeded and chopped

2 Peppadew peppers

2 tablespoons mint leaves, plus more for garnish (optional)

Juice of ½ lime

1 clove garlic, minced

¼ teaspoon kosher or sea salt

In a blender, combine the raspberries, tomato, cucumber, peppers, mint, lime juice, garlic, and salt. Blend until smooth. Strain through a mesh sieve. Serve immediately in chilled bowls, or refrigerate until cold. Garnish with extra raspberries, cucumber, and mint leaves, if desired.

Nutrition (per serving) • 77 calories, 2 g protein, 17 g carbohydrates, 7 g fiber, 8 g sugars, 1 g fat, 0 g saturated fat, 218 mg sodium

Spiced Peanut Soup

GLUTEN-FREE | PACK FOR LUNCH

Pull out this soup recipe on a cold day—bonus points if it's snowing—since the creamy, hearty texture and little burst of chili powder will warm you up. Use the second half of your sweet potato in Kale Quesadillas (page 95) or Winter Squash Pudding (page 221), or to add more bulk to Hearty Miso Soup (page 160) or Spicy Thai Curry Soup (page 164).

Prep time: 5 minutes

Total time: 20 minutes

Makes 1 serving

½ teaspoon canola oil

1 teaspoon chili powder

⅔ cup low-sodium chicken broth

2 tablespoons well-stirred canned lite coconut milk

1½ tablespoons regular or reduced-fat creamy peanut butter

½ small sweet potato, peeled and chopped

¼ teaspoon grated fresh ginger or ½ teaspoon ground ginger

½ teaspoon fresh lime juice

1 teaspoon chopped cilantro (optional)

1. In a medium saucepan, heat the oil over medium heat. Add the chili powder and stir for 1 minute. Stir in the broth, coconut milk, and peanut butter and bring to a simmer. Add the sweet potato, partially cover the saucepan, and cook for 10 to 12 minutes, or until the sweet potato is tender.

2. Stir in the ginger and lime juice until heated through. Transfer to a blender and puree until smooth. Serve, garnished with cilantro, if desired.

Nutrition (per serving) • 224 calories, 8 g protein, 13 g carbohydrates, 2 g fiber, 5 g sugars, 16 g fat, 4 g saturated fat, 175 mg sodium

Avgolemono Soup

ONE PAN

Show off your adventurous side and cook this deceptively simple soup in front of an audience. Your dining partner will be amazed when you effortlessly stir raw eggs into the broth to create a creamy, delicious base for your chicken and rice.

Prep time: 5 minutes

Total time: 15 minutes

Makes 2 servings

½ **cup frozen cooked brown or white rice**

2 cups low-sodium chicken broth

2 eggs

½ **packed cup shredded rotisserie chicken**

Juice and zest of ½ **lemon**

⅛ **teaspoon kosher salt**

⅛ **teaspoon ground black pepper**

2 teaspoons chopped fresh flat-leaf parsley

1. Prepare the rice according to package directions.

2. In a medium saucepan, heat the broth over medium-high heat until simmering.

3. In a medium bowl, whisk the eggs. Slowly drizzle in up to ¾ cup of the hot broth, whisking constantly. Reduce the heat to low. Slowly pour the egg mixture back into the saucepan, stirring constantly, and cook until thickened (the soup should be smooth and the eggs shouldn't curdle).

4. Add the rice, chicken, lemon juice and zest, salt, and pepper. Increase the heat to medium-high and cook for 2 minutes, or until heated through. Serve topped with the parsley.

Nutrition (per serving) • 238 calories, 25 g protein, 16 g carbohydrates, 1 g fiber, 1 g sugars, 8 g fat, 2.5 g saturated fat, 296 mg sodium

Hearty Miso Soup

VEGAN | GLUTEN-FREE | PACK FOR LUNCH

Napa or Savoy cabbage is heartier and holds up better to boiling, so make sure to get one of those varieties when you're making this soup. Use the remaining cabbage to substitute for the plain cabbage in Pork Lettuce Wraps (page 184) or Tuna Burger with Miso Mayo (page 176).

Prep time: 5 minutes

Total time: 20 minutes

Makes 2 servings

3 cups water

1 sweet potato, peeled and cut into ½" cubes

½ small head (about 1 pound) Napa or Savoy cabbage, coarsely chopped

3 tablespoons white (shiro) or light yellow miso paste

¾ cup canned white beans, rinsed and drained

1 scallion, sliced

1 teaspoon toasted sesame oil

1. In a large saucepan, bring the water to a boil over medium-high heat. Cook the sweet potato for 10 to 12 minutes, or until tender. Add the cabbage and cook for 1 minute, or until barely tender.

2. In a bowl, whisk ½ cup of the cooking water with the miso. Return to the saucepan. Add the beans. Reduce the heat to medium and cook until heated through. Divide between 2 bowls and garnish with the scallions and a drizzle of the oil.

Nutrition (per serving) • 280 calories, 13 g protein, 52 g carbohydrates, 10 g fiber, 12 g sugars, 3 g fat, 0.5 g saturated fat, 772 mg sodium

Shrimp Corn Chowder

ONE PAN | PACK FOR LUNCH

It might seem strange to pull out flour when you're making soup, but the little dose of gluten thickens the broth and transforms this recipe from a soup into a hearty chowder without the added fat in heavy cream.

Prep time: 5 minutes

Total time: 20 minutes

Makes 1 serving

---

1 cup low-sodium chicken broth

Kernels from 1 husked ear corn or 1 cup frozen corn kernels

1 medium red potato, chopped

2 tablespoons whole wheat or all-purpose flour

¼ teaspoon paprika

6 large shrimp, peeled and deveined

⅛ teaspoon kosher salt

⅛ teaspoon ground black pepper

1 lime wedge

1. In a small saucepan, bring the broth to a simmer over medium-high heat. Add the corn, potato, flour, and paprika. Reduce the heat to low, cover, and simmer, stirring occasionally, for 10 minutes, or until the potato is just barely tender.

2. Add the shrimp, salt, and pepper and cook, uncovered, for 5 minutes, or until the potato is completely tender and the shrimp are pink and curled. Serve with the lime wedge.

Nutrition (per serving) • 362 calories, 21 g protein, 67 g carbohydrates, 7 g fiber, 8 g sugars, 5 g fat, 0.5 g saturated fat, 589 mg sodium

TAKE YOUR TIME

Potato Leek Soup

GLUTEN-FREE | PACK FOR LUNCH

Leeks add onionlike flavor to this soup, but they're more delicate and they won't make you cry when you chop them! If you're packing this soup for lunch, either skip the yogurt topping or pack it separately to add after reheating.

Prep time: 10 minutes

Total time: 40 minutes

Makes 2 servings

1 tablespoon unsalted butter

2 leeks, white and light green parts only, halved, rinsed, and sliced

2 cups low-sodium chicken broth

1 pound gold potatoes, chopped into ½" cubes

1 sprig fresh thyme

½ teaspoon kosher salt

Pinch of ground black pepper

2 tablespoons chopped chives

2 tablespoons low-fat plain regular or Greek yogurt

1. In a medium saucepan, melt the butter over medium heat. Cook the leeks for 10 minutes, or until softened.

2. Add the broth, potatoes, thyme, salt, and pepper and bring to a boil. Reduce the heat to medium-low and simmer, partially covered, for 15 to 20 minutes, or until the potatoes are extremely tender.

3. Remove and discard the thyme sprig and puree the soup in a blender until smooth. To serve, sprinkle with the chives and top with a dollop of yogurt.

Nutrition (per serving) • 318 calories, 11 g protein, 58 g carbohydrates, 6 g fiber, 7 g sugars, 8 g fat, 4 g saturated fat, 651 mg sodium

Asparagus Soup with Mustard Croutons

VEGETARIAN | PACK FOR LUNCH | FREEZER FRIENDLY

Since you're taking time to make this delicious soup, go ahead and make this 4-serving batch for freezing. Freeze the croutons separately and give them a quick toast in a dry skillet to crisp them up before using. But go ahead and freeze the asparagus tips directly in the soup. Portion out the soup before freezing so you have individual servings ready to thaw and eat.

Prep time: 10 minutes

Total time: 30 minutes

Makes 4 servings

1 tablespoon + 1 teaspoon extra-virgin olive oil, divided

1 shallot, finely chopped

1 clove garlic, minced

1 quart low-sodium vegetable or chicken broth

1 pound asparagus, trimmed, tips reserved, and stalks cut into 1" pieces

1 russet potato (10–12 ounces), peeled and cut into 1" cubes

1 teaspoon whole grain mustard

1 teaspoon unsalted butter, melted

½ teaspoon kosher salt, divided

¼ baguette, cut into 1" cubes

½ cup fat-free milk or fat-free plain Greek yogurt

¼ teaspoon ground black pepper

1. Preheat the oven to 350°F. In a medium saucepan, heat 1 tablespoon of the oil over medium heat. Cook the shallot, stirring, for 2 to 3 minutes, or until soft. Add the garlic and cook for 1 minute. Add the broth and bring to a boil.

2. Blanch the asparagus tips in the broth for 1 minute. Remove with a slotted spoon and set aside. Add the remaining asparagus and the potato. Simmer, partially covered, for 12 to 15 minutes, or until the potato is tender.

3. Meanwhile, in a small bowl, combine the mustard, remaining 1 teaspoon oil, butter, and ¼ teaspoon of the salt. On a baking sheet, toss the bread cubes with the mustard mixture until evenly coated. Bake for 7 to 8 minutes, or until crisp and golden.

4. Carefully pour the soup into a blender, in batches if necessary, and puree until smooth. Return the soup to the saucepan. Stir in the milk or yogurt and the remaining ¼ teaspoon salt and pepper; heat through. Garnish each serving with the reserved asparagus tips and croutons.

Nutrition (per serving) • 232 calories, 7 g protein, 37 g carbohydrates, 4 g fiber, 6 g sugars, 6 g fat, 1.5 g saturated fat, 570 mg sodium

Spicy Thai Curry Soup

VEGAN | PACK FOR LUNCH | GLUTEN-FREE

If you have coconut oil, use that to enhance the delicious coconut and curry flavors in this soup. Add the leftover bell pepper to the Roasted Veggie Sandwich (page 114) or use it in Greek Salad-Tabbouleh Mash Up (page 120).

Prep time: 15 minutes

Total time: 40 minutes

Makes 2 servings

2 teaspoons coconut oil or olive oil

½ pound carrots, peeled and cut into 1" cubes

1 sweet potato (6 ounces), peeled and cut into 1" cubes

½ yellow onion, coarsely chopped

1½ teaspoons peeled and chopped fresh ginger

1½ cups low-sodium vegetable or chicken broth

1 cup coconut water

1 tablespoon fresh lime juice

½–1 teaspoon curry powder (to taste)

Pinch of ground cardamom or cinnamon

½ red bell pepper, sliced

1 scallion, sliced

2 tablespoons sliced basil leaves

2 tablespoons toasted pumpkin seeds

1. In a medium saucepan, heat the oil over medium heat. Add the carrots, sweet potato, and onion. Cover and cook, stirring occasionally, for 10 minutes, or until the vegetables begin to soften and slightly brown. Add the ginger, stir, and cook for 1 minute. Add the broth and bring to a boil. Reduce the heat to a simmer, partially cover, and cook for 10 minutes, or until the vegetables are completely soft.

2. Transfer the soup to a blender and carefully puree, in batches if necessary, until smooth. Add the coconut water and blend to combine. Return the soup to the saucepan. Stir in the lime juice, curry, and cardamom or cinnamon and heat through. Divide between 2 bowls and top each serving with the bell pepper, scallion, basil, and pumpkin seeds.

Nutrition (per serving) • 262 calories, 6 g protein, 45 g carbohydrates, 9 g fiber, 18 g sugars, 9 g fat, 4.5 g saturated fat, 266 mg sodium

DELICIOUS AND NUTRITIOUS

COCONUT OIL | Believe it or not, fat can actually be a good thing! Coconut oil is high in natural saturated fats, which pack a one-two punch for cholesterol—they increase your healthy (HDL) cholesterol while turning the bad (LDL) cholesterol into the good HDL variety.

Creamy Vegetable Soup

VEGAN | GLUTEN-FREE | PACK FOR LUNCH

Don't let the name fool you—this creamy soup contains no cream, or any dairy for that matter, and is deliciously vegan. The dried chile pepper is crucial to the flavor of this soup, so don't substitute with a fresh one; the flavor in a dried chile is much more concentrated.

Prep time: 10 minutes

Total time: 50 minutes

Makes 2 servings

1 tablespoon olive oil

1 small dried chile pepper (such as chile de arbol)

1 small clove garlic, smashed

1 small leek, white and light green parts only, halved, rinsed, and chopped

1½ cups cauliflower florets

½ pound baby Yukon gold potatoes, larger ones halved or quartered

2 cups low-sodium vegetable broth

1 cup water

½ teaspoon kosher salt

½ teaspoon ground black pepper

2 tablespoons chopped chives

2 tablespoons cashews, finely chopped

½ teaspoon smoked sea salt, such as Maldon (optional)

1. In a medium saucepan, heat the oil, chile pepper, and garlic over medium-high heat. Add the leek and cook for 5 minutes, or until soft. Add the cauliflower, potatoes, broth, water, salt, and black pepper. Bring to a boil, reduce the heat to low, and simmer for 30 minutes, or until the potatoes are tender.

2. Remove and discard the chile pepper and puree the soup in a blender, in batches if necessary, until smooth. Return the soup to the saucepan and heat through. Divide between 2 bowls and serve topped with the chives, cashews, and smoked salt (if using).

Nutrition (per serving) • 263 calories, 6 g protein, 38 g carbohydrates, 5 g fiber, 6 g sugars, 11 g fat, 2 g saturated fat, 749 mg sodium

Minestrone

VEGAN | ONE PAN | FREEZER FRIENDLY | PACK FOR LUNCH

Cook this soup on the stovetop or, if you have a slow cooker, you can start the soup in the morning and let it cook all day. It also freezes perfectly, so just portion cooled servings into freezer-safe containers and freeze for later. Thaw overnight in the refrigerator and warm in a medium saucepan over medium heat.

Prep time: 15 minutes

Total time: 1 hour 5 minutes

Makes 6 servings

---

2 tablespoons olive oil

2 carrots, thinly sliced

2 ribs celery, thinly sliced

1 onion, chopped

3 cloves garlic, sliced

1 tablespoon dried oregano

1 bay leaf

1/2 teaspoon kosher salt

1/2 teaspoon ground black pepper

1 quart low-sodium vegetable broth

1 can (14 1/2 ounces) diced tomatoes with their juice

2 cans (14 –15 ounces each) beans (such as kidney, chickpea, or cranberry), rinsed and drained

1 small zucchini, halved lengthwise and sliced 1/4" thick

1 1/2 cups whole grain ditalini or elbow pasta

6 tablespoons finely grated Parmesan cheese

3 tablespoons shredded fresh basil leaves

ON THE STOVETOP:

1. In a large saucepan, heat the oil over medium-high heat. Cook the carrots, celery, and onion for 5 minutes, or until softened. Add the garlic, oregano, bay leaf, salt, and pepper and cook for 1 minute. Add the broth and tomatoes, and bring to a boil. Cover, reduce the heat to a simmer, and cook for 30 minutes, or until the vegetables are tender.

2. Add the beans, zucchini, and pasta and cook for 10 minutes, or until the pasta is al dente. Remove and discard the bay leaf. Garnish each serving with the cheese and basil.

IN A SLOW COOKER:

1. In a 4- or 6-quart slow cooker, combine the broth, tomatoes (with their juice), carrots, celery, onion, garlic, oregano, bay leaf, salt, and pepper. Cover and cook on low for 6 to 8 hours or on high for 3 to 4 hours, or until the vegetables are tender.

2. Remove the lid and add the beans, zucchini, and pasta. Cook, uncovered, on high for 30 minutes, or until the pasta is tender. Remove and discard the bay leaf. Garnish each serving with the cheese and basil.

Nutrition (per serving) • 255 calories, 14 g protein, 42 g carbohydrates, 10 g fiber, 8 g sugars, 3 g fat, 1 g saturated fat, 891 mg sodium

MAIN DISHES

AND NOW WE COME TO THE MAIN EVENT: MEALS THAT ARE FUN TO COOK, ARE full of flavor, and will satisfy your hunger for the rest of the night. We know how tempting it is, after a long day at work and maybe a stop at the gym, to opt for a quick single-ingredient dinner. That's one of the dangers of cooking for yourself: Suddenly popcorn, a bowl of buttery noodles, or even just a bag of frozen tater tots seems like a good meal option. But as we discussed in the beginning of this book, why serve yourself a meal you wouldn't serve to other people? Especially since our delicious **Prep It Ahead** meals take about as long to cook as that bag of popcorn. Hmmm . . . Cinnamon Chili Rubbed Pork with Raw Sprout Slaw (page 169) or slightly burned low-fat popcorn? We know our choice.

For a quick meal, making dinner in advance is a great choice. But if you have a little bit of time, and are making a **Throw It Together** dinner, take the time to get your next day in order as well. If you've prepped your vegetables in advance, you'll have extra time to work. Cooking dinner is the perfect time to check in on the breakfast and lunch you've planned for the next day and prep anything that needs prepping. Put overnight oats in the refrigerator, chop the vegetables you'll be dipping in your snack hummus, gather the ingredients for making your lunch sandwich. Use the boiling, baking, or resting time in your dinner recipe to make tomorrow even easier.

The **Take Your Time** recipes offer an even better opportunity to enjoy cooking for yourself. Spending the same amount of time it takes to watch a crime drama making a delicious meal is certainly time well spent. Plus, lots of our recipes include fun techniques that, once you learn, you'll be able to use all the time. Ever wondered what *en papillote* is, or how eggplant rollatini gets all rolled up? Well, put on your apron, blast some Adele, and get cooking with our fun, simple-to-follow recipes in this section. Trust us, if we can master these recipes, you can, too!

PREP IT AHEAD

169 | Cinnamon Chili Rubbed Pork with Raw Sprout Slaw

170 | Rhubarb-Roasted Chicken

171 | Apple and Chicken Curry

172 | Hearty Greens Pesto Pasta

173 | Rosemary-Roasted Vegetables with Manchego Cheese and Serrano Ham

174 | Spicy Tempeh Chili

THROW IT TOGETHER

175 | Salmon Cakes with Horseradish Sauce

176 | Tuna Burger with Miso Mayo

177 | Halibut with Bean Puree

178 | Broiled Steak and Smashed Potatoes

179 | Cod with Fennel and Pineapple Salsa

180 | Five Fast Pasta Sauces

183 | Lamb Meatball Skewers with Tahini–Goat Cheese Sauce

184 | Pork Lettuce Wraps

185 | Black Bean Burgers over Mexicali Slaw

186 | Broiled Lamb with Charred Asparagus and Leeks

187 | Baked Coconut Shrimp

188 | Orange Chicken and Broccoli Stir-Fry

189 | Honey-Cayenne Grilled Pork Chops

190 | Maple, Bourbon, and Mustard–Glazed Salmon with Slaw

191 | Yogurt and Parmesan Fettuccine Alfredo

192 | Cashew and Pepper Stir-Fry

TAKE YOUR TIME

193 | Seared Steak and Roasted Veggie Bowl

194 | Blueberry Turkey Burgers

195 | Apple and Butternut Squash Pasta with Brown Butter–Sage Sauce

196 | Beef Tenderloin with Spinach Chimichurri

197 | Blackberry Pork Tenderloin

198 | Chickpea Chard Eggplant Rolls

199 | Kale Pesto Pasta with Meatballs

200 | Spring Faux Risotto

201 | Spicy Chipotle Peach Ribs

202 | Chicken Breasts Stuffed with Cilantro and Walnuts

203 | Pan-Roasted Chicken with Mushroom and Herb Gravy

204 | Trout Ratatouille *en Papillote*

205 | Pan-Seared Pork Chops and Spiced Apples

168   MAIN DISHES

Cinnamon Chili Rubbed Pork with Raw Sprout Slaw

GLUTEN-FREE

Eliminate about half of the cooking time in this recipe by prepping the slaw ahead of time. It will keep in the refrigerator in an airtight container for up to 3 days.

Prep time: 5 minutes

Total time: 35 minutes

Makes 2 servings

2 grapefruits

2 scallions, thinly sliced, greens and whites kept separate

2 tablespoons + 1 teaspoon olive oil, divided

Kosher salt and ground black pepper

3 cups shredded Brussels sprouts

½ cup shredded carrot

½ teaspoon brown sugar

½ teaspoon chili powder

¼ teaspoon ground cinnamon

8 ounces pork tenderloin

1. Preheat the oven to 400°F. Juice 1 grapefruit to yield 6 tablespoons. Set the juice aside. Segment the second grapefruit: With a sharp knife, cut off enough of the top and bottom of the grapefruit to reveal a circle of flesh. Cut away the peel, following the contours of the grapefruit and removing all the pith. With the grapefruit in 1 hand and a paring knife in the other, slide the knife down in between the membranes to release the flesh into a small bowl.

2. In a large bowl, whisk together the reserved grapefruit juice, the scallion whites, 2 tablespoons of the oil, and a pinch of salt and pepper. Toss in the Brussels sprouts, carrot, the grapefruit segments, and the scallion greens until completely coated in the dressing. Season to taste with additional salt and pepper.

3. In a small bowl, combine the remaining 1 teaspoon oil, the brown sugar, chili powder, cinnamon, and ½ teaspoon salt. Rub all over the pork tenderloin and transfer to a baking sheet. Roast for 15 minutes, or until a thermometer inserted in the center reaches 145°F. Let rest for 5 minutes before slicing and serving with the slaw.

Nutrition (per serving) • 394 calories, 30 g protein, 31 g carbohydrates, 7 g fiber, 14 g sugars, 19 g fat, 3 g saturated fat, 664 mg sodium

Rhubarb-Roasted Chicken

GLUTEN-FREE | PACK FOR LUNCH

This recipe reheats well, so make the whole meal in advance as a heat-and-serve lunch or dinner; you can even double or triple the recipe for extra meals on the go.

Prep time: 5 minutes

Total time: 30 minutes

Makes 1 serving

¼ **cup quinoa**

1 **cup chopped rhubarb**

1 **small shallot, chopped**

1¼ **teaspoons olive oil, divided**

¼ **teaspoon kosher salt, divided**

¼ **teaspoon ground black pepper, divided**

1 **boneless, skinless chicken thigh**

¼ **cup chopped parsley**

1 **teaspoon grated orange zest**

1. Preheat the oven to 400°F. Prepare the quinoa according to package directions.

2. Meanwhile, in a small baking dish, toss the rhubarb, shallot, 1 teaspoon of the oil, and ⅛ teaspoon of the salt and pepper. Brush the remaining ¼ teaspoon oil on the chicken, season with the remaining ⅛ teaspoon salt and pepper, and place on top of the rhubarb in the dish.

3. Bake for 25 minutes, or until the chicken is golden and a thermometer inserted in the thickest portion registers 165°F. Transfer the chicken to a plate and slice. Stir the parsley into the rhubarb mixture. Stir the orange zest into the quinoa. Serve the chicken with the quinoa and rhubarb mixture.

Nutrition (per serving) • 385 calories, 29 g protein, 40 g carbohydrates, 6 g fiber, 5 g sugars, 13 g fat, 2 g saturated fat, 551 mg sodium

Apple and Chicken Curry

GLUTEN-FREE | PACK FOR LUNCH

The flavors in curry taste better as the dish sits, so make this for dinner and have the tasty leftovers for lunch the day after! Serve over brown basmati rice or multi-colored quinoa to sop up the juices.

Prep time: 10 minutes

Total time: 1 hour

Makes 2 servings

½ **cup brown basmati rice**

1 teaspoon olive oil

½ **medium yellow onion, chopped**

1 clove garlic, minced

1 teaspoon grated fresh ginger

8 ounces boneless, skinless chicken breast, cut into 1½" cubes

Kosher salt and ground black pepper

1 medium tomato, chopped

1 teaspoon curry powder

1 sweet-tart apple, such as Honeycrisp or Sweet Tango, halved, cored, and cut into 1" cubes

⅓ **cup low-sodium chicken broth**

2 tablespoons well-stirred lite coconut milk

2 cups baby spinach

1. Prepare the rice according to package directions.

2. Meanwhile, in a large nonstick skillet, heat the oil over medium heat until shimmering. Cook the onion for 5 minutes, or until tender. Stir in the garlic and ginger, and cook for 1 minute, or until fragrant.

3. Season the chicken generously with salt and pepper. Add to the skillet and cook for 5 minutes, or until golden. Stir in the tomato and curry powder, and cook for 1 minute, or until fragrant. Add the apple, broth, and coconut milk and simmer for 10 minutes, or until the sauce thickens slightly and the chicken is no longer pink. Stir in the spinach until wilted, and season to taste with salt and pepper. Serve the curry over the brown rice.

Nutrition (per serving) • 364 calories, 30 g protein, 45 g carbohydrates, 7 g fiber, 13 g sugars, 8 g fat, 2 g saturated fat, 443 mg sodium

Hearty Greens Pesto Pasta

VEGETARIAN | PACK FOR LUNCH

This dish is the perfect canvas for additional add-ins—try throwing in white beans, chickpeas, or shredded rotisserie chicken. To prep ahead, make the pesto sauce in advance and store in the refrigerator for up to 5 days, or freeze it in ice cube trays. You can defrost the pesto cubes in the refrigerator overnight or add them to hot sauces to pump up flavor! Use nutritional yeast in place of the parmesan for a vegan dish!

Prep time: 5 minutes

Total time: 15 minutes

Makes 2 servings

4 ounces short pasta, such as rotini, cavatappi, or orecchiette

½ cup hearty greens, such as kale, spinach, chard, or escarole

1 tablespoon olive oil

1 tablespoon lemon juice

1 tablespoon grated Parmesan cheese + more for serving

1 tablespoon chopped nuts, such as almonds, pine nuts, pistachios, or walnuts

1 clove garlic

Kosher salt and ground black pepper

1 cup halved cherry tomatoes

1. Prepare the pasta according to package directions. Reserve ½ cup of the pasta cooking water and drain the pasta.

2. Meanwhile, in a food processor, combine the hearty green, oil, lemon juice, cheese, nuts, and garlic. Pulse together until smooth. Season to taste with salt and pepper.

3. Toss the pesto with the pasta and tomatoes, adding splashes of the reserved cooking water if needed to reach desired consistency. Sprinkle with a little more cheese, if desired.

Nutrition (per serving) • 323 calories, 12 g protein, 49 g carbohydrates, 7 g fiber, 2 g sugars, 11 g fat, 2 g saturated fat, 113 mg sodium

Rosemary-Roasted Vegetables with Manchego Cheese and Serrano Ham

GLUTEN-FREE | PACK FOR LUNCH

You can make this whole dish in advance, saving the cheese for when you're ready to eat it. It makes a filling lunch or dinner that you can easily reheat in the microwave.

Prep time: 10 minutes

Total time: 35 minutes

Makes 1 serving

½ **pound asparagus, trimmed and cut into 2″ pieces**

½ **pound small Brussels sprouts, trimmed and cut in half**

2 teaspoons coarsely chopped fresh rosemary

2 teaspoons olive oil

Pinch of ground black pepper

1 ounce Serrano ham, torn into small pieces

1 tablespoon sherry vinegar

2 tablespoons grated manchego cheese

1. Preheat the oven to 425°F. On a baking sheet, toss together the asparagus, Brussels sprouts, rosemary, oil, and pepper.

2. Roast the vegetables, stirring once, for 20 minutes, or until tender and charred. Toss in the ham and vinegar and roast for 2 minutes.

3. Serve sprinkled with the cheese on top.

Nutrition (per serving) • 322 calories, 21 g protein, 24 g carbohydrates, 11 g fiber, 7 g sugars, 19 g fat, 6 g saturated fat, 935 mg sodium

Spicy Tempeh Chili

VEGAN | FREEZER FRIENDLY | ONE PAN | PACK FOR LUNCH

Look for tempeh in the refrigerated section in the natural foods department of your grocery store. If tempeh is not your thing, you can substitute lean ground turkey. To prep this ahead, make the chili and portion it out, allow it to cool completely, and freeze in airtight containers for up to 3 months. Thaw overnight in the refrigerator and gently reheat in a saucepan or in the microwave when you are ready to eat.

Prep time: 5 minutes

Total time: 35 minutes

Makes 2 servings

2 teaspoons canola oil

3 ounces non-GMO tempeh, crumbled

½ small onion, chopped

½ red bell pepper, seeded and chopped

½ green bell pepper, seeded and chopped

½ serrano pepper, seeded and chopped

¼ teaspoon kosher salt

¼ teaspoon ground black pepper

½ cup canned black beans, rinsed and drained

½ cup canned pinto beans, rinsed and drained

1 teaspoon chili powder

1 teaspoon ground cumin

½ teaspoon garlic powder

½ cup crushed tomatoes

1¼ cups water

½ avocado, peeled and chopped

1. In a medium saucepan, heat the oil over medium heat until shimmering. Cook the tempeh, onion, peppers, salt, and black pepper, stirring, for 10 minutes, or until the vegetables begin to brown.

2. Stir in the beans, chili powder, cumin, garlic powder, tomatoes, and water. Simmer for 20 to 25 minutes, or until the flavors have melded. Serve hot, topped with the avocado.

Nutrition (per serving) • 279 calories, 16 g protein, 36 g carbohydrates, 9 g fiber, 7 g sugars, 10 g fat, 1 g saturated fat, 770 mg sodium

Salmon Cakes with Horseradish Sauce

PACK FOR LUNCH

Simplify the prep by precooking, or buying precooked, rice. Use the leftover rice in Kale Salad with Wild Rice, Grilled Chicken, and Apples (page 144).

Prep time: 5 minutes
Total time: 15 minutes
Makes 2 servings

1 can (6 ounces) salmon, drained and flaked with a fork

⅓ cup soft whole wheat bread crumbs

¼ cup cooked wild rice or brown rice

1 egg white

½ teaspoon toasted sesame oil

¼ cup 2% plain Greek yogurt

1½ teaspoons drained prepared horseradish

2½ teaspoons olive oil, divided

2 cups baby spinach

2 cups arugula

1 tablespoon lemon juice + lemon wedges, for serving

Kosher salt and ground black pepper

1. In a medium bowl, combine the salmon, bread crumbs, rice, egg white, and sesame oil. Form the mixture into 2 patties about 3″ in diameter. In a small bowl, mix the yogurt and horseradish.

2. In a nonstick skillet, heat 1 teaspoon of the olive oil over medium heat. Cook the patties for 6 minutes, turning once, or until golden on both sides.

3. In a medium bowl, toss the spinach and arugula with the lemon juice and the remaining 1½ teaspoons olive oil. Season the salad to taste with salt and pepper.

4. Serve the cakes with the salad, lemon wedges, and sauce.

Nutrition (per serving) • 356 calories, 29 g protein, 19 g carbohydrates, 3 g fiber, 3 g sugars, 19 g fat, 3 g saturated fat, 475 mg sodium

DELICIOUS AND NUTRITIOUS

SALMON | Research has linked the omega-3 fatty acids that you get from salmon to everything from better heart health to reduced risks of cancer and dementia. Researchers find new benefits all the time, but what we do know is this: Salmon is a tasty way to get an essential fatty acid that your body can't produce on its own.

Tuna Burger with Miso Mayo

GLUTEN-FREE

Replace the beef with tuna and the bun with cabbage leaves, and you've got a healthier burger—now with Asian-inspired flavors and fresh vegetables and herbs mixed in. Don't skip the chopped almonds, which add a nice crunch to the dish.

Prep time: 10 minutes

Total time: 15 minutes

Makes 1 serving

1 can (5 ounces) albacore tuna, drained

1 egg white

2 tablespoons grated carrot

1 tablespoon chopped cilantro

1 teaspoon pickled or fresh jalapeño chile pepper

1 tablespoon mayonnaise

1 teaspoon white miso

2 red or green cabbage leaves

1 teaspoon chopped almonds

1. In a medium bowl, combine the tuna, egg white, carrot, cilantro, and jalapeño pepper. Form the mixture into 2 patties.

2. Coat a nonstick skillet with cooking spray and heat over medium heat. Cook the patties for 4 minutes, turning once, or until golden on both sides.

3. Meanwhile, in a small bowl, mix the mayonnaise and miso. Transfer the patties to the cabbage leaves, dollop the miso mayo on top, and sprinkle with the almonds.

Nutrition (per serving) • 336 calories, 32 g protein, 6 g carbohydrates, 2 g fiber, 2 g sugars, 19 g fat, 4 g saturated fat, 809 mg sodium

Halibut with Bean Puree

GLUTEN-FREE

A great starter for those who are beginners when it comes to cooking fish, halibut has a light flavor and cooks quickly and easily.

Prep time: 5 minutes

Total time: 15 minutes

Makes 2 servings

1 teaspoon canola oil

2 Alaskan halibut fillets (5–6 ounces each)

Kosher salt and ground black pepper

½ cup frozen lima beans

⅓ cup low-sodium fish or vegetable broth

2 tablespoons fresh flat-leaf parsley leaves

1 teaspoon finely grated lemon zest

1 clove garlic, chopped

⅛ teaspoon crushed red-pepper flakes

2 teaspoons extra-virgin olive oil

2 tablespoons chopped chives

Lemon wedges, for serving

1. In a large nonstick skillet, heat the canola oil over medium-high heat until shimmering. Season the fish with ¼ teaspoon each salt and black pepper. Cook the fish for 7 minutes, turning once, or until it flakes easily and is golden brown. Remove from the heat.

2. Meanwhile, in a small saucepan, combine the lima beans and broth. Bring to a boil, reduce the heat, and simmer for 5 minutes, or until the lima beans are tender. Transfer to a blender and add the parsley, lemon zest, garlic, red-pepper flakes, and ⅛ teaspoon salt. Blend for 1 minute, or until completely smooth. With the blender running on low, slowly drizzle in the olive oil.

3. Divide the bean puree between 2 plates, top with the halibut, and sprinkle with the chives. Serve with the lemon wedges.

Nutrition (per serving) • 290 calories, 33 g protein, 15 g carbohydrates, 3 g fiber, 0 g sugars, 11 g fat, 2 g saturated fat, 518 mg sodium

Broiled Steak and Smashed Potatoes

GLUTEN-FREE

Steak without a grill is heresy to some people, but there is a way to cook steak in your kitchen—no matter how tiny—that results in a dish just as delicious as a summer barbecue. The secret is your broiler! Turn that fire or very hot coil on to get that steak browning.

Prep time: 5 minutes

Total time: 20 minutes

Makes 1 serving

4 ounces baby potatoes

4 ounces flank steak

4 ounces green beans, trimmed

4 ounces cherry tomatoes

Kosher salt and ground black pepper

2 teaspoons olive oil

1. Place the potatoes in a medium saucepan, cover with water, and bring to a boil. Cook for 7 minutes, or until just fork-tender. Drain.

2. Heat the broiler to high. On a baking sheet, arrange the steak, green beans, cherry tomatoes, and the boiled potatoes. Season the steak with salt and pepper. Toss the vegetables with the oil and season with salt and pepper. Using the bottom of a mug or juice glass, press the potatoes to flatten.

3. Broil for 5 minutes, turning the steak and vegetables once, or until the vegetables are golden and a thermometer inserted in the center of the steak registers 145°F for medium-rare.

Nutrition (per serving) • 373 calories, 28 g protein, 31 g carbohydrates, 7 g fiber, 8 g sugars, 16 g fat, 4 g saturated fat, 660 mg sodium

Cod with Fennel and Pineapple Salsa

GLUTEN-FREE

If this is the only pineapple you're cooking with all week, there is no need to buy a whole can or even a whole fruit (unless you enjoy snacking on it!). Just grab exactly as much as you need from the salad bar at your grocery store.

Prep time: 5 minutes

Total time: 15 minutes

Makes 1 serving

¼ **cup chopped pineapple**

¼ **cup chopped fennel**

¼ **cup chopped red bell pepper**

1 teaspoon fresh lime juice

¼ **teaspoon crushed red-pepper flakes**

1 teaspoon olive oil

4 ounces cod fillet

Pinch of kosher salt

Pinch of ground black pepper

1. In a small bowl, combine the pineapple, fennel, bell pepper, lime juice, and red-pepper flakes. Set aside.

2. In a small nonstick skillet, heat the oil over medium heat until shimmering. Season the cod with salt and black pepper and cook for 6 minutes, turning once, or until it flakes easily and the outside is golden. Serve topped with the reserved salsa.

Nutrition (per serving) • 189 calories, 22 g protein, 14 g carbohydrates, 3 g fiber, 6 g sugars, 6 g fat, 1 g saturated fat, 676 mg sodium

Five Fast Pasta Sauces

Pasta is one of the easiest meals you can throw together. But don't reach for that same old boring (and expensive!) jar of sauce; give these quick, delicious recipes a shot! Each of the recipes that follow makes two servings and the nutrition facts assume four ounces of whole wheat pasta, prepared according to package directions and split.

Butternut Squash Sauce

GLUTEN-FREE | VEGETARIAN | 5 INGREDIENTS OR FEWER

Prep time: 5 minutes

Total time: 20 minutes

3 cups warm leftover roasted butternut squash or frozen butternut squash, cooked according to package directions, or 1 cup canned butternut squash puree

½ cup pasta cooking water

Kosher salt and ground black pepper

2 tablespoons grated Pecorino Romano cheese

In a blender, combine the squash with the pasta cooking water. Blend until pureed. Season to taste with salt and pepper. Toss with the pasta and sprinkle the cheese over the top. Best with rigatoni or orecchiette.

Nutrition (per serving) • 359 calories, 12 g protein, 75 g carbohydrates, 15 g fiber, 8 g sugars, 3 g fat, 1 g saturated fat, 581 mg sodium

Chickpea Sauce

VEGAN | GLUTEN-FREE

Prep time: 5 minutes

Total time: 20 minutes

1 cup canned chickpeas, rinsed and drained

1 cup low-sodium chicken or vegetable broth

1 bay leaf

1 tablespoon olive oil

1 tablespoon fresh lemon juice

¼ cup pasta cooking water

2 tablespoons chopped fresh flat-leaf parsley

Ground black pepper

1. In a small saucepan, combine the chickpeas, broth, and bay leaf. Cook over medium heat for 10 minutes, or until the chickpeas are heated through. Remove the bay leaf and discard.

2. With a fork or potato masher, mash the chickpeas until almost smooth. Stir in the oil and lemon juice and toss with the pasta, adding splashes of pasta cooking water as needed to loosen the sauce. Stir in the parsley and top with the pepper to taste. Best with mafalda or farfalle.

Nutrition (per serving) • 416 calories, 16 g protein, 67 g carbohydrates, 11 g fiber, 3 g sugars, 10 g fat, 1 g saturated fat, 428 mg sodium

Salsa Cruda

VEGAN | GLUTEN-FREE

Prep time: 10 minutes

Total time: 20 minutes

2 medium tomatoes, chopped

½ small red onion, chopped

1 small clove garlic, minced

2 tablespoons chopped fresh basil

Kosher salt and ground black pepper

2 tablespoons olive oil

In a medium bowl, combine the tomatoes, onion, garlic, basil, and salt and pepper to taste. In a small skillet, heat the oil over medium-high heat for 3 minutes, or until shimmering. Pour the oil over the vegetables and toss in the pasta. Best with cavatappi or penne.

Nutrition (per serving) • 374 calories, 9 g protein, 52 g carbohydrates, 7 g fiber, 7 g sugars, 16 g fat, 2 g saturated fat, 498 mg sodium

Super Simple Marinara

GLUTEN-FREE | 5 INGREDIENTS OR FEWER | VEGAN | FREEZER FRIENDLY

Prep time: 5 minutes

Total time: 20 minutes

2 tablespoons olive oil

2 small cloves garlic, smashed

1 can (28 ounces) whole peeled San Marzano tomatoes

1 sprig fresh basil

Kosher salt and ground black pepper

In a medium saucepan, heat the oil and garlic over medium heat for 3 minutes, or until sizzling. Carefully pour in the tomatoes and add the sprig of basil. Bring to a simmer and, using a wooden spoon, break up the tomatoes. Cook until your desired consistency—for medium thickness, simmer about 15 minutes. Season to taste with salt and pepper. Remove and discard the basil sprig. Good with all pasta, but let's keep it traditional and use spaghetti.

Nutrition (per serving) • 391 calories, 12 g protein, 60 g carbohydrates, 11 g fiber, 12 g sugars, 15 g fat, 2 g saturated fat, 813 mg sodium

Lazy Bolognese

GLUTEN-FREE

Prep time: 5 minutes

Total time: 20 minutes

6 ounces lean ground beef

½ recipe Super Simple Marinara (above)

In a medium saucepan over medium heat, cook the meat, breaking it up with a wooden spoon, for 10 minutes, or until no longer pink. Stir in the marinara sauce and cook for 5 minutes, or until heated through and the flavors meld. Best with pappardelle or campanelle.

Nutrition (per serving) • 392 calories, 27 g protein, 51 g carbohydrates, 9 g fiber, 7 g sugars, 11 g fat, 2 g saturated fat, 457 mg sodium

Lamb Meatball Skewers with Tahini–Goat Cheese Sauce

GLUTEN-FREE | PACK FOR LUNCH

Keep these meatballs gluten-free by replacing bread crumbs with sesame seeds, which also complement the flavor of the lamb nicely. If you're packing these skewers for lunch, keep the sauce separate and add it after you reheat the meatballs.

Prep time: 5 minutes

Total time: 20 minutes

Makes 2 servings

8 ounces ground lamb

1 egg white

1 tablespoon dried Italian seasoning

1 teaspoon toasted sesame seeds

¼ teaspoon + pinch of kosher salt, divided

1 tablespoon soft goat cheese

1½ teaspoons fresh lemon juice

1 teaspoon tahini

1 teaspoon water

1. Position an oven rack 4" from the broiler element and heat the broiler. Place a rack in the center of a rimmed baking sheet and coat with cooking spray.

2. In a medium bowl, mix together the lamb, egg white, Italian seasoning, sesame seeds, and ¼ teaspoon of the salt. Portion the lamb mixture into eight 1" balls. Skewer 4 meatballs on each of 2 skewers. Place on the rack. Broil the skewers for 8 minutes, or until no longer pink.

3. In a small bowl, combine the goat cheese, lemon juice, tahini, water, and the remaining pinch of salt. Serve the skewers with the sauce.

Nutrition (per serving) • 269 calories, 23 g protein, 1 g carbohydrates, 0 g fiber, 0 g sugars, 19 g fat, 7.5 g saturated fat, 481 mg sodium

Pork Lettuce Wraps

GLUTEN-FREE | PACK FOR LUNCH

Lean pork is a great option when you want the indulgent flavor of pork, but you don't want all of the fat. Sauté it in this delicious peanut sauce, and you won't even taste the difference.

Prep time: 5 minutes

Total time: 15 minutes

Makes 2 servings

1½ **teaspoons canola oil**

8 **ounces lean ground pork**

1½ **tablespoons creamy peanut butter**

1½ **tablespoons hoisin sauce**

1 **teaspoon chili powder**

8 **large Bibb lettuce leaves**

1 **carrot, grated**

½ **cup shredded red cabbage**

1. In a medium nonstick skillet, heat the oil over medium-high heat. Cook the pork for 5 minutes, or until no longer pink.

2. In a small bowl, stir together the peanut butter, hoisin sauce, and chili powder and add it to the skillet. Stir, cover, and reduce the heat to medium. Cook, stirring once, for 3 minutes, or until the flavors have melded.

3. Overlap 2 lettuce leaves, making 1 larger leaf, and spread one-quarter of the pork filling along the bottom edge. Sprinkle with a quarter of the carrot and cabbage and roll like a burrito. Repeat with the remaining ingredients.

Nutrition (per serving) • 295 calories, 28 g protein, 14 g carbohydrates, 3 g fiber, 7 g sugars, 15 g fat, 3 g saturated fat, 344 mg sodium

Black Bean Burgers over Mexicali Slaw

VEGETARIAN

Make your own veggie burger for a tasty high-protein, low-fat meal. Serve over a veggie-packed Mexicali slaw for a light, fresh dish so tasty that it'll make you glad it comes with 2 portions.

Prep time: 5 minutes

Total time: 20 minutes

Makes 2 servings

1 medium yellow onion

2 tablespoons rolled oats

2 cloves garlic

1 can (15½ ounces) black beans, rinsed and drained

1 teaspoon ground cumin

1 teaspoon grated lime zest

Kosher salt and ground black pepper

1 teaspoon olive oil

¼ cup low-fat plain yogurt

2 tablespoons store-bought salsa

2 cups coleslaw mix

¼ cup corn kernels

1 jalapeño chile pepper, chopped (seeded for less heat)

2 tablespoons chopped cilantro

1. In a food processor, pulse together half the onion, the oats, and garlic until finely chopped. Add the beans, cumin, lime zest, and a pinch of salt and black pepper. Form the mixture into four ½"-thick patties.

2. In a medium nonstick skillet, heat the oil over medium heat until shimmering. Cook the patties for 8 minutes, turning once, or until golden on both sides.

3. Meanwhile, in a medium bowl, combine the yogurt and salsa. Thinly slice the remaining onion and add it to the bowl with the coleslaw, corn, and jalapeño pepper. Toss well to combine.

4. Serve the burgers over the slaw and sprinkle with the cilantro.

Nutrition (per serving) • 233 calories, 12 g protein, 41 g carbohydrates, 11 g fiber, 9 g sugars, 4 g fat, 1 g saturated fat, 765 mg sodium

Broiled Lamb with Charred Asparagus and Leeks

GLUTEN-FREE

Lamb chop lollipops don't come on a stick—they're a special cut of lamb with a long bone that adds a ton of flavor when left in for cooking. If you're not sure what to look for, ask the butcher at your grocery store for help, since your store might label them differently or keep them in the back.

Prep time: 5 minutes

Total time: 20 minutes

Makes 1 serving

4 spears asparagus, trimmed and halved

1 leek, white and light green parts only, quartered

2 teaspoons olive oil, divided

Kosher salt and ground black pepper

½ teaspoon chopped fresh rosemary

1 small clove garlic, minced

3 lamb chop lollipops

1. Preheat the oven to 450°F. In a cast-iron skillet, toss the asparagus, leek, 1 teaspoon of the oil, and a pinch of salt and pepper. Roast for 8 minutes, or until the vegetables are tender.

2. Meanwhile, in a small bowl, combine the remaining 1 teaspoon oil with the rosemary and garlic. Spread all over the lamb chops and season with salt and pepper.

3. Remove the skillet from the oven, push the vegetables to the edges, and place the lamb chops in the center. Turn the oven on to broil and cook for 5 minutes, turning the lamb chops once, until the vegetables are charred and a thermometer inserted in the center of a chop registers 160°F for medium doneness.

Nutrition (per serving) • 432 calories, 44 g protein, 17 g carbohydrates, 3 g fiber, 5 g sugars, 21 g fat, 5.5 g saturated fat, 391 mg sodium

Baked Coconut Shrimp

Crispy shrimp is a delicious meal, but it's usually deep-fried and filled with fat—a shame, because on its own, shrimp is one of the healthiest forms of protein out there! By baking our shrimp instead of frying, you'll get the same great crunch without the excess fat.

Prep time: 5 minutes

Total time: 20 minutes

Makes 2 servings

¼ **cup panko bread crumbs**

¼ **cup unsweetened coconut flakes (or shredded coconut)**

⅛ **teaspoon ground red pepper**

⅛ **teaspoon chili powder**

2 tablespoons all-purpose flour

1 egg white, beaten

12 large shrimp, peeled and deveined

2 tablespoons sweet chili sauce

2 tablespoons pineapple or mango jam or preserves

1. Preheat the oven to 425°F. Line a baking sheet with foil or parchment paper and coat with cooking spray.

2. In a medium resealable plastic bag, combine the panko, coconut, pepper, and chili powder. Shake to mix. In separate small dishes, put the flour and beaten egg white.

3. Dredge 4 shrimp at a time first in the flour, followed by a dip in the egg. Place the shrimp in the bag with the panko-coconut mixture and close. Shake until each shrimp is completely coated. Transfer the shrimp to the baking sheet. Repeat with the remaining shrimp.

4. Lightly coat the shrimp with cooking spray and bake for 10 minutes, or until they are firm to the touch and the coconut begins to brown.

5. Meanwhile, in a small saucepan or microwaveable bowl, combine the chili sauce and jam. Heat over medium-low heat for 5 minutes, or microwave on high power for 30 seconds, until the jam has melted. Stir to combine, and serve with the shrimp.

Nutrition (per serving) • 242 calories, 9 g protein, 32 g carbohydrates, 2 g fiber, 19 g sugars, 8 g fat, 6 g saturated fat, 389 mg sodium

Orange Chicken and Broccoli Stir-Fry

GLUTEN-FREE

We all have those nights when we just *crave* Chinese delivery. For nights like that, turn to this recipe, which gives you all of the flavors you love from takeout, without the high saturated fat and sodium.

Prep time: 10 minutes

Total time: 20 minutes

Makes 2 servings

¼ **cup fresh orange juice**

1 tablespoon reduced-sodium soy sauce

1 tablespoon orange marmalade

1 teaspoon cornstarch

2 tablespoons canola oil

½ **pound chicken tenders, trimmed and cut into 1" pieces**

2 scallions, sliced

1 clove garlic, minced

1½ **teaspoons minced fresh ginger**

Pinch of crushed red-pepper flakes

¼ **cup reduced-sodium chicken broth**

1 pound broccoli crowns, chopped into florets

½ **red bell pepper, thinly sliced**

1. In a small bowl, stir together the orange juice, soy sauce, marmalade, and cornstarch. Set aside.

2. In a wok or large nonstick skillet, heat the oil over medium-high heat. Cook the chicken, stirring frequently, for 2 minutes, or until no longer pink. With a slotted spoon, remove the chicken to a plate. Add the scallions, garlic, ginger, and red-pepper flakes to the wok and toss together.

3. Reduce the heat to medium. Add the broth and broccoli to the wok. Cover and cook for 2 minutes. Increase the heat to high and add the bell pepper. Cook, stirring frequently, for 2 minutes, or until the broth evaporates and the vegetables are tender-crisp. Stir the reserved sauce and add to the wok along with the chicken. Cook, stirring constantly, for 2 minutes, or until the sauce thickens and the chicken is heated through.

Nutrition (per serving) • 375 calories, 34 g protein, 30 g carbohydrates, 7 g fiber, 14 g sugars, 16 g fat, 1 g saturated fat, 593 mg sodium

Honey-Cayenne Grilled Pork Chops

GLUTEN-FREE

To prep this recipe in advance, pre-make the spice seasoning mix. Then when it's time to make dinner, just sprinkle the seasoning on the pork chop, and you're ready to cook! You can also make extra spice mix and use it on any other protein you want to cook.

Prep time: 5 minutes

Total time: 20 minutes

Makes 2 servings

1 teaspoon garlic powder

1 teaspoon onion powder

1 teaspoon ancho chili powder or New Mexican red chili powder

1 teaspoon ground red (cayenne) pepper

¼ teaspoon kosher salt

¼ teaspoon ground black pepper

2 pork chops (1" thick)

2 tablespoons honey

1. In a small bowl, combine the garlic powder, onion powder, chili powder, red pepper, salt, and black pepper. Lightly coat the pork chops all over with cooking spray and season both sides with the spice mixture. Drizzle the honey evenly over both sides.

2. Preheat a grill or grill pan to medium-high heat. Grill the chops for 10 to 14 minutes, turning once, or until a thermometer inserted in the center registers 160°F. Let the chops rest for 5 minutes before serving.

Nutrition (per serving) • 303 calories, 40 g protein, 21 g carbohydrates, 1 g fiber, 18 g sugars, 7 g fat, 2 g saturated fat, 397 mg sodium

Maple, Bourbon, and Mustard–Glazed Salmon with Slaw

GLUTEN-FREE

The bourbon in this recipe is optional, but we don't recommend skipping it. If you don't regularly keep bourbon around, pick up one of the small shot bottles sold at liquor stores. The alcohol will cook off when you simmer the sauce, but the yummy oaky flavor of the bourbon will stay in the sauce.

Prep time: 5 minutes

Total time: 20 minutes

Makes 2 servings

2 tablespoons Dijon mustard

1½ tablespoons maple syrup

1 tablespoon olive oil

1 tablespoon bourbon or whiskey (optional)

1 tablespoon white wine vinegar

1½ cups coleslaw mix

2 skin-on salmon fillets (about 6 ounces each)

Kosher salt and ground black pepper

1. In a small saucepan, combine the mustard, maple syrup, oil, and bourbon or whiskey (if using). Bring to a simmer over medium heat, stirring occasionally, and cook for 1 minute. Remove from the heat and cool slightly.

2. Transfer 1 tablespoon of the glaze to a large bowl, whisk with the vinegar, and toss with the coleslaw mix.

3. Preheat a grill or grill pan to medium heat. Lightly season the salmon with salt and pepper and lay the salmon, skin side down, on the grill. Cook, covered, for 3 minutes, or until nearly opaque. Brush with the remaining glaze and cook for 2 to 4 minutes, or until the fish flakes. Serve with the slaw.

Nutrition (per serving) • 481 calories, 35 g protein, 16 g carbohydrates, 1 g fiber, 12 g sugars, 30 g fat, 6 g saturated fat, 592 mg sodium

Yogurt and Parmesan Fettuccine Alfredo

VEGETARIAN

Fettuccine Alfredo is total comfort food, and usually it's packed with fat and calories when you order it from a restaurant. We've slimmed it down in this recipe, but not too much. We still kept the healthy fat of full-fat Greek yogurt and plenty of Parmesan cheese, and added grated lemon zest and fresh herbs for zippy flavor.

Prep time: 5 minutes

Total time: 20 minutes

Makes 2 servings

4 ounces fettuccine

1 teaspoon unsalted butter

1 small clove garlic, minced

¼ cup full-fat plain Greek yogurt

½ cup grated Parmesan cheese

1 teaspoon grated lemon zest

1 tablespoon chopped fresh flat-leaf parsley

Fresh basil, torn, for garnish

1. Prepare the pasta according to package directions. Reserve ¼ cup of the pasta cooking water and drain.

2. In a large skillet, melt the butter over medium heat. Cook the garlic for 1 minute, or until fragrant. Whisk in the yogurt, cheese, lemon zest, and parsley. Add the fettuccine to the skillet and toss to coat, adding reserved pasta water as necessary to thin the sauce. Garnish with basil and serve.

Nutrition (per serving) • 342 calories, 19 g protein, 45 g carbohydrates, 2 g fiber, 5 g sugars, 10 g fat, 6 g saturated fat, 271 mg sodium

Cashew and Pepper Stir-Fry

VEGETARIAN | PACK FOR LUNCH

Vegetable stir-fry is a perfect lunch or dinner for days when you want something hearty but light. Pack this for lunch with the cashews on top and enjoy the second-day flavors of the vegetables after they've marinated overnight in the sauce. Replace the honey with maple syrup to make the recipe vegan.

Prep time: 10 minutes

Total time: 20 minutes

Makes 2 servings

3 tablespoons reduced-sodium soy sauce

1 tablespoon seasoned rice vinegar

2 teaspoons honey

2 teaspoons cornstarch

2 teaspoons vegetable oil

1 piece (1½″) fresh ginger, peeled and cut into matchsticks

2 cloves garlic, minced

1 large red bell pepper, sliced

1 medium red onion, sliced into ½″ wedges

1 cup snap peas, trimmed

6 tablespoons roasted cashews

1 tablespoon sliced chives, for serving

1. In a small bowl, stir together the soy sauce, vinegar, honey, and cornstarch. Set aside.

2. In a wok or large nonstick skillet, heat the oil over high heat. Cook the ginger and garlic for 1 minute, or until lightly browned. Add the pepper, onion, and snap peas and cook, stirring occasionally, for 3 minutes, or until tender-crisp.

3. Add the reserved sauce mixture and cook for 30 seconds, or until slightly thickened. Toss to combine and serve topped with the cashews and chives.

Nutrition (per serving) • 313 calories, 8 g protein, 35 g carbohydrates, 5 g fiber, 15 g sugars, 17 g fat, 3 g saturated fat, 811 mg sodium

TAKE YOUR TIME

Seared Steak and Roasted Veggie Bowl

PACK FOR LUNCH

Great chefs say that each bite of a meal should combine every single element on the plate. By layering the components of this recipe in a bowl, you guarantee that every bite you take will include a little bit of barley, steak, and roasted veggies.

Prep time: 10 minutes

Total time: 30 minutes

Makes 2 servings

½ cup barley

½ cup (3 ounces) Brussels sprouts, halved

½ cup chopped sweet potato

½ cup cauliflower florets

½ cup sliced beets

1 teaspoon + 1 tablespoon extra-virgin olive oil, divided

6 ounces skirt steak

Kosher salt and ground black pepper

3 tablespoons chopped fresh parsley + more for serving

3 tablespoons chopped fresh dill + more for serving

1 small shallot, finely chopped

2 tablespoons fresh lemon juice

1. Preheat the oven to 425°F. Prepare the barley according to package directions.

2. Meanwhile, lightly coat a baking sheet with cooking spray and add the Brussels sprouts, sweet potato, and cauliflower. Make a little space on the sheet and add the beets, keeping them separate (otherwise, their color will bleed onto everything else). Roast, turning occasionally, for 20 minutes, or until the vegetables are browned and tender.

3. In a large skillet, heat 1 teaspoon of the oil over medium-high heat. Season the steak with salt and pepper and add to the hot skillet. Cook for 6 to 8 minutes, turning once, or until a thermometer inserted in the center registers 145°F for medium-rare. Transfer to a cutting board and let rest for 5 minutes before slicing against the grain.

4. Stir the parsley, dill, shallot, lemon juice, and remaining 1 tablespoon oil into the cooked barley and season with salt and pepper. Divide the barley between 2 bowls and top each with half of the roasted vegetables, sliced steak, and more herbs, if desired.

Nutrition (per serving) • 493 calories, 27 g protein, 61 g carbohydrates, 12 g fiber, 7 g sugars, 17 g fat, 4 g saturated fat, 604 mg sodium

Blueberry Turkey Burgers

PACK FOR LUNCH

One small change will make all of the difference for this recipe: Instead of conventional blueberries, look for wild blueberries. Wild blueberries work best in this burger because they are smaller and blend better with the turkey.

Prep time: 10 minutes

Total time: 30 minutes

Makes 2 servings

2 teaspoons olive oil

2 medium shallots, thinly sliced

1 teaspoon red wine vinegar

½ pound ground turkey

3 ounces fresh blueberries, preferably wild

1½ tablespoons plain whole wheat bread crumbs

1 teaspoon fresh lemon juice

½ teaspoon Dijon mustard

1 clove garlic, minced

⅛ teaspoon kosher salt

⅛ teaspoon ground black pepper

2 multigrain burger buns

1 ounce Gruyère cheese, coarsely grated

2 small lettuce leaves

2 slices tomato

1. In a medium skillet, heat the oil over medium heat until shimmering. Cook the shallots, stirring, for 8 minutes, or until they begin to soften and color slightly. Reduce the heat to low, cover, and cook, stirring occasionally, for 10 minutes, or until the shallots become dark brown and very soft. (If the pan becomes too dry during cooking, add 1 to 2 tablespoons water.) Stir in the vinegar.

2. Meanwhile, in a large bowl, combine the turkey, blueberries, bread crumbs, lemon juice, mustard, garlic, salt, and pepper. Form into two ¾"-thick patties. Preheat a grill pan over medium-high heat until smoking. Coat with cooking spray. Grill the burgers, turning once, for 8 minutes, or until grill marks form on both sides, a thermometer inserted in the center registers 165°F, and the meat is no longer pink.

3. Toast the buns in a toaster oven or under the broiler.

4. Add the cheese to the burgers, cover, and cook for 1 minute, or until melted. Top the bottom half of each bun with a lettuce leaf, tomato slice, burger, half of the caramelized shallots, and top bun.

Nutrition (per serving) • 399 calories, 32 g protein, 32 g carbohydrates, 3 g fiber, 10 g sugars, 18 g fat, 5 g saturated fat, 390 mg sodium

DELICIOUS AND NUTRITIOUS

BLUEBERRIES | Aging is a beautiful thing, and a diet rich in blueberries ensures that the process is beautiful on the inside and out. As the world's best source of antioxidants, they protect your body against free radicals that damage cell structure.

Apple and Butternut Squash Pasta with Brown Butter–Sage Sauce

GLUTEN-FREE | VEGETARIAN

You can find pre-spiralized vegetables in most grocery store produce sections, but if you want to make these noodles at home and don't have a spiralizer, use a vegetable peeler to make ribbons. To store the unused bottom half of the squash, lay a damp paper towel on the cut side, then store in a resealable plastic bag in the refrigerator. Use the remaining squash in the Butternut Squash and Chard Mini Taco Bites (page 83), Kale Quesadillas (page 95), Butternut Squash Sauce (page 180), Butternut Squash Soufflé (page 217), or Winter Squash Pudding (page 221).

Prep time: 5 minutes

Total time: 25 minutes

Makes 2 servings

1 small (about 2½ pounds) butternut squash, top part cut off and peeled, bottom saved for another use

½ teaspoon olive oil

Kosher salt and ground black pepper

1½ tablespoons unsalted butter

1 tablespoon chopped fresh sage

1 large tart, crisp apple, such as Braeburn, Cripps Pink, Jazz, or Granny Smith

Parmigiano-Reggiano or aged white Cheddar, grated, for serving (optional)

1. Preheat the oven to 400°F. Using a spiralizer or vegetable peeler, make noodles or ribbons out of the top of the squash and cut into 6″ to 8″ lengths. On a baking sheet, toss the squash noodles with the oil and season with ¼ teaspoon each salt and pepper. Roast for 10 minutes, or until tender.

2. Meanwhile, in a large skillet, melt the butter over low heat. When it's no longer foaming, add the sage and cook for 2 minutes, or until the butter turns golden and the sage becomes fragrant. Remove from the heat.

3. Add the butternut squash to the butter in the skillet and toss. Spiralize the apple and toss with the squash in the skillet. Season to taste with more salt and pepper, sprinkle with cheese, if using, and serve immediately.

Nutrition (per serving) • 297 calories, 4 g protein, 55 g carbohydrates, 10 g fiber, 19 g sugars, 10 g fat, 6 g saturated fat, 496 mg sodium

Beef Tenderloin with Spinach Chimichurri

PACK FOR LUNCH

We believe in buying the best versions of ingredients, so if you're already buying beef tenderloin, grass fed is the best choice—it is leaner, tastes better, and is more ethical. So go ahead and splurge a little—the price you pay is going to be only 25 percent of the per-pound price anyway!

Prep time: 10 minutes

Total time: 25 minutes

Makes 1 serving

⅓ **cup quick-cooking barley**

2 tablespoons fresh lime juice (from 1 lime)

2 tablespoons finely chopped baby spinach

4 teaspoons finely chopped cilantro

2 cloves garlic, minced

2 teaspoons olive oil, divided

4 ounces grass-fed beef tenderloin medallion

Kosher salt and ground black pepper

Pinch of ground coriander

1. Prepare the barley according to package directions.

2. In a small bowl, whisk together the lime juice, spinach, cilantro, garlic, and 1 teaspoon of the oil.

3. Heat a small nonstick skillet over medium-high heat. Rub the beef with ½ teaspoon of the oil and sprinkle with a pinch of salt and pepper. Cook the beef, turning it once when a rich brown crust forms on the bottom, for 6 minutes, or until a thermometer inserted in the center registers 145°F for medium-rare. Remove from the skillet and let rest for 5 minutes.

4. Toss the barley with the remaining ½ teaspoon oil and a pinch of coriander and salt. Serve alongside the beef drizzled with the chimichurri.

Nutrition (per serving) • 338 calories, 25 g protein, 21 g carbohydrates, 3 g fiber, 1 g sugars, 18 g fat, 5 g saturated fat, 558 mg sodium

Blackberry Pork Tenderloin

GLUTEN-FREE

Make sure you choose pork tenderloin that is not marinated or brined, and is labeled as natural. Normally, pork tenderloin comes with 2 in a pack; cut in half crosswise for an 8-ounce portion, and freeze the halves separately for future use.

Prep time: 5 minutes

Total time: 30 minutes

Makes 2 servings

½ **pound pork tenderloin**

Kosher salt and ground black pepper

2 teaspoons olive oil, divided

½ **red onion, sliced**

1 container (6 ounces) fresh blackberries, divided

½ **cup grape tomatoes, halved**

¼ **cup pomegranate juice**

1 teaspoon balsamic vinegar

¼ **teaspoon fresh thyme leaves**

1. Preheat the oven to 425°F. Pat the pork dry and season with salt and pepper. In a medium ovenproof skillet, heat 1 teaspoon of the oil over medium-high heat. Brown the pork on all sides, 2 to 3 minutes per side. Place the skillet in the oven and cook for 20 minutes, or until a thermometer inserted in the center registers 145°F in the thickest part of the pork. Let rest for 5 minutes before slicing.

2. Meanwhile, in a medium skillet, heat the remaining 1 teaspoon oil over medium heat. Cook the onion and a pinch of salt and pepper for 5 minutes, or until soft. Add half of the blackberries and all of the tomatoes and cook for 10 minutes, or until they break down. Add the pomegranate juice and vinegar, and bring to a boil. Reduce the heat to a simmer and cook for 3 minutes, or until thickened. Stir in the remaining blackberries. Serve the pork with the sauce, sprinkled with the thyme leaves.

Nutrition (per serving) • 258 calories, 26 g protein, 17 g carbohydrates, 5 g fiber, 11 g sugars, 10 g fat, 2 g saturated fat, 265 mg sodium

Chickpea Chard Eggplant Rolls

VEGAN | GLUTEN-FREE | PACK FOR LUNCH

The "vegan" version of anything is likely to be met with a little bit of doubt—but trust us, this vegan, gluten-free version of the classic eggplant rollatini is its own delicious dish. Try adding marinara sauce before reheating it the second day to trick your tastebuds into thinking you're eating something new.

Prep time: 5 minutes

Total time: 35 minutes

Makes 2 servings

1 small eggplant

Kosher salt

1½ teaspoons olive oil, divided

2 leaves Swiss chard

1 clove garlic, minced

1 can (14½ ounces) diced tomatoes

1 can (14½ ounces) chickpeas, rinsed and drained

½ teaspoon fresh thyme leaves

Ground black pepper

1 tablespoon thinly sliced basil

Lemon wedges, for serving

1. Slice the eggplant lengthwise into six ⅛"-thick slabs and season with salt. In a large nonstick skillet, heat ½ teaspoon of the oil over medium heat. Cook the eggplant slabs for 2 minutes, turning once, or until they are pliable. Set aside on a plate.

2. Remove the leaves from the chard stems and finely chop the stems. Roll the leaves and thinly slice them. Add the remaining 1 teaspoon oil to the skillet with the garlic and cook for 1 minute, or until fragrant. Toss in the stems, leaves, tomatoes, chickpeas, thyme, and a pinch of salt and pepper. Cook, stirring, for 5 minutes, or until the flavors meld.

3. Using a slotted spoon, place some of the chickpea mixture onto the lower edge of each eggplant slab and roll. Nestle each roll, seam side down, into the sauce. Cover and cook for 5 minutes, or until the eggplant is completely tender. Top with the basil and serve with the lemon wedges.

Nutrition (per serving) • 246 calories, 10 g protein, 42 g carbohydrates, 12 g fiber, 11 g sugars, 5 g fat, 0.5 g saturated fat, 604 mg sodium

Kale Pesto Pasta with Meatballs

PACK FOR LUNCH

For a cheaper version of pesto with extra nutrients and its own special flavor, we've replaced the basil with kale. And our simple roasted meatballs come together in a snap for a hearty, but nutritious, meal.

Prep time: 10 minutes

Total time: 35 minutes

Makes 2 servings

4 ounces whole wheat rotini

2 cloves garlic

4 ounces ground pork

1 tablespoon chopped onion

Kosher salt and ground black pepper

½ cup torn kale leaves

1 tablespoon olive oil

1 tablespoon raw almonds

1 tablespoon fresh lemon juice

1. Prepare the pasta according to package directions. Preheat the oven to 425°F. Coat a baking sheet with cooking spray.

2. Meanwhile, mince 1 clove of the garlic. In a medium bowl, combine the pork, onion, the minced garlic, and ¼ teaspoon each salt and pepper. Roll the mixture into 6 meatballs. Place the meatballs on the baking sheet with about 1″ of space around each meatball. Roast, turning once, for 15 minutes, or until browned on the outside and no longer pink on the inside.

3. In a food processor, combine the kale, oil, almonds, lemon juice, and the remaining clove of garlic. Pulse until smooth. Season to taste with salt and pepper, toss with the pasta, and serve with the meatballs.

Nutrition (per serving) • 370 calories, 22 g protein, 47 g carbohydrates, 8 g fiber, 3 g sugars, 12 g fat, 2 g saturated fat, 530 mg sodium

Spring Faux Risotto

VEGETARIAN

Risotto is great—when someone else makes it. We always wilt around the third addition of broth when our stirring arm is finally worn out. That's why we love this faux risotto—replacing the Arborio rice with wheat berries eliminates the need for slowly adding broth. The wheat berries are plump on their own, absorb the broth quickly, and hold up well to the ricotta cheese. Since they take a while to cook, make extra wheat berries, portion into $1/2$ cup servings, and freeze in freezer-safe containers.

Prep time: 5 minutes

Total time: 40 minutes

Makes 1 serving

$1/4$ **cup wheat berries**

1 teaspoon olive oil

1 portobello mushroom cap, gills removed and discarded, cap sliced

1 tablespoon finely chopped shallot

$1/8$ **teaspoon kosher salt**

$1/4$ **cup frozen green peas, thawed**

2 tablespoons low-sodium chicken or vegetable broth

3 tablespoons part-skim ricotta cheese

1 teaspoon grated Parmesan cheese

1 teaspoon chopped fresh dill

1. Prepare the wheat berries according to package directions.

2. In a small skillet, heat the oil over medium heat until shimmering. Cook the mushroom, shallot, and salt, stirring, for 5 minutes, or until the shallot is golden and the mushroom is soft.

3. Stir in the wheat berries, peas, and broth and cook for 2 minutes, or until warmed through.

4. Remove from the heat and stir in the ricotta, Parmesan, and dill.

Nutrition (per serving) • 500 calories, 23 g protein, 82 g carbohydrates, 15 g fiber, 5 g sugars, 10 g fat, 3 g saturated fat, 102 mg sodium

Spicy Chipotle Peach Ribs

GLUTEN-FREE

If you don't have access to an outdoor grill, you can still make these finger-licking ribs. Just make sure you have a lid for your grill pan. If you don't, pull out some foil and fashion a tent over your ribs while they cook. The key is covering them enough that the heat circulates all around the ribs.

Prep time: 5 minutes

Total time: 40 minutes

Makes 2 servings

½ cup frozen peach slices, thawed and chopped

¼ cup ketchup

2 tablespoons apple cider vinegar

1 teaspoon chipotle chile powder

Pinch of black pepper

4 boneless country-style ribs (1 pound, not spare ribs), trimmed

2 teaspoons reduced-sodium taco seasoning

1. Preheat a grill to medium heat. In a small saucepan, combine the peach, ketchup, vinegar, chipotle, and black pepper. Bring to a boil over medium heat. Reduce the heat and simmer, stirring occasionally, for 10 minutes. Transfer to a blender and process until smooth. Transfer half to a small bowl and set aside; transfer the remainder to a separate bowl to use for basting the ribs.

2. Meanwhile, rub the ribs with the taco seasoning. Place the ribs on the grill and baste with the sauce. Close the lid and grill for 5 minutes. Turn the ribs, baste, cover, and grill for 5 minutes. Turn the ribs and grill, covered, for 5 minutes, or until a thermometer inserted in the center of a rib registers 145°F. Remove to a plate, cover with foil, and let rest for 5 minutes. Serve with the reserved sauce (discard basting sauce).

Nutrition (per serving) • 373 calories, 48 g protein, 14 g carbohydrates, 1 g fiber, 11 g sugars, 13 g fat, 5 g saturated fat, 698 mg sodium

Chicken Breasts Stuffed with Cilantro and Walnuts

Make sure you have an instant-read thermometer before cooking stuffed chicken; since your ingredients are coming in contact with the raw chicken, you want to make sure that everything you eat reaches 165°F to ensure any salmonella or bad bacteria has been cooked out before you enjoy this couscous-stuffed chicken breast.

Prep time: 10 minutes

Total time: 45 minutes

Makes 2 servings

2 tablespoons whole wheat couscous

¼ cup cilantro, chopped

2 tablespoons chopped walnuts

2 unsweetened, dried apricots, finely chopped

2 tablespoons finely chopped shallot

½ teaspoon ras el hanout (Moroccan spice)

Kosher salt and ground black pepper

2 boneless, skinless chicken breasts

1 tablespoon olive oil

1. Preheat the oven to 375°F. Prepare the couscous according to package directions. Fluff with a fork, and stir in the cilantro, walnuts, apricots, shallot, ras el hanout, and a pinch of salt and pepper.

2. With a paring knife, cut a lengthwise slit into the side of the thickest part of the chicken breasts, being careful not to poke through the other side. Use the knife to enlarge the pocket. Spoon as much of the couscous mixture into the chicken as you can. Season the chicken with salt and pepper.

3. In a large ovenproof skillet, heat the oil over medium heat. Cook the chicken for 3 minutes, or until golden brown. Carefully turn the chicken and transfer the skillet to the oven. Bake for 7 minutes, or until a thermometer inserted in the thickest portion registers 165°F. Let rest for 5 minutes before serving.

Nutrition (per serving) • 294 calories, 28 g protein, 15 g carbohydrates, 3 g fiber, 3 g sugars, 14 g fat, 2 g saturated fat, 616 mg sodium

Pan-Roasted Chicken with Mushroom and Herb Gravy

ONE PAN

This recipe calls for bone-in, skin-on chicken breasts because they are so much juicier and more flavorful than boneless, skinless breasts and hold up well to roasting in the oven. Plus, the skin will be crispy and delicious from pan searing when it's done.

Prep time: 10 minutes

Total time: 45 minutes

Makes 2 servings

2 teaspoons olive oil

2 sprigs thyme, plus 1 teaspoon chopped fresh thyme

2 bone-in, skin-on chicken breasts (about 1 pound)

Kosher salt and ground black pepper

3 ounces shiitake mushrooms, trimmed and sliced

1 shallot, finely chopped

2 teaspoons all-purpose flour

2 tablespoons white wine

¾ cup low-sodium chicken broth

1. Preheat the oven to 425°F. In a large ovenproof skillet, heat the oil and thyme sprigs over medium-high heat.

2. Season the chicken with ½ teaspoon each salt and pepper. Cook, skin side down, for 4 minutes, or until the skin is crisp and golden. Turn the chicken, transfer the skillet to the oven, and roast for 20 minutes, or until a thermometer inserted in the thickest portion registers 165°F. Carefully remove the skillet from the oven, transfer the chicken to a platter, and cover to keep warm.

3. Place the skillet over medium-high heat and add the mushrooms. Cook for 5 minutes, adding 1 to 2 tablespoons broth if the skillet seems dry, or until the mushrooms are tender. Add the shallot and cook for 3 minutes, or until softened. Stir in the flour and cook for 1 minute. Add the wine, scraping the bottom of the pan with a wooden spoon, and cook until the wine evaporates and only 2 tablespoons of wine remain. Add remaining broth and cook for 3 minutes, or until the mixture thickens. Stir in the chopped thyme, season to taste with salt and pepper, and serve over the chicken.

Nutrition (per serving) • 266 calories, 34 g protein, 10 g carbohydrates, 2 g fiber, 3 g sugars, 9 g fat, 1.5 g saturated fat, 685 mg sodium

Trout Ratatouille *en Papillote*

GLUTEN-FREE | ONE PAN

This recipe is great for two main reasons aside from its delicious flavors and taste: It's an impressive meal to cook for someone, and if you wrap the parchment tight enough, there's practically zero cleanup. Count us in!

Prep time: 25 minutes

Total time: 35 minutes

Makes 2 servings

2 trout fillets (about 4 ounces each)

Kosher salt and ground black pepper

1 small zucchini, thinly sliced

1 small yellow squash, thinly sliced

1 small eggplant, thinly sliced

1 Roma tomato, thinly sliced

1 tablespoon olive oil, divided

2 teaspoons chopped fresh thyme

Fresh basil leaves

1. Preheat the oven to 375°F. Cut 2 pieces of parchment paper, each measuring approximately 12" x 18", and lay them on a clean work surface. Fold each in half crosswise, then open and lay flat.

2. Lightly season the trout on both sides with salt and pepper. Divide the vegetables among the parchment, shingling them in alternating layers on 1 side of the fold. Drizzle with half of the oil and sprinkle with some of the thyme and salt and pepper to taste. Lay a fillet on top of the vegetables and drizzle with the remaining oil and a sprinkling of thyme. Fold over the parchment and form a half-moon shape: Beginning at 1 corner, make small overlapping pleats all the way around to seal the edges completely.

3. Transfer the packets to a baking sheet and bake for 10 minutes, or until the parchment puffs up and browns lightly.

4. Immediately place a packet on each of 2 plates and use kitchen shears to cut open the packets at the table. Top with the basil.

Nutrition (per serving) • 282 calories, 26 g protein, 12 g carbohydrates, 5 g fiber, 7 g sugars, 15 g fat, 2 g saturated fat, 192 mg sodium

Pan-Seared Pork Chops and Spiced Apples

GLUTEN-FREE

Pork chops and applesauce are a classic for a reason—the flavors of pork and apple go together beautifully. This recipe adds a tiny bit of pumpkin pie spice, so it's great for when you want a meal that really tastes like fall.

Prep time: 5 minutes

Total time: 35 minutes

Makes 2 servings

2 bone-in pork chops (¾" thick)

½ teaspoon kosher salt

½ teaspoon ground black pepper

1 tablespoon unsalted butter

1 tablespoon olive oil

2 Pink Lady or Honeycrisp apples, halved, cored, peeled, and cut into 1" wedges

1 teaspoon pumpkin pie spice

¼ cup low-sodium chicken broth

2 tablespoons thinly sliced chives

1. Preheat the oven to 400°F. Season the pork chops with the salt and pepper. In a large ovenproof skillet, preferably cast iron, heat the butter and oil over medium-high heat. Sear the pork chops for 8 minutes, turning once, or until a golden crust forms on each side. Transfer to a plate.

2. Reduce the heat to medium, add the apples and pumpkin pie spice to the skillet, and stir to combine. Add the chicken broth, stirring with a wooden spoon to scrape up any of the brown bits, and cook for 2 minutes, or until the apples begin to soften. Nestle the pork chops back in the skillet. Transfer to the oven and roast for 8 minutes, or until the apples are tender and a thermometer inserted in the center of a chop registers 145°F.

3. Remove from the oven and let rest for 10 minutes before sprinkling with the chives and serving.

Nutrition (per serving) • 425 calories, 38 g protein, 24 g carbohydrates, 4 g fiber, 16 g sugars, 20 g fat, 4 g saturated fat, 399 mg sodium

DESSERTS

AFTER ALL OF THE WORK YOU'VE PUT INTO PLANNING, PREPPING, AND making delicious meals for yourself, you deserve a treat! In moderation, a little indulgence for your sweet tooth can be a great thing and can keep the late-night cravings at bay!

Dessert is where cookbooks and online recipes let down single cooks the most. Not only is making a batch of two dozen cookies for one person wasteful, it leads to lots of unnecessary snacking. The goal is a little sweet treat, not a day's worth of calories in a pan of brownies. And sorry, but there's no way we're pulling out (or buying) an ice cream maker to home-churn a half cup of the sweet stuff.

For long days, when dinner happens at 9:00 p.m. and you need a little sugar to treat your stressed-out brain, our **Prep It Ahead** recipes are perfect. Most of the time you know when those days are coming (quarterly meetings, any-one?), and a premade treat is the perfect gift to your future self. If you were blindsided by one of those days, however, our **Throw It Together** recipes will let you treat yourself in a snap, with just a few simple ingredients.

But then there are the nights when plans were cancelled, or an awards show is on TV. You've cooked delicious, healthy meals all day, and the urge to keep your apron on and play baker is strong. For those nights, we love our **Take Your Time** desserts. We think that after a few attempts, you'll find that making a soufflé is almost as much fun as eating it! And with these nutrition-conscious recipes, you won't even have to make a guilty run to the gym the next day!

Aloha Bowl

VEGAN | GLUTEN-FREE | ONE PAN

Prep this treat ahead by toasting the macadamia nuts and the coconut chips in a dry skillet over medium heat for 5 minutes, or just until they take on color, and portion the frozen fruit in a container. If macadamia nuts are out of your price range, cashews make a good substitute. Store nuts and coconut in the refrigerator for a longer shelf life.

Prep time: 5 minutes

Total time: 10 minutes

Makes 1 serving

½ **frozen banana, cut into chunks**

⅓ **cup frozen pineapple or mango chunks**

2 tablespoons unsweetened almond milk + more as needed

2 tablespoons toasted macadamia nuts, coarsely chopped

2 tablespoons toasted coconut chips

1 teaspoon honey (optional)

In a blender, combine the banana, pineapple or mango, and almond milk. Pulse and blend, adding more almond milk as needed, until the mixture reaches a thick, soft-serve consistency. Pour into a chilled bowl and top with the nuts, coconut chips, and honey (if using). Serve immediately.

Nutrition (per serving) • 289 calories, 3 g protein, 27 g carbohydrates, 5 g fiber, 15 g sugars, 21 g fat, 8.5 g saturated fat, 86 mg sodium

Chocolate Citrus Ricotta Pot

VEGETARIAN | GLUTEN-FREE

This dessert, made through step 1, can be stored for up to 4 days in the refrigerator. So prep ahead by making it in advance and storing, covered, in the refrigerator until ready to eat. Use leftover ricotta in the Portobello "Bacon" and Eggs (page 44), Maple Ricotta Cream (page 57), or Ricotta, Lemon, and Basil Stuffed Cherry Tomatoes (page 76).

Prep time: 5 minutes

Total time: 5 minutes

Makes 1 serving

1½ **tablespoons semisweet chocolate chips**

¼ **teaspoon grated lemon or orange zest**

Pinch of kosher salt

⅓ **cup part-skim ricotta cheese**

2 **tablespoons puffed brown rice cereal**

1 **teaspoon cacao nibs, coarsely chopped**

1. Place the chocolate in a microwaveable bowl and microwave on high power in 20-second intervals, stirring between each interval, until the chocolate is melted. Stir in the zest and salt. Fold in the ricotta until completely combined.

2. To serve, top the ricotta mixture with the cereal and cacao nibs.

Nutrition (per serving) • 230 calories, 11 g protein, 19 g carbohydrates, 2 g fiber, 10 g sugars, 14 g fat, 8 g saturated fat, 251 mg sodium

Pear-Ginger Muffins

VEGETARIAN | FREEZER FRIENDLY

Try using whole wheat flour instead of all-purpose to bump up the fiber in these muffins. Once they are cool, you can store the muffins in an airtight container at room temperature for up to 3 days or freeze them in a freezer-safe storage bag for an easy grab-and-go snack or dessert.

Prep time: 10 minutes

Total time: 35 minutes +
cooling time

Makes 12

2 cups all-purpose flour

1 tablespoon baking powder

1 cup fat-free plain yogurt

⅓ cup firmly packed brown sugar

⅓ cup vegetable oil

2 eggs, lightly beaten

1 teaspoon grated fresh ginger

2 large pears, halved, peeled, cored, and shredded

¼ cup chopped crystallized ginger

1. Preheat the oven to 400°F. Line a 12-cup muffin pan with paper liners and coat lightly with cooking spray.

2. In a large bowl, combine the flour and baking powder. In a separate bowl, whisk together the yogurt, brown sugar, oil, eggs, and fresh ginger. Add to the dry ingredients and stir until moistened. Fold in the pears and crystallized ginger.

3. Divide the batter among the muffin cups, filling each about two-thirds full. Bake for 18 to 20 minutes, or until golden on top and a tooth pick inserted in the center of a muffin comes out clean. Cool for 5 minutes in the pan before transferring the muffins to a rack to cool completely.

Nutrition (per muffin) • 212 calories, 5 g protein, 33 g carbohydrates, 2 g fiber, 14 g sugars, 7g fat, 0.5 g saturated fat, 152 mg sodium

Spicy Peanut Butter Cookies

VEGETARIAN | GLUTEN-FREE | FREEZER FRIENDLY

There's no need to eat these cookies right out of the oven—you can store cooled cookies in an airtight container at room temperature for up to 1 week or freeze them, individually wrapped in plastic wrap, for up to 2 months. Let them defrost at room temperature for 30 minutes before eating.

Prep time: 5 minutes

Total time: 35 minutes

Makes 18

1 cup natural peanut butter

¾ cup firmly packed brown sugar

1 egg

4 teaspoons chili powder

¾ teaspoon baking soda

Pinch of kosher salt

18 large dark chocolate chips

1. Preheat the oven to 350°F. Line a baking sheet with parchment paper.

2. In a food processor, combine the peanut butter, brown sugar, egg, chili powder, baking soda, and salt. Process until combined and smooth.

3. Scoop out balls (about 2 tablespoons each) and place on the baking sheet. Press with the tines of a fork. Bake for 10 minutes, or until lightly browned around the edges.

4. Remove from the oven and press a chocolate chip into the center of each cookie. Let the cookies rest on the baking sheet for 2 minutes, then remove to a rack to cool completely.

Nutrition (per cookie) • 140 calories, 4 g protein, 14 g carbohydrates, 1 g fiber, 11 g sugars, 8 g fat, 1 g saturated fat, 121 mg sodium

Chocolate Candy Coins

VEGAN | GLUTEN-FREE | 5 INGREDIENTS OR FEWER

You won't believe how simple it is to make this homemade version of nonpareils. To prep it ahead, chop the chocolate ahead of time and store, covered, at room temperature until you're ready to make the candies.

Prep time: 2 minutes

Total time: 15 minutes

Makes 8 servings
---

4 ounces dark chocolate (70% cacao), chopped

1 tablespoon round sprinkles

1. Line a plate or baking sheet with parchment paper.

2. Place the chocolate in a microwaveable bowl and microwave on high power in 30-second intervals, stirring between each interval, until melted. Pour quarter-size circles onto the sheet of parchment.

3. Top with the sprinkles and refrigerate for 10 minutes before peeling off the parchment. Store in an airtight container in the refrigerator for up to 2 months.

Nutrition (per serving) • 37 calories, 0 g protein, 3 g carbohydrates, 1 g fiber, 2 g sugars, 3 g fat, 1 g saturated fat, 1 mg sodium

Broiled Pineapple with Boozy Yogurt

VEGETARIAN | GLUTEN-FREE | 5 INGREDIENTS OR FEWER

The teaspoon of rum in this dessert adds tropical flavor to the yogurt, but since it doesn't cook off, make sure to share it only with people over 21. Freeze any leftover pineapple, whether fresh or canned, to use in the Aloha Bowl (page 208) or Hawaiian Pizza Sandwich (page 109).

Prep time: 5 minutes

Total time: 15 minutes

Makes 1 serving

2 pineapple wedges

2 teaspoons firmly packed brown sugar

2 tablespoons 2% plain Greek yogurt

1 teaspoon rum

3 small mint leaves

1. Heat the broiler to high. Place the pineapple on a baking sheet and top each wedge with 1 teaspoon of the brown sugar. Broil for 6 minutes, or until the pineapple is brown and bubbly.

2. In a small bowl, stir together the yogurt and rum. Serve the pineapple topped with the yogurt and mint.

Nutrition (per serving) • 122 calories, 3 g protein, 25 g carbohydrates, 2 g fiber, 21 g sugars, 1 g fat, 0.5 g saturated fat, 13 mg sodium

Lemon Whip

VEGETARIAN | GLUTEN-FREE | 5 INGREDIENTS OR FEWER | ONE PAN

This light treat is similar to a milkshake, without all of the fat and calories. If you don't typically keep seltzer water on hand, just buy a single can so you're not left with a large bottle that will go flat.

Prep time: 5 minutes

Total time: 5 minutes

Makes 1 serving

¾ **cup seltzer water**

½ **cup ice cubes**

½ **cup vanilla frozen yogurt**

2½ **tablespoons fresh lemon juice**

1 **lemon wedge, for garnish**

In a blender, combine the seltzer water, ice cubes, frozen yogurt, and lemon juice. Blend until smooth. Serve in a frosted glass with the lemon wedge and a straw.

Nutrition (per serving) • 108 calories, 2 g protein, 20 g carbohydrates, 0 g fiber, 14 g sugars, 3 g fat, 1.5 g saturated fat, 39 mg sodium

Minty Cantaloupe Salad

VEGAN | GLUTEN-FREE | 5 INGREDIENTS OR FEWER | ONE PAN

If you can't wait 20 minutes, go ahead and eat this salad right away. But if you can, the wait time in the refrigerator allows the flavors to meld.

Prep time: 5 minutes

Total time: 20 minutes

Makes 1 serving

½ **small cantaloupe, rind removed**

1 **tablespoon sweet white wine, such as Moscato, Riesling, or rosé**

1 **teaspoon chopped fresh mint**

Use a vegetable peeler to strip ½ cup of ribbons from the cantaloupe. Transfer to a small bowl and toss with the wine and mint. Refrigerate for at least 15 to 20 minutes before eating.

Nutrition (per serving) • 39 calories, 1 g protein, 7 g carbohydrates, 1 g fiber, 6 g sugars, 0 g fat, 0 g saturated fat, 13 mg sodium

Chocolate-Dipped Cherries or Oranges

VEGAN | GLUTEN-FREE | ONE PAN | 5 INGREDIENTS OR FEWER>

This dessert looks like it came straight from a confectionary, but it requires minimal effort and only a little microwaving! Make sure you buy unsweetened coconut flakes; the cherries or orange segments have plenty of their own sweetness.

Prep time: 2 minutes

Total time: 15 minutes

Makes 1 serving

1 ounce dark chocolate, chopped or broken

4 whole cherries with stems, or 1 mandarin orange, peeled (all pits removed) and separated

1 heaping teaspoon unsweetened coconut flakes

1. Place the chocolate in a microwaveable bowl and microwave on high power in 15-second increments, stirring after each increment, until smooth.

2. Dip a cherry or half of an orange segment in the chocolate and place on a plate. Repeat with the remaining fruit. Immediately sprinkle with the coconut flakes. Let set for 10 minutes before eating.

Nutrition (per serving, for cherries) • 112 calories, 1 g protein, 14 g carbohydrates, 2 g fiber, 11 g sugars, 6 g fat, 4 g saturated fat, 4 mg sodium

Nutrition (per serving, for orange) • 138 calories, 2 g protein, 21 g carbohydrates, 3 g fiber, 16 g sugars, 6 g fat, 4 g saturated fat, 6 mg sodium

Frozen Banana and Peanut Butter Ice Cream

VEGAN | GLUTEN-FREE | 5 INGREDIENTS OR FEWER

This dairy-free imitation of soft-serve ice cream is almost better than the real thing—and it gives you one of your daily servings of fruit! The cherry is optional, but it makes the whole dish feel like a special treat.

Prep time: 5 minutes

Total time: 5 minutes

Makes 1 serving

1 frozen banana, sliced

1 tablespoon natural creamy peanut butter

2 tablespoons dark chocolate chips

1 maraschino cherry (optional)

1. In a blender, blend the banana until finely chopped and icy. Add the peanut butter and blend until creamy, about 30 seconds. Transfer to a bowl.

2. Place the chocolate chips in a microwaveable bowl and microwave on high power for 15 seconds, or until melted. Stir. Drizzle over the ice cream and top with the cherry, if using.

Nutrition (per serving) • 344 calories, 7 g protein, 48 g carbohydrates, 7 g fiber, 28 g sugars, 18 g fat, 8 g saturated fat, 73 mg sodium

KALE SALAD WITH WILD RICE, GRILLED
CHICKEN, AND APPLES | PAGE 144

JICAMA ORANGE SALAD WITH SCALLION AND RADISH | PAGE 132

BLACK BEAN BURRITO SALAD | PAGE 135

TUNA TACOS | PAGE 94

PEACH AND ARUGULA GRILLED CHEESE | PAGE 106

ROASTED VEGGIE SANDWICH | PAGE 114

ROSEMARY-ROASTED VEGETABLES WITH MANCHEGO CHEESE
AND SERRANO HAM | PAGE 173

BLUEBERRY TURKEY BURGERS | PAGE 194

ORANGE CHICKEN AND BROCCOLI STIR-FRY | PAGE 188

**Seared Steak and Roasted
Veggie Bowl | page 193**

PAN-SEARED PORK CHOPS AND SPICED
APPLES | PAGE 205

BAKED COCONUT SHRIMP | PAGE 187

BROILED PINEAPPLE WITH BOOZY YOGURT | PAGE 213

SPICY PEANUT BUTTER COOKIES | PAGE 211

FROZEN BANANA AND PEANUT BUTTER ICE CREAM | PAGE 216

APPLE GALETTE WITH CHÈVRE AND
TAHINI-HONEY DRIZZLE | PAGE 220

Butternut Squash Soufflé

VEGETARIAN | GLUTEN-FREE

You can also make this recipe with pumpkin or sweet potatoes, and you can even make it with leftovers from dinner if your meal had extra pureed squash. But take your puffy, just-from-the-oven soufflé pictures quickly—the puff will start to go down almost immediately after it finishes cooking.

Prep time: 5 minutes

Total time: 40 minutes

Makes 1 serving

½ **cup mashed, cooked butternut squash (from fresh squash, frozen cubes, or canned puree)**

2 **teaspoons honey**

½ **teaspoon vanilla extract**

¼ **teaspoon ground cinnamon**

¼ **teaspoon ground nutmeg**

Pinch of kosher salt

1 **egg, beaten**

1 **tablespoon sliced almonds**

1. Preheat the oven to 325°F.

2. In a bowl, combine the squash, honey, vanilla, cinnamon, nutmeg, and salt. Add the egg and mix together. Pour into an 8- to 10-ounce ramekin and bake for 30 minutes, or until set.

3. Meanwhile, in a dry skillet over medium heat, toast the almonds for 5 minutes, or until they just turn golden.

4. Top the soufflé with the almonds and serve immediately. (The soufflé will start to sink once it's removed from the oven.)

Nutrition (per serving) • 204 calories, 9 g protein, 26 g carbohydrates, 5 g fiber, 12 g sugars, 8 g fat, 2 g saturated fat, 229 mg sodium

Ginger-Poached Pear with Pomegranate

VEGETARIAN

This is a deceptively simple dessert to serve a crowd—just multiply the recipe per person! Poached pears can be refrigerated overnight in their syrup and served cold with the hot, reduced syrup. Use the leftover pomegranate seeds in the Spinach Salad with Pomegranate, Lentils, and Pistachios (page 140), sprinkle them as a garnish for Peanut Butter Pancakes with Pomegranate Syrup (page 42), or freeze them scattered on a plate or baking sheet until frozen, then transferred to a freezer-safe container. For a vegan version, replace the honey with brown sugar or agave.

Prep time: 5 minutes

Total time: 40 minutes

Makes 1 or 2 servings

¼ cup pomegranate juice or red wine

2 teaspoons honey

1 piece (½") ginger, sliced

¾ cup water

1 firm pear, halved, peeled, and cored

2 tablespoons pomegranate seeds

1. In a small saucepan, combine the pomegranate juice or wine, honey, ginger, and water. Bring to a boil. Add the pear, ensuring the halves are covered with the liquid. Reduce the heat and simmer, covered, for 20 minutes, or until the pear is very tender. Transfer the pear to a bowl, cover with foil, and remove and discard the ginger from the liquid.

2. Return the liquid to high heat and cook for 10 minutes, or until syrupy and reduced to about ¼ cup. Pour the liquid over the pear and garnish with the pomegranate seeds.

Nutrition (per serving, for 1) • 197 calories, 1 g protein, 51 g carbohydrates, 6 g fiber, 40 g sugars, 1 g fat, 0 g saturated fat, 18 mg sodium

Nutrition (per serving, for 2) • 99 calories, 1 g protein, 26 g carbohydrates, 3 g fiber, 20 g sugars, 0 g fat, 0 g saturated fat, 9 mg sodium

Honey Lime Cantaloupe Pops

VEGETARIAN | GLUTEN-FREE | 5 INGREDIENTS OR FEWER
FREEZER FRIENDLY | ONE PAN

Ice pop molds can be found at any dollar store in the summer months, or if you're in a pinch, you can use craft store Popsicle sticks and small paper cups. If you have any leftover cantaloupe, use it for Minty Cantaloupe Salad (page 214).

Prep time: 10 minutes

Total time: 15 minutes + freezing time

Makes about 10

4 cups cubed ripe cantaloupe (from a 3- to 4-pound melon)

¼-⅓ cup honey, depending on the ripeness of your melon

¼ cup fresh lime juice

¼ teaspoon kosher salt

¾ cup water

1. In a blender, combine the cantaloupe, ¼ cup of the honey, the lime juice, salt, and water. Blend until completely smooth. Taste and add more honey as needed; you want the base to taste a touch on the sweeter side, as it will taste less sweet after freezing.

2. Transfer to ice pop molds and freeze for 3 hours, or until set. Pops will keep in the freezer for up to 1 month.

Nutrition (per serving) • 49 calories, 1 g protein, 13 g carbohydrates, 1 g fiber, 12 g sugars, 0 g fat, 0 g saturated fat, 59 mg sodium

Apple Galette with Chèvre and Tahini-Honey Drizzle

VEGETARIAN

This dessert is deceptively simple—it's the perfect dish to take when a friend invites you over to dinner and asks you to bring dessert. Or just make it for yourself and enjoy a slice after dinner every night! Store extra tahini in the refrigerator and use it in Baba Ghanoush (page 69), Beet and Dill Hummus (page 72), or Lamb Meatball Skewers with Tahini–Goat Cheese Sauce (page 183).

Prep time: 5 minutes

Total time: 35 minutes

Makes 4 servings

½ an 8-ounce sheet frozen puff pastry, thawed

1 apple, halved, cored, and very thinly sliced

1½ teaspoons tahini

1½ teaspoons honey

½ teaspoon water

2 tablespoons crumbled goat cheese

¼ teaspoon sesame seeds (optional)

1. Preheat the oven to 400°F. Line a baking sheet with parchment paper.

2. Lay the pastry on the parchment. Shingle the apple slices around the pastry in 2 layers, leaving about a 1″ border. Fold up and crimp the edges of the pastry around the apple slices.

3. Bake for 20 minutes, or until the pastry is puffed and golden and the apple slices are tender.

4. Meanwhile, in a small bowl, combine the tahini, honey, and water.

5. Remove the galette from the oven and crumble the goat cheese over the top. Drizzle with the tahini-honey mixture, then garnish with the sesame seeds, if using.

6. Serve warm or let the galette cool completely before storing in an airtight container in the refrigerator for up to 4 days. Gently reheat in a warm oven.

Nutrition (per serving) • 170 calories, 3 g protein, 19 g carbohydrates, 2 g fiber, 8 g sugars, 9 g fat, 3 g saturated fat, 153 mg sodium

Winter Squash Pudding

VEGETARIAN

Homemade pudding is shockingly easy to make and so much tastier than the instant version. You can use canned puree if you like, or make your own in advance: Just halve a small pumpkin, remove the seeds, wrap each half in foil, and roast on a baking sheet at 350°F for 35 to 45 minutes, or until the flesh is very tender. Then scoop the flesh into a food processor and puree until smooth. If you use butternut squash, repurpose it in various recipes during the week, including the Butternut-Maple Amaranth Porridge (page 43) or Butternut Squash Sauce (page 180).

Prep time: 5 minutes

Total time: 15 minutes + cooling time

Makes 2 servings

1 cup 1% milk (or other milk)

¼ cup sugar

1 egg

1½ tablespoons cornstarch

Pinch of kosher salt

½ cup canned or homemade pumpkin, sweet potato, or butternut squash puree

½ teaspoon vanilla extract

⅛ teaspoon ground cinnamon

1. In a medium saucepan, whisk together the milk, sugar, egg, cornstarch, and salt. Cook over medium-high heat, whisking constantly, for 6 to 8 minutes, or until the mixture thickens and bubbles. Reduce the heat to low and cook, whisking, for 1 minute.

2. Remove the pan from the heat and quickly whisk in the puree, vanilla, and cinnamon. Pour the mixture through a mesh sieve set over a bowl. Press plastic wrap on the surface of the pudding to prevent a skin from forming and refrigerate for 3 hours, or until cold, or up to 3 days.

3. To serve, whisk again until smooth and divide between 2 bowls.

Nutrition (per serving) • 232 calories, 8 g protein, 42 g carbohydrates, 2 g fiber, 33 g sugars, 4 g fat, 1.5 g saturated fat, 153 mg sodium

PART

3

Plans
&
Resources

10 MEAL PLANS FOR EVERY KIND OF WEEK

Every week is a new and unique challenge, and it's incredibly important to plan your meals around your life and your schedule (instead of planning your week around your meals). This is one of the best parts of cooking for one or two—you can craft a meal plan based solely on what you want and need! We gave you tips on making your own plan on page 6, but here we've made a collection of plans for you. Each plan includes tips on what to prep on Sunday. We've included options for every meal of the week, so be sure to skip buying ingredients for the meals you'll instead be eating out.

Busy at Work Week

We all have these weeks—a million meetings, maybe a big project deadline or a late-night event that threatens to throw everything out of whack. These are the weeks when a solid meal plan, with a lot of recipes that can be prepped in advance, will be your saving grace. Premade salads, simple snacks, and wholesome dinners are on the menu this week, with some fun weekend recipes to treat yourself.

SUNDAY PREP PLAN

- Bake a batch of Blueberry, Flax, and Cardamom Muffins *(page 31)*.

- Make the Rosemary-Apricot "Jam" *(page 27)*.

- Make Pumpkin Seed Clusters *(page 70)* for snacking all week long.

- Make the Bulgur Salad with Cucumber and Tomatoes *(page 117)* and the Light and Lemony Chicken Salad *(page 119)*.

- Make the Roasted Cherry Tomatoes *(page 68)*.

- Make the Apple and Chicken Curry *(page 171)*.

- Make the pesto for Hearty Greens Pesto Pasta *(page 172)*.

- Make the Rosemary-Roasted Vegetables with Manchego Cheese and Serrano Ham *(page 173)*.

- Make the Chocolate Citrus Ricotta Pot *(page 209)*.

MONDAY

BREAKFAST •
Blueberry, Flax, and Cardamom Muffins *(page 31)*

LUNCH •
Light and Lemony Chicken Salad *(page 119)*

SNACK •
Roasted Cherry Tomatoes *(page 68)*

DINNER •
Apple and Chicken Curry *(page 171)*

TUESDAY

BREAKFAST •
Bagel with Rosemary-Apricot "Jam" *(page 27)* *(You'll use the other half of this bagel on Thursday.)*

LUNCH •
Bulgur Salad with Cucumber and Tomatoes *(page 117)*

SNACK •
Pumpkin Seed Clusters *(page 70)*

DINNER •
Hearty Greens Pesto Pasta *(page 172)*

DESSERT •
Chocolate Citrus Ricotta Pot *(page 209)*

WEDNESDAY

BREAKFAST •
Blueberry, Flax, and Cardamom Muffins *(page 31)*

LUNCH •
Apple and Chicken Curry *(page 171)*

SNACK •
Roasted Cherry Tomatoes *(page 68)*

DINNER •
Rosemary-Roasted Vegetables with Manchego Cheese and Serrano Ham *(page 173)*

THURSDAY	FRIDAY	SATURDAY	SUNDAY
BREAKFAST • **Bagel with Rosemary-Apricot "Jam"** *(page 27)*	BREAKFAST • **Blueberry, Flax, and Cardamom Muffins** *(page 31)*	BREAKFAST • **Goat Cheese and Mint Omelet** *(page 37)*	BREAKFAST • **Steak and Eggs with Watermelon Chimichurri** *(page 41)*
LUNCH • **Light and Lemony Chicken Salad** *(page 119)*	LUNCH • **Bulgur Salad with Cucumber and Tomatoes** *(page 117)*	LUNCH • **Kale Quesadillas** *(page 95)*	LUNCH • **Goat Cheese and Sesame Tartine** *(page 104)*
SNACK • **Pumpkin Seed Clusters** *(page 70)*	SNACK • **Honey Black Pepper Snack Mix** *(page 73)*	SNACK • **Avocado Deviled Eggs** *(page 90)*	SNACK • **Ricotta, Lemon, and Basil Stuffed Cherry Tomatoes** *(page 76)*
DINNER • **Fried Egg Sandwich** *(page 101)*	DINNER • **Udon Soup with Broccoli, Tofu, and Ginger** *(page 156)*	DINNER • **Broiled Steak and Smashed Potatoes** *(page 178)*	DINNER • **Orange Chicken and Broccoli Stir-Fry** *(page 188)*
DESSERT • **Chocolate Citrus Ricotta Pot** *(page 209)*			

Get Fit Week

The goal for this week isn't to diet or eat reduced calories—it's to power your body with lots of protein and complex carbohydrates so you can go for runs, climb that mountain, or hold your pose longer in yoga. Whatever your fitness goal is, this meal plan is here to support it.

SUNDAY PREP PLAN

- Make smoothie bags.
- Chop vegetables for Waldorf Chicken Salad Cups (page 124) and Thai Beef Salad with Mint (page 134).
- Cook chicken for Waldorf Chicken Salad Cups (page 124).
- Make Harvest Chicken Salad (page 130).
- Make Honey Black Pepper Snack Mix (page 73).

MONDAY

BREAKFAST •
Berry Cobbler Smoothie (page 50)

LUNCH •
Waldorf Chicken Salad Cups (page 124)

SNACK •
Pineapple Ham Tostada (page 78)

DINNER •
Tuna Burger with Miso Mayo (page 176)

TUESDAY

BREAKFAST •
Cherry-Vanilla Smoothie (page 59)

LUNCH •
Harvest Chicken Salad (page 130)

SNACK •
Honey Black Pepper Snack Mix (page 73)

DINNER •
Halibut with Bean Puree (page 177)

WEDNESDAY

BREAKFAST •
Berry Cobbler Smoothie (page 50)

LUNCH •
Asparagus, Tuna, and Chickpea Salad (page 125)

SNACK •
Pineapple Ham Tostada (page 78)

DINNER •
Orange Chicken and Broccoli Stir-Fry (page 188)

THURSDAY	FRIDAY	SATURDAY	SUNDAY
BREAKFAST • **PB&J Smoothie** *(page 59)*	**BREAKFAST •** **Cherry-Vanilla Smoothie** *(page 59)*	**BREAKFAST •** **Egg Baked in Avocado** *(page 45)*	**BREAKFAST •** **Egg Baked in Avocado** *(page 45)*
LUNCH • **Waldorf Chicken Salad Cups** *(page 124)*	**LUNCH •** **Asparagus, Tuna, and Chickpea Salad** *(page 125)*	**LUNCH •** **Thai Beef Salad with Mint** *(page 134)*	**LUNCH •** **Maple, Bourbon, and Mustard–Glazed Salmon with Slaw** *(page 190)*
SNACK • **Honey Black Pepper Snack Mix** *(page 73)*	**SNACK •** **Veggies with Green Goddess Dip** *(page 71)*	**SNACK •** **Honey Black Pepper Snack Mix** *(page 73)*	**SNACK •** **Veggies with Green Goddess Dip** *(page 71)*
DINNER • **Broiled Lamb with Charred Asparagus and Leeks** *(page 186)*	**DINNER •** **Maple, Bourbon, and Mustard–Glazed Salmon with Slaw** *(page 190)*	**DINNER •** **Blackberry Pork Tenderloin** *(page 197)*	**DINNER •** **Thai Beef Salad with Mint** *(page 134)*

Budget Week

Maybe you attended a bachelorette party last weekend or finally bought *that* pair of shoes. It doesn't matter why you want to save a little cash this week; we're here with some inexpensive but delicious options. When saving cash is the name of the game, repeat ingredients often so you can buy large packs and pay less per pound. This week, you'll get a lot of your protein from eggs, chicken, and beans—our favorite low-cost protein superstars.

SUNDAY PREP PLAN

- Make a large batch of oatmeal.
- Cook brown rice for Crispy Garlic Fried Rice *(page 29)*.
- Cook chicken breasts for Buffalo Chicken Sandwich *(page 100)*, Thai Chicken Sandwich *(page 112)*, and Waldorf Chicken Salad Cups *(page 124)*.
- Make Black Bean Dip *(page 67)*.
- Make pesto for Hearty Greens Pesto Pasta *(page 172)*.
- Cook wheat berries for Spring Faux Risotto *(page 200)*.
- Bake a batch of Spicy Peanut Butter Cookies *(page 211)* for desserts.

MONDAY

BREAKFAST •
Oatmeal with Brown Sugar Pineapple Swirl *(page 28)*

LUNCH •
Thai Chicken Sandwich *(page 112)*

SNACK •
Carrots and Black Bean Dip *(page 67)*

DINNER •
Hearty Greens Pesto Pasta *(page 172)*

DESSERT •
Spicy Peanut Butter Cookies *(page 211)*

TUESDAY

BREAKFAST •
Crispy Garlic Fried Rice *(page 29)*

LUNCH •
Waldorf Chicken Salad Cups *(page 124)*

SNACK •
Mashed Pea Tartine *(page 80)*

DINNER •
Black Bean Soup with Mango *(page 155)*

WEDNESDAY

BREAKFAST •
Oatmeal with Brown Sugar Pineapple Swirl *(page 28)*

LUNCH •
Buffalo Chicken Sandwich *(page 100)*

SNACK •
Carrots and Black Bean Dip *(page 67)*

DINNER •
Spring Faux Risotto *(page 200)*

DESSERT •
Spicy Peanut Butter Cookies *(page 211)*

THURSDAY	FRIDAY	SATURDAY	SUNDAY
BREAKFAST • **Crispy Garlic Fried Rice** *(page 29)*	**BREAKFAST •** **Oatmeal with Brown Sugar Pineapple Swirl** *(page 28)*	**BREAKFAST •** **Broiled Grapefruit** *(page 38)*	**BREAKFAST •** **Broiled Grapefruit** *(page 38)*
LUNCH • **Thai Chicken Sandwich** *(page 112)*	**LUNCH •** **Waldorf Chicken Salad Cups** *(page 124)*	**LUNCH •** **French Lentil and Fennel Soup** *(page 148)*	**LUNCH •** **Lentil Hot Pot** *(page 150)*
SNACK • **Mashed Pea Tartine** *(page 80)*	**SNACK •** **Carrots and Black Bean Dip** *(page 67)*	**SNACK •** **Steamed Broccoli with Miso Peanut Butter Dip** *(page 82)*	**SNACK •** **Steamed Broccoli with Miso Peanut Butter Dip** *(page 82)*
DINNER • **Hearty Miso Soup** *(page 160)*	**DINNER •** **Chicken Breasts Stuffed with Cilantro and Walnuts** *(page 202)*	**DINNER •** **Chickpea Chard Eggplant Rolls** *(page 198)*	**DINNER •** **Black Bean and Brussels Sprouts Burritos** *(page 98)*
	DESSERT • **Spicy Peanut Butter Cookies** *(page 211)*		

Super Chef Week

Some weeks you just want to tie on your apron, pull out your chef's knife, and really enjoy cooking. This is your meal plan for that week when you have visitors you want to impress, or when you just need to treat yourself with care. You can do some prep on Sunday, but a lot of these recipes are meant to be cooked from start to finish!

SUNDAY PREP WORK PLAN	MONDAY	TUESDAY	WEDNESDAY
• Cook beets for Beets with Goat Cheese and Chermoula *(page 143)* and Beet and Dill Hummus *(page 72)*. • Make Ultimate Tuna Salad *(page 129)*.	BREAKFAST • **Eggs with Crab and Tomato on Toast** *(page 36)* LUNCH • **Beets with Goat Cheese and Chermoula** *(page 143)* SNACK • **Caramelized Leek Dip with Asparagus** *(page 79)* DINNER • **Shaved Asparagus and Lamb Salad** *(page 133)* DESSERT • **Lemon Whip** *(page 214)*	BREAKFAST • **Goat Cheese and Mint Omelet** *(page 37)* LUNCH • **Ultimate Tuna Salad** *(page 129)* SNACK • **Sliced veggies and Beet and Dill Hummus** *(page 72)* DINNER • **Asparagus Soup with Mustard Croutons** *(page 163)*	BREAKFAST • **Blueberry Muffin Breakfast Parfait** *(page 40)* LUNCH • **Spicy Crab Melt** *(page 102)* SNACK • **Caramelized Leek Dip with Asparagus** *(page 79)* DINNER • **Broiled Lamb with Charred Asparagus and Leeks** *(page 186)* DESSERT • **Chocolate-Dipped Cherries** *(page 215)*

THURSDAY	FRIDAY	SATURDAY	SUNDAY
BREAKFAST •	BREAKFAST •	BREAKFAST •	BREAKFAST •
Eggs with Crab and Tomato on Toast *(page 36)*	**Blueberry Muffin Breakfast Parfait** *(page 40)*	**Poached Egg over Asparagus with Mustard Sauce** *(page 46)*	**Goat Cheese and Mint Omelet** *(page 37)*
LUNCH •	LUNCH •	LUNCH •	LUNCH •
Goat Cheese and Sesame Tartine *(page 104)*	**Ultimate Tuna Salad** *(page 129)*	**Tuna Tacos** *(page 94)*	**Asparagus, Tuna, and Chickpea Salad** *(page 125)*
SNACK •	SNACK •	SNACK •	SNACK •
Sliced veggies and Beet and Dill Hummus *(page 72)*	**Caramelized Leek Dip with Asparagus** *(page 79)*	**Sliced veggies and Beet and Dill Hummus** *(page 72)*	**Blackberry-Corn Salsa** *(page 75)*
DINNER •	DINNER •	DINNER •	DINNER •
Trout Ratatouille en Papillote *(page 204)*	**Lamb Meatball Skewers with Tahini–Goat Cheese Sauce** *(page 183)*	**Pan-Roasted Chicken with Mushroom and Herb Gravy** *(page 203)*	**Blackberry Pork Tenderloin** *(page 197)*
	DESSERT •		
	Butternut Squash Soufflé *(page 217)*		

Detox Week

Do you ever just feel bloated and sluggish? Maybe last week involved a few too many beers and appetizers? We love this plan to detox your body and reinfuse it with lots of great nutrients. This week isn't about losing weight; it's about feeling refreshed and fueled by your diet. This week's recipes include lots of water-based foods to reduce the sodium in your body and very little oil and meat.

SUNDAY PREP PLAN

- Make Walnut Slaw with Cilantro *(page 118)*.
- Make Quick Fridge Pickles *(page 86)*.
- Make Chocolate-Dipped Grapefruit *(page 66)*.
- Slice the vegetables for the Spicy Watermelon Salad *(page 138)*, Creamy Vegetable Soup *(page 165)*, and Seared Steak and Roasted Veggie Bowl *(page 193)*.
- Slice the watermelon and cucumber for the Spicy Cool Mini Watermelon Skewers *(page 77)*.
- Make smoothie bags for the week's smoothies.

MONDAY

BREAKFAST •
Kickin' Green Smoothie *(page 52)*

LUNCH •
Walnut Slaw with Cilantro *(page 118)*

SNACK •
Quick Fridge Pickles *(page 86)*

DINNER •
Udon Soup with Broccoli, Tofu, and Ginger *(page 156)*

TUESDAY

BREAKFAST •
Gingered Winter Greens Smoothie *(page 54)*

LUNCH •
Spicy Watermelon Salad *(page 138)*

SNACK •
Chocolate-Dipped Grapefruit *(page 66)*

DINNER •
Baked Coconut Shrimp *(page 187)*

WEDNESDAY

BREAKFAST •
Peach-Chard Smoothie *(page 60)*

LUNCH •
Walnut Slaw with Cilantro *(page 118)*

SNACK •
Spicy Cool Mini Watermelon Skewers *(page 77)*

DINNER •
Salmon Cakes with Horseradish Sauce *(page 175)*

THURSDAY	FRIDAY	SATURDAY	SUNDAY
BREAKFAST •	**BREAKFAST •**	**BREAKFAST •**	**BREAKFAST •**
Pear-Ginger Smoothie *(page 62)*	**Berry Cobbler Smoothie** *(page 50)*	**Broiled Grapefruit** *(page 38)*	**Broiled Grapefruit** *(page 38)*
LUNCH •	**LUNCH •**	**LUNCH •**	**LUNCH •**
Spicy Watermelon Salad *(page 138)*	**Walnut Slaw with Cilantro** *(page 118)*	**Mashed Pea Tartine** *(page 80)*	**Spinach Salad with Pomegranate, Lentils, and Pistachios** *(page 140)*
SNACK •	**SNACK •**	**SNACK •**	**SNACK •**
Quick Fridge Pickles *(page 86)*	**Chocolate-Dipped Grapefruit** *(page 66)*	**Spicy Cool Mini Watermelon Skewers** *(page 77)*	**Chocolate-Dipped Grapefruit** *(page 66)*
DINNER •	**DINNER •**	**DINNER •**	**DINNER •**
Creamy Vegetable Soup *(page 165)*	**Rhubarb-Roasted Chicken** *(page 170)*	**Seared Steak and Roasted Veggie Bowl** *(page 193)*	**Trout Ratatouille en Papillote** *(page 204)*

Vegan Week

Even if you don't regularly follow a vegan diet, occasionally eliminating animal products from your diet can have amazing benefits for your skin, hair, and waistline. By shifting your focus from meats and cheeses to fruits and vegetables, you'll find a whole new world of flavors and cooking styles.

SUNDAY PREP PLAN

- Make the Homemade Granola (*page 32*).
- Make the Ramen in a Jar (*page 153*).
- Make the Baba Ghanoush (*page 69*).
- Make the Bulgur Salad with Cucumber and Tomatoes (*page 117*).
- Cook the wheat berries for the Spring Faux Risotto (*page 200*).
- Chop the vegetables for the Cashew and Pepper Stir-Fry (*page 192*), Fennel, Carrot, and Tarragon Salad (*page 126*), Spicy Cool Mini Watermelon Skewers (*page 77*), and Strawberry-Avocado Scallion Salsa (*page 81*).
- Freeze bananas for Frozen Banana and Peanut Butter Ice Cream (*page 216*).

MONDAY

BREAKFAST •
Homemade Granola (*page 32*)

LUNCH •
Ramen in a Jar (*page 153*)

SNACK •
Baba Ghanoush (*page 69*)

DINNER •
Spring Faux Risotto (*page 200*)

TUESDAY

BREAKFAST •
Butternut-Maple Amaranth Porridge (*page 43*)

LUNCH •
Bulgur Salad with Cucumber and Tomatoes (*page 117*)

SNACK •
Chips with Strawberry-Avocado Scallion Salsa (*page 81*)

DINNER •
Chickpea Chard Eggplant Rolls (*page 198*)

DESSERT •
Frozen Banana and Peanut Butter Ice Cream (*page 216*)

WEDNESDAY

BREAKFAST •
Homemade Granola (*page 32*)

LUNCH •
Spiced Peanut Soup (*page 158*)

SNACK •
Baba Ghanoush (*page 69*)

DINNER •
Cashew and Pepper Stir-Fry (*page 192*)

THURSDAY	FRIDAY	SATURDAY	SUNDAY
BREAKFAST • **Broiled Grapefruit** *(page 38)*	**BREAKFAST •** **Homemade Granola** *(page 32)*	**BREAKFAST •** **Butternut-Maple Amaranth Porridge** *(page 43)*	**BREAKFAST •** **Broiled Grapefruit** *(page 38)*
LUNCH • **Bulgur Salad with Cucumber and Tomatoes** *(page 117)*	**LUNCH •** **Fennel, Carrot, and Tarragon Salad** *(page 126)*	**LUNCH •** **Jicama Orange Salad with Scallion and Radish** *(page 132)*	**LUNCH •** **Spicy Watermelon Salad** *(page 138)*
SNACK • **Spicy Cool Mini Watermelon Skewers** *(page 77)*	**SNACK •** **Chips with Strawberry-Avocado Scallion Salsa** *(page 81)*	**SNACK •** **Steamed Broccoli with Miso Peanut Butter Dip** *(page 82)*	**SNACK •** **Spiced Sweet Potato Fries with Creamy Avocado Dip** *(page 91)*
DINNER • **Spicy Tempeh Chili** *(page 174)*	**DINNER •** **Creamy Vegetable Soup** *(page 165)*	**DINNER •** **Minestrone** *(page 166)*	**DINNER •** **Spicy Thai Curry Soup** *(page 164)*
DESSERT • **Frozen Banana and Peanut Butter Ice Cream** *(page 216)*			

Spring Week

From March through June (approximately, depending on where you live), the farmers' markets are full of delicate spring produce with the perfect light flavors for both the weather and prepping for bikini season. In the spring, enjoy eating perennial favorites like asparagus, radishes, leeks, peas, onions, and more.

SUNDAY PREP PLAN

- Make the Caramelized Leek Dip (*page 79*).
- Chop the vegetables for Jicama Orange Salad with Scallion and Radish (*page 132*).
- Cook the wheat berries for Spring Faux Risotto (*page 200*).
- Make smoothie bags for Peach-Chard Smoothie (*page 60*).

MONDAY

BREAKFAST •
Green Tea French Toast with Mandarin Orange Preserves (*page 35*)

LUNCH •
Jicama Orange Salad with Scallion and Radish (*page 132*)

SNACK •
Caramelized Leek Dip with Asparagus (*page 79*)

DINNER •
Spring Faux Risotto (*page 200*)

TUESDAY

BREAKFAST •
Peach-Chard Smoothie (*page 60*)

LUNCH •
Chicken and Asparagus Soup (*page 147*)

SNACK •
Steamed Broccoli with Miso Peanut Butter Dip (*page 82*)

DINNER •
Broiled Lamb with Charred Asparagus and Leeks (*page 186*)

DESSERT •
Aloha Bowl (*page 208*)

WEDNESDAY

BREAKFAST •
Smoked Salmon and Egg Tartine (*page 39*)

LUNCH •
Potato Leek Soup (*page 162*)

SNACK •
Caramelized Leek Dip with Asparagus (*page 79*)

DINNER •
Mashed Pea Tartine (*page 80*)

THURSDAY	FRIDAY	SATURDAY	SUNDAY
BREAKFAST • **Peach-Chard Smoothie** *(page 60)*	**BREAKFAST •** **Smoked Salmon and Egg Tartine** *(page 39)*	**BREAKFAST •** **Green Tea French Toast with Mandarin Orange Preserves** *(page 35)*	**BRUNCH •** **Bacon, Egg, and Asparagus Brunch Salad** *(page 139)*
LUNCH • **Jicama Orange Salad with Scallion and Radish** *(page 132)*	**LUNCH •** **Potato Leek Salad** *(page 162)*	**LUNCH •** **Asparagus, Tuna, and Chickpea Salad** *(page 125)*	**SNACK •** **Steamed Broccoli with Miso Peanut Butter Dip** *(page 82)*
SNACK • **Steamed Broccoli with Miso Peanut Butter Dip** *(page 82)*	**SNACK •** **Caramelized Leek Dip with Asparagus** *(page 79)*	**SNACK •** **Steamed Broccoli with Miso Peanut Butter Dip** *(page 82)*	**DINNER •** **Orange Chicken and Broccoli Stir-Fry** *(page 188)*
DINNER • **Asparagus Soup with Mustard Croutons** *(page 163)*	**DINNER •** **Tuna with Snap Peas and Watermelon Radish** *(page 136)*	**DINNER •** **Black Bean Burgers over Mexicali Slaw** *(page 185)*	
DESSERT • **Aloha Bowl** *(page 208)*			

Summer Week

Oh, the sweet summertime—fresh fruit and vegetables are in abundance, and the vegetables you love year-round taste even better than usual. This week, we celebrate tomatoes, corn, berries, melons, beets, peppers, green beans, eggplant, and more.

SUNDAY PREP PLAN

- Make Blueberry, Flax, and Cardamom Muffins *(page 31)*.
- Make Bulgur Salad with Cucumber and Tomatoes *(page 117)*.
- Make Blackberry-Corn Salsa *(page 75)*.
- Make Roasted Cherry Tomatoes *(page 68)*.
- Chop vegetables for Pork Lettuce Wraps *(page 184)*, Spicy Watermelon Salad *(page 138)*, Seared Steak and Roasted Veggie Bowl *(page 193)*, and Cashew and Pepper Stir-Fry *(page 192)*.
- Make Honey Lime Cantaloupe Pops *(page 219)*.

MONDAY

BREAKFAST •
Blueberry, Flax, and Cardamom Muffins *(page 31)*

LUNCH •
Bulgur Salad with Cucumber and Tomatoes *(page 117)*

SNACK •
Tortilla chips with Blackberry-Corn Salsa *(page 75)*

DINNER •
Pork Lettuce Wraps *(page 184)*

DESSERT •
Honey Lime Cantaloupe Pops *(page 219)*

TUESDAY

BREAKFAST •
Eggs with Crab and Tomato on Toast *(page 36)*

LUNCH •
Spicy Watermelon Salad *(page 138)*

SNACK •
Roasted Cherry Tomatoes *(page 68)*

DINNER •
Shrimp Corn Chowder *(page 161)*

WEDNESDAY

BREAKFAST •
Blueberry Muffin Breakfast Parfait *(page 40)*

LUNCH •
Raspberry Gazpacho *(page 157)*

SNACK •
Tortilla chips with Blackberry-Corn Salsa *(page 75)*

DINNER •
Blueberry Turkey Burgers *(page 194)*

DESSERT •
Honey Lime Cantaloupe Pops *(page 219)*

THURSDAY	FRIDAY	SATURDAY	SUNDAY
BREAKFAST •	**BREAKFAST •**	**BREAKFAST •**	**BRUNCH •**
Blueberry, Flax, and Cardamom Muffins *(page 31)*	**Eggs with Crab and Tomato on Toast** *(page 36)*	**Blueberry Muffin Breakfast Parfait** *(page 40)*	**Amaranth Huevos Rancheros** *(page 47)*
LUNCH •	**LUNCH •**	**LUNCH •**	**SNACK •**
Bulgur Salad with Cucumber and Tomatoes *(page 117)*	**Raspberry Gazpacho** *(page 157)*	**Spicy Watermelon Salad** *(page 138)*	**Ricotta, Lemon, and Basil Stuffed Cherry Tomatoes** *(page 76)*
SNACK •	**SNACK •**	**SNACK •**	**DINNER •**
Roasted Cherry Tomatoes *(page 68)*	**Tortilla chips with Blackberry-Corn Salsa** *(page 75)*	**Ricotta, Lemon, and Basil Stuffed Cherry Tomatoes** *(page 76)*	**Blackberry Pork Tenderloin** *(page 197)*
DINNER •	**DINNER •**	**DINNER •**	
Seared Steak and Roasted Veggie Bowl *(page 193)*	**Chickpea Chard Eggplant Rolls** *(page 198)*	**Cashew and Pepper Stir-Fry** *(page 192)*	
	DESSERT •		
	Honey Lime Cantaloupe Pops *(page 219)*		

Fall Week

Fall is a great, cozy time for delicious, warm food. These recipes are hearty but still healthy, featuring lots of butternut squash, apples, kale, potatoes, Swiss chard, and more.

SUNDAY PREP PLAN

- Make Sausage, Kale, and Apple Frittata *(page 30)*.
- Make Kale Salad with Wild Rice, Grilled Chicken, and Apples *(page 144)*.
- Make Tamari-Almond Cauliflower Bites *(page 88)*.
- Make smoothie bags for Peach-Chard Smoothies *(page 60)*.
- Make Kale Quesadillas *(page 95)*.
- Make Pumpkin Seed Clusters *(page 70)*.
- Make Apple and Chicken Curry *(page 171)*.
- Make Kale Pesto for Kale Pesto Pasta with Meatballs *(page 199)*.
- Make Spicy Peanut Butter Cookies *(page 211)*.

MONDAY

BREAKFAST •
Sausage, Kale, and Apple Frittata *(page 30)*

LUNCH •
Kale Salad with Wild Rice, Grilled Chicken, and Apples *(page 144)*

SNACK •
Tamari-Almond Cauliflower Bites *(page 88)*

DINNER •
Pan-Seared Pork Chops and Spiced Apples *(page 205)*

TUESDAY

BREAKFAST •
Peach-Chard Smoothie *(page 60)*

LUNCH •
Kale Quesadillas *(page 95)*

SNACK •
Pumpkin Seed Clusters *(page 70)*

DINNER •
Broiled Steak and Smashed Potatoes *(page 178)*

DESSERT •
Spicy Peanut Butter Cookies *(page 211)*

WEDNESDAY

BREAKFAST •
Sausage, Kale, and Apple Frittata *(page 30)*

LUNCH •
Kale Salad with Wild Rice, Grilled Chicken, and Apples *(page 144)*

SNACK •
Tamari-Almond Cauliflower Bites *(page 88)*

DINNER •
Apple and Butternut Squash Pasta with Brown Butter–Sage Sauce *(page 195)*

THURSDAY	FRIDAY	SATURDAY	SUNDAY
BREAKFAST •	BREAKFAST •	BREAKFAST •	BRUNCH •
Peach-Chard Smoothie *(page 60)*	**Sausage, Kale, and Apple Frittata** *(page 30)*	**Portobello "Bacon" and Eggs** *(page 44)*	**Butternut-Maple Amaranth Porridge** *(page 43)*
LUNCH •	LUNCH •	LUNCH •	SNACK •
Kale Quesadillas *(page 95)*	**Spicy Baby Potato Salad** *(page 141)*	**Baja Apple Salsa Burrito** *(page 111)*	**Butternut Squash and Chard Mini Taco Bites** *(page 83)*
SNACK •	SNACK •	SNACK •	DINNER •
Pumpkin Seed Clusters *(page 70)*	**Tamari-Almond Cauliflower Bites** *(page 88)*	**Butternut Squash and Chard Mini Taco Bites** *(page 83)*	**Pan-Roasted Chicken with Mushroom and Herb Gravy** *(page 203)*
DINNER •	DINNER •	DINNER •	
Apple and Chicken Curry *(page 171)*	**Kale Pesto Pasta with Meatballs** *(page 199)*	**Spicy Chipotle Peach Ribs** *(page 201)*	
DESSERT •			
Spicy Peanut Butter Cookies *(page 211)*			

Winter Week

'Tis the season for root vegetables and citrus, and we have you covered. Winter is also the perfect time to experiment with hearty soups to keep you warm even when it's chilly outside. So sit back and enjoy the best grapefruits, oranges, cabbage, pineapple, and leeks of the year.

SUNDAY PREP PLAN

Hard-cook eggs for Avocado Deviled Eggs (*page 90*).

Chop produce for Jicama Orange Salad with Scallion and Radish (*page 132*).

Make oatmeal for Oatmeal with Brown Sugar Pineapple Swirl (*page 28*).

Make Chocolate-Dipped Grapefruit (*page 66*).

Make Walnut Slaw with Cilantro (*page 118*).

Make Winter Squash Pudding (*page 221*).

MONDAY

BREAKFAST •
Broiled Grapefruit (*page 38*)

LUNCH •
Jicama Orange Salad with Scallion and Radish (*page 132*)

SNACK •
Avocado Deviled Eggs (*page 90*)

DINNER •
Cod with Fennel and Pineapple Salsa (*page 179*)

DESSERT •
Winter Squash Pudding (*page 221*)

TUESDAY

BREAKFAST •
Oatmeal with Brown Sugar Pineapple Swirl (*page 28*)

LUNCH •
Orange Beef Sandwich (*page 97*)

SNACK •
Chocolate-Dipped Grapefruit (*page 66*)

DINNER •
Black Bean Soup with Mango (*page 155*)

WEDNESDAY

BREAKFAST •
Broiled Grapefruit (*page 38*)

LUNCH •
Orange-Cranberry Turkey Club Lettuce Wrap with Jicama (*page 110*)

SNACK •
Avocado Deviled Eggs (*page 90*)

DINNER •
Orange Chicken and Broccoli Stir-Fry (*page 188*)

THURSDAY	FRIDAY	SATURDAY	SUNDAY
BREAKFAST • Oatmeal with Brown Sugar Pineapple Swirl *(page 28)*	**BREAKFAST •** Broiled Grapefruit *(page 38)*	**BREAKFAST •** Portobello "Bacon" and Eggs *(page 44)*	**BRUNCH •** Green Tea French Toast with Mandarin Orange Preserves *(page 35)*
LUNCH • Jicama Orange Salad with Scallion and Radish *(page 132)*	**LUNCH •** Orange-Cranberry Turkey Club Lettuce Wrap with Jicama *(page 110)*	**LUNCH •** Avgolemono Soup *(page 159)*	**SNACK •** Veggie Chips *(page 84)*
SNACK • Chocolate-Dipped Grapefruit *(page 66)*	**SNACK •** Avocado Deviled Eggs *(page 90)*	**SNACK •** Veggie Chips *(page 84)*	**DINNER •** French Lentil and Fennel Soup *(page 148)*
DINNER • Walnut Slaw with Cilantro *(page 118)*	**DINNER •** Cinnamon Chili Rubbed Pork with Raw Sprout Slaw *(page 169)*	**DINNER •** Maple, Bourbon, and Mustard–Glazed Salmon with Slaw *(page 190)*	
DESSERT • Winter Squash Pudding *(page 221)*			

Healthy Meals
Q&A

EVEN THE MOST CAREFULLY DETAILED PLANS CAN RUN INTO UNEXPECTED changes—you shopped for the ingredients, you chopped and refrigerated and prepped, but life gets in the way. Here are some questions from real women who wanted answers to the roadblocks that they have come up against while trying to cook for one.

"I got stuck at work and won't be able to eat the meal that I planned for tonight. What should I do so it doesn't go to waste?"—Stephanie Farrell, Philadelphia, PA

First of all, take a deep breath and make sure that whatever you're feeding yourself tonight is as healthful as what you were going to cook. Sometimes when we get overwhelmed, we want to treat ourselves with food, but grabbing greasy pizza or fast food on the run is only going to make you feel worse. Now, take a look at your schedule for the rest of the week. Are you crazy busy? Is there a night where you might have a lot of extra time and could cook two meals so you could freeze one of them for later? Maybe you're getting close to the end of the week—if your recipe serves two, you could reschedule a dinner date you had planned out to stay in. Or, could these ingredients turn into a different meal entirely? Maybe they would all be yummy mixed into a breakfast frittata. Think of this as a chance to cook and plan creatively, and not as a big road bump that will leave you with wasted food.

"It's difficult for me to find the time to prep my lunches in the morning when I'm running around getting ready for work. This is even harder when I have an early exercise class that I want to go to, meaning my meal won't go right to my work fridge."—Deborah Binko Meehan, Stamford, CT

How much do you trust your coworkers? We have a great list of meals that can be made in advance for lunch, some of them even a few days before, so you can stock up your work fridge at the beginning of the week. This does mean that you don't want big, bulky lunches (we wouldn't want to take up too much space!)—a few Mason jar salads or soups would be perfect for this. Just put them all in a bag labeled clearly with your name, and be sure to clean them out at the end of the week.

"Having to cook a meal just for myself and then spend a ton of time washing dishes discourages me from cooking at all (particularly before I had a dishwasher). Even now that I have a dishwasher, it's something I still try to be mindful of. I avoid cooking because one meal generally requires the use of practically all of the bowls I own."—Becca Chazin, Philadelphia, PA

You could start eating your meals straight out of the pot over the kitchen sink to avoid cleaning an extra plate, but that just doesn't sound like a very enjoyable dinner! There are a few tricks you can use to minimize the cleanup required after a meal. First, if you've done the prep that we talked about earlier in the book, then you should have a lot fewer knives and cutting boards to deal with over the course of the week. Also, try to be conscientious about using only one pot or pan, which you can do by cooking ingredients in shifts and cooking the recipes that we have designated as "one pan." If there are a lot of herbs or vegetables to chop, put them in finished piles on your cutting board, instead of moving them to individual bowls (just make sure you don't cut raw meat on the same board).

Most of the recipes in this book have already minimized the amount of kitchen tools you'll need to use, but we'll leave you with one of our favorite kitchen cleanup tips: For any baking or roasting (under 400°F), parchment paper or foil are your best friends! Line your pan or dish before cooking, then simply toss the liner when your meal is done. The pan might require a quick rinse if any crumbs or oil got through, but this trick will save a lot of cleanup time—we promise!

"It's so tempting to use the more expensive pre-cut vegetables from the grocery store—frozen rice, pre-chopped onions, and especially cubed butternut squash. They really make cooking feel less daunting. How can I break this habit and save myself some money?"—Bethy Atkins, Boston, MA

Cheers to you for finding something that works to help you cook and save time! But you are right, those pre-cut vegetables are sometimes five times more expensive than their whole counterparts. You're essentially paying someone else to do the prep work that we covered earlier in the book. We think you'll find that once you prep your veggies a couple of weeks in a row, it will become a habit, and the idea of spending money to avoid a half hour of work won't be so tempting. But some weeks, you might not have the time to prep, and in that case, these are a great substitute to help you continue cooking at home. Just make sure the only ingredients are the vegetables you're buying, and you're not accidentally eating a bunch of extra preservatives. And definitely avoid bagged salad mixes—the greens in them can be up to 2 weeks old before you even buy them, and one study found that many bagged salad mixes contain bacteria consistent with poor sanitation and even fecal contamination.[1]

"I love using herbs; they make a dish feel full, green, and fancy. But you have to buy a bunch of herbs all at once, way more than I need for a week's worth of meals for myself. How can I put the herbs to good use and avoid wasting them?"—Melissa Kowalcyzk, Mt. Airy, PA

Herbs really do make a meal taste better, don't they? But you're right, they don't last long, and unlike produce, you can't buy them individually at the grocery store. The first step to solving this dilemma is to plan meals that use similar herbs throughout the week. For example, don't just have one meal that features basil; add basil into your eggs or even a smoothie. But if it gets to the end of the week and you think your herbs have only a couple of good days left in them, turn to your freezer. Chop up your herbs either separately or in yummy blends, and fill an ice cube tray with them. Then cover the herbs in olive oil, pouring into each section until it's almost full. Freeze your herb cubes until they're solid, then pop them out and store them in the freezer in a resealable plastic bag (you can put multiple cubes in one bag). You can add them to all sorts of recipes for a yummy burst of flavor. You could even try growing some of your own herbs in little pots on your windowsill or in your garden if you are lucky enough to have outdoor space of your own! That way, you would always have fresh herbs at your fingertips.

"My produce always seems to go bad. Either it rots quickly outside of the refrigerator, or I refrigerate it and it comes out tasting mealy (I'm looking at you, tomatoes!). How do I know where to store everything so that it lasts the longest time possible?"—Haley Whitchurch, Louisville, KY

Mealy refrigerator tomatoes are the worst! But even worse than that is produce going bad before you get to use it, so we can feel your pain. We could write out a list for you of where to store everything you could possibly buy, or you could scour Google and all of its conflicting information, but the answer you seek is already in front of you (yes, we are produce gurus sometimes) at your grocery store! Who is more interested in keeping produce tasting and looking good for as long as possible than the people trying to sell it to you? It doesn't matter if you're in Georgia or Wyoming, a grocery store produce section is always laid out the same way—a line of cold storage on the walls, with room temperature storage in the middle. There's your guide! Did you get it from the edges of the store (greens, carrots, herbs)? To the refrigerator it goes! Produce items from the middle of the store—potatoes, onions, citrus fruit, and yes, tomatoes—are happy campers right at room temperature. Some, like onions and citrus, will do just fine in the refrigerator, if your counter space is limited.

"I'm always starving when I get home, and I think it affects my cooking and eating choices. Sometimes I'm so hungry I can't imagine cooking and end up ordering food. If I do cook, I make way more than I should. Help!"—Amy Palmer, Washington, DC

Cooking is always going to be faster than ordering in, unless your favorite Indian place is literally downstairs (in which case, wow are we jealous!). So you're right, hunger is causing you to make irrational decisions, and you know what the better choices are, so let's focus on eliminating this hunger. You can make many of the snack recipes in this book in advance so that you can take some to work with you every day and make sure you have an afternoon snack. Your body needs to eat every few hours, but the gap between lunch and dinner is sometimes as many as 8 or 9 hours depending on your hectic and ever-changing schedule. But let's say you missed the snack and you're starving and you need to cook and the delivery app is looking very tempting. Take a deep breath and drink a full glass of water. If you still need to nosh, try a handful of nuts or a slice of whole grain bread dipped in a tablespoon of olive oil. It's okay to give yourself a little snack—like some carrot sticks or a piece of fruit—before dinner; it's much healthier than ordering in. Now you can cook your dinner in peace without the grumble of your stomach leading you astray.

"I love onions, but there are times I find myself just leaving them out because every time I start to cut one, my eyes tear up! Is there anything that I can do to make this stop?"—Danielle Curtis, New York, NY

It's the worst, right? Don't tell anyone, but sometimes we skip onions in recipes, too, because crying in the kitchen is the worst (for reasons other than burnt casseroles). Or, we used to skip them, before we learned a few secret tricks for keeping your eyes dry while cutting onions. First, never cut the root end of the onion (the gnarly brown part). Cutting that releases most of the gas that makes your eyes tear up. Then, always keep a glass of ice water by your side; besides being refreshing and hydrating, sipping on the water will help flush your system and keep the tears at bay. If you try both of these and still find your eyes getting watery, it's time to go nuclear. Grab a piece of bread and stick it in your mouth, with most of the piece sitting outside your mouth. You might feel a little crazy, but the bread will absorb the gas before it gets to your eyes. And trust us, the flavor that onions add to any dish will be worth the effort!

Cooking Glossary: from A to Zest

AROMATICS. Food that is added to a recipe to enhance the natural flavor of other ingredients in the recipe. Most often, this is a combination of herbs, spices, and light-flavor vegetables like onions and celery that are sautéed in fat at the beginning of a recipe. Most soups begin by cooking aromatics.

BAKE. Cooking in dry heat (like an oven) without direct exposure to flame. Generally, the oven temperature is between 250° and 400°F. Baking generally involves taking unstructured food (a batter, a casserole, dough) and cooking it until it takes its desired shape and becomes solid.

BASTE. Using liquid (fat, pan juices, stock) to keep an item moist during cooking. This usually involves brushing or pouring liquid over meat, but this is also a great technique for cooking lots of vegetables.

BLANCHE. A process to quickly cook vegetables and then stop the cooking process so they remain crisp and full of color. This involves a couple of minutes in boiling water, then dunking the vegetables in a bowl of ice water. Great for crudités, salads, and prepping vegetables so they're ready for snacking whenever you want!

BOIL. Bringing liquid to the temperature at which it bubbles and becomes vapor. For water, and most cooking purposes, this temperature is 212°F. If left at a boil, the water will evaporate from the recipe, reducing the liquid content (see **Reduce** on page 253).

BOUQUET GARNI. A bag of herbs that cook with a dish and are removed before serving. It saves your fingers from being scalded while you're trying to pick herbs like bay leaves and rosemary out of soup!

BROIL. Cooking under direct heat. The broiler in your oven or toaster oven radiates heat from the top of the unit. When broiling meat, vegetables, or any dish, you want to adjust the cooking rack to one of the highest settings so that the top of your food is within a few inches of the broiler. The heat from broiling is too much for some kitchen tools (such as parchment paper and some pans), so be sure to check the temperature restrictions before putting them under the broiler. But if you're looking for nice crisp and color on your meat, vegetables, or cheese dishes (yum!), the broiler is your best friend.

BROWN. Quickly cooking the outside of a raw piece of meat until it is (duh!) brown in color. This is a great way to maintain delicious flavor and works to "seal" some of the juices inside the meat. If you're cooking beef in a slow cooker, this is a great first step before the long cooking process.

CARAMELIZE. To cook food with natural sugars or added sugars at a low temperature so that the sugars turn into caramel. Slowing cooking onions until they're caramelized is a great way to enhance the natural sweetness of onions without adding sugar.

CHOP. Cutting fruits or vegetables into roughly bite-size pieces. When a recipe calls for an ingredient to be "chopped," it should be big enough that it's visible in the dish and won't disappear while cooking. As you develop your prepping skills, focus on trying to make all of your chopped pieces around the same size. This will help ensure that when you cook the pieces, they'll all be done at the same time. If some of your chopped carrots are $1/2$-inch pieces, and some are 2 inches, you'll end up with some hard and some soggy pieces (not appetizing!). Consistency is your BFF when it comes to cooking.

DASH. Cooking terms like *dash* are where home cooks tend to separate into two groups: scientific cooks and artistic cooks. If you worry about leveling off $1/4$ teaspoon of salt, you're a scientific cook. If you read a recipe once and then start cooking from memory, you're more of an artistic cook. For an artistic cook, a dash is a little less than a pinch and a little more than a tad. But this glossary is for our scientific friends, so here are some loose guidelines: If you're adding a dash of a liquid ingredient, you want about four or five drops. For a dash of dry ingredients, such as herbs, it's usually in the $1/8$ teaspoon to $1/4$ teaspoon range, depending on your taste.

DEGLAZE. Removing the residue left in a pan from cooking with liquid. It might sound fancy, but this technique is actually really easy, adds lots of flavor to your food, and (shhh!) makes cleanup easier later! After cooking meat and removing it from the pan, just add about $1/4$ cup of water to the still hot pan; it should bubble and boil when it hits the pan. Quickly stir the water around, pulling up the fond—a word for the residue left over, which is full of great flavor—and creating what will look like a sauce. You can pour this over your meat before serving it for extra juiciness.

DICE. Cutting food into small cubes. Even more than chopping, diced pieces should be very consistent in size, and smaller than a chop. If a recipe calls for diced vegetables, try to make the cubes about $\frac{1}{4}$ inch to $\frac{1}{2}$ inch in size. The easiest way to dice an ingredient is to cut it into consistently sized strips, then gather a few strips at a time and cut them about as long as the strip is wide, working your way down the piece. If this feels uncomfortable, you can cut them one piece at a time.

FOLD. Gently adding an ingredient into an already mixed or combined bowl of food. This is most commonly done when you add an ingredient to a batter or whipped mixture. To fold an ingredient in, you add it to the top of the mixture and then, using a rubber spatula, cut through the center of the bowl to the bottom. Then guide your spatula up the side of the bowl, flipping it over and back to the center of the mixture. Do this a few times, working your way around the bowl as you gently fold the ingredient in.

GARNISH. A final decoration or edible element that is added as the very last step before eating a dish. Most often, herbs are used to garnish food. The benefit of a garnish is that it is usually uncooked and fresh, adding a bright, crisp touch of flavor to cooked food. Even if a recipe doesn't call for a garnish, setting aside a little extra of herbs or citrus to top your finished dish right at the end can make even a simple meal feel special—and isn't that what cooking for yourself is all about?

JULIENNE. Cutting vegetables into short, thin strips of consistent size, about the shape of a matchstick. This is a great way to cut vegetables that take a while to cook, like carrots or potatoes, so that they stay substantial and flavorful, but cook much faster than if they were whole.

KNEAD. Working bread dough by stretching, pressing, and folding to help form the gluten in the dough. Kneading usually requires a little extra flour to keep the dough from sticking to the surface you're using. If you're feeling adventurous, making your own bread is a cheap and fun project for a lazy Sunday.

MARINATE. Soaking food in a liquid or *marinade*—which is usually acidic in order to penetrate the food—in order to add flavor before cooking. Marinating overnight is a great way to prep meat before the next day's dinner. Just make sure you don't marinate meat and vegetables in the same liquid, which risks cross-contamination between the raw meat bacteria and the vegetables, and always marinate in the refrigerator and not at room temperature.

MEASUREMENTS. Knowing how measurements relate to each other makes cooking for one (or two!) a lot easier because it allows you to quickly cut down recipes to the portion you want. So here is your ultimate conversion guide!

1 tablespoon = 3 teaspoons	**1 pint = 2 cups**
$\frac{1}{16}$ cup = 1 tablespoon	**1 quart = 2 pints = 4 cups**
$\frac{1}{4}$ cup = 4 tablespoons = 12 teaspoons	**1 gallon = 4 quarts = 8 pints = 16 cups**
$\frac{1}{3}$ cup = 5 tablespoons + 1 teaspoon	**16 ounces = 1 pound**
8 fluid ounces = 1 cup	

MEAT TEMPERATURES. One of the cheapest and best kitchen tools you can buy is a meat thermometer. Cooking meat to the right temperature ensures that it is safe to eat and delicious. When testing for temperature, try to insert the thermometer into the center, meatiest part of the meat (the last place the heat reaches). Here's a guide to minimum meat temperatures from our friends at the USDA; any temperature below the guide is considered unsafe to eat.

PORK, VEAL, LAMB •
145°F and allow to rest for at least 3 minutes

GROUND MEAT • 160°F

HAM, FRESH OR SMOKED •
145°F

ALL POULTRY (breasts, whole bird, legs, thighs, and wings, ground poultry, and stuffing) •
165°F

FISH AND SHELLFISH •
145°F

BEEF •
Medium-rare: **145°F**

Medium: **160°F**

Medium-well: **165°F**

Well: **170°F**

MINCE. The smaller cousin to dice (page 251). Still consistent in size, mince is the smallest size of cutting. Less than $\frac{1}{4}$ inch, minced produce will disappear into a recipe almost as soon as it is added. Just watch your fingers while mincing, and be patient— small cuts like this take time to master.

PARE. Trimming the outer edges with a knife—usually a paring knife. This is the more precise version of peeling, but it takes some skill and technique to keep your fingers safe! And check your directions—sometimes paring involves leaving some of the outer skin on.

PEEL. Removing all of the skin from fruit or produce, usually with a vegetable peeler. Always make sure to peel away from your body to avoid nicks and cuts. If you're shaky, it helps to peel vertically, with the end of the vegetable resting on a cutting board.

PICKLE. A pickle is any vegetable (or fruit!) that is preserved in vinegar, brine, or other solution. Pickled vegetables are crisp, flavorful, and ready to eat whenever you want, which is why they've become so popular in farm-to-table restaurants.

PINCH. More than a dash (page 250), a pinch is a healthy addition of flavor to a dish. For artistic cooks, a pinch is the amount that you can grasp between your thumb and forefinger (hence the name!). For scientific cooks, you want to add anywhere between $\frac{1}{8}$ and $\frac{1}{4}$ teaspoon. But isn't pinching salt so much more fun?

PREHEAT. Warming an oven, pan, or cooking surface to the exact temperature you want for cooking before adding food. For baking in the oven, this is very important for making sure your food cooks correctly. For stovetop cooking, most food cooks better and keeps more flavor when added to a hot pan, as opposed to starting in a cold pan and slowly getting warmer.

PUREE. Cooked food that is mashed or blended into a consistent texture, without lumps. A puree can be made from a single ingredient or multiple ingredients.

REDUCE. Cooking liquid, or ingredients in liquid, over high heat in order to let some of the water in the liquid evaporate. This concentrates the flavor of the liquid and thickens the consistency of the sauce. A lot of recipes will call for you to wait until the liquid is reduced by half, but the amount of time this takes varies a lot based on your stove and other factors, so don't stress if it takes a while!

RESTING. The time between when your meat is taken off its heat source and when it is sliced or served. Resting is really important for meat, as it will actually continue to cook and get warmer as it sits on the plate or cutting board. Most meat needs only a couple of minutes to rest, but steak should sit for 10 to 15 minutes. This lets the juices in the steak reabsorb, rather than running out of the steak when it is cut.

ROAST. Cooking food in dry, consistent heat at a higher temperature than baking, usually more than 400°F. Roasting is usually used to cook whole ingredients, such as meat or vegetables. When food with high amounts of natural sugar is roasted, it can result in caramelization or browning. Roasting is an ideal technique for foods where the desired end result is a crispy or crunchy texture.

ROOM TEMPERATURE. About 70°F, although it can vary based on access to an air conditioner (or spotty radiators!). Some ingredients, such as eggs or butter, might need to be brought to room temperature before being used in a recipe. Our rule of thumb is just to set them out about an hour before.

ROUX. A mixture of fat (such as butter or oil) and flour, which works as a thickener for sauces, soups, and gravy. If you've ever made homemade macaroni and cheese, then you've made a roux! Melt or heat the fat in a pot, add an equal amount of flour, whisk quickly until smooth, and then continue whisking over heat until it just turns brown. Then you can add broth, milk, or whatever your recipe calls for. So if you see a roux in a recipe, don't fear—you can make it!

SEAR. The cooking technique of using a very hot pan to brown meat quickly (see **Brown** on page 250).

SEASONALITY. Buying and cooking with produce that is currently being grown in your area of the country. Produce that is in-season is more likely to be local (and therefore hasn't taken a plane ride or round-the-world trip to get to your plate) and is more nutritious and generally more flavorful. In-season produce is also way cheaper because there is more of it to go around. The perfect example of seasonality is tomatoes. For most of the country, grocery-store tomatoes are mealy, perfectly round, limited in variety, and expensive in the winter because they are out of season. In the summer, when tomatoes are in season, there are more varieties and they are cheaper and more flavorful. When planning your weekly meals, try to keep an eye to seasonality. You can also try one of our in-season meal plans (see page 236), because while it may vary slightly, most produce has the same seasonality no matter where you live.

SIMMER. Cooking a liquid, or food in a liquid, just below the boiling point (see **Boil** on page 249), usually for an extended period of time. As a rule of thumb, if you're simmering a recipe, you want to avoid large bubbles—that usually means you've reached a boil.

SMOKE POINT. The temperature at which an oil or fat used for cooking starts producing a light smoke, which also means it has started developing carcinogens and a bad, burned taste. But some recipes, like stir-fries, are better when cooked at higher temperatures. So when choosing your cooking fat, follow this temperature guide to pick the right one for your recipe.[1]

Peanut, safflower, soybean oils: 450°F

Grapeseed oil: 445°F

Canola oil: 435°F

Corn, olive, sesame seed, sunflower oils: 410°F

Extra-virgin olive oil: 375°F

Butter: 350°F

Coconut oil: 350°F

SWEAT. Gently heating vegetables to allow them to release their natural water content. This softens the vegetables and brings out delicious flavor. This is commonly done to aromatics (page 249) at the beginning of a recipe, especially onions.

ZEST. The outer skin of citrus fruit including oranges, lemons, and limes. Also the resulting finely separated peel from using a rasp or grater on the skin of citrus.

Endnotes

Introduction

1   "Families, Ages 25-34." *United States Census Bureau.* http://www.census.gov/hhes/families/files/ad3-25-34.xlsx&sa=D&ust=1492834599105000&usg=AFQjCNGjImpoj5iP5KtF0wAF3vlyurzV0w. Accessed April 10, 2017.

2   Katherine L. Hanna, Peter F. Collins. "Relationship between living alone and food and nutrient intake." *Nutrition Reviews 2015*, vol. 73, no. 9, pp. 594-611, https://doi.org/10.1093/nutrit/nuv024. Accessed May 24, 2017.

3   "U.S. food-away-from-home sales topped food-at-home sales in 2014." *United States Department of Agriculture.* 12 April 2016, https://www.ers.usda.gov/data-products/chart-gallery/gallery/chart-detail/?chartId=58364. Accessed May 24, 2017.

4   Urban, Lorien E. et al. "Energy Contents of Frequently Ordered Restaurant Meals and Comparison with Human Energy Requirements and US Department of Agriculture Database Information: A Multisite Randomized Study." *Journal of the Academy of Nutrition and Dietetics*, vol. 116, issue 4, pp.590–598, http://www.andjrnl.org/article/S2212-2672(15)01736-0/abstract. Accessed May 24, 2017.

Prepping for the Week

1   Zerbe, Leah. "8 Natural Cleaning Products You Can Easily Make." Rodale's Organic Life, October 15, 2015, http://www.rodalesorganiclife.com/home/8-natural-cleaning-products-you-can-easily-make?slide=1/slide/8. Accessed May 24, 2017.

2   "Food Product Dating." USDA Food Safety and Inspection Service, USDA, December 14, 2016, https://www.fsis.usda.gov/wps/portal/fsis/topics/food-safety-education/get-answers/food-safety-fact-sheets/food-labeling/food-product-dating/food-product-dating/!ut/p/a1/jZFfT4MwFMU_DY-lF5kL842QmA0duCw61hdTRltISkvaTqKf3vrvYWbo2qd7-ju5955igitMFH3pBHWdVlR-1GT-DBuYR4sM8nlR3cKqeNqUd1kGyfbaA_s_gCK-0D9xUvjPn1_Q4Mqss7XAZKCuRZ3iGleCOUSVHZmxuOJaN8hSztwr4vTgkG0Zcz8PktZMdkp8l4PRzdEzjY9oStxhcjoWRP6uing7W-ZFDOXsN3Amty9gOhi_uZC6_vykfarqOPErGsaZYSY8Gi-3zg32JoAAxnEMhdZCsvCg-wDOWVptHa5OSTz0j9XbfbqE7qHfJTZ9B_9fjN8!/#6. Accessed May 24, 2017.

Breakfast

1   Moriarty, Kate. "The Surprising Danger of Skipping Breakfast." *Women's Health*, June 25, 2013, http://www.womenshealthmag.com/food/the-surprising-danger-of-skipping-breakfast. Accessed May 24, 2017.

Snacks

1   Moriarty, Kate. "The Surprising Danger of Skipping Breakfast." *Women's Health*, June 25, 2013, http://www.womenshealthmag.com/food/the-surprising-danger-of-skipping-breakfast. Accessed May 24, 2017.

Soups

1   "Chicken Stock." Rodale's Organic Life, 2017, http://www.rodalesorganiclife.com/recipes/chicken-stock. Accessed May 24, 2017.

Healthy Meals Q&A

1   "How Clean Is Bagged Salad?" *Consumer Reports,* March 2010, http://www.consumerreports.org/cro/2012/05/how-clean-is-bagged-salad/index.htm. Accessed May 24, 2017.

Cooking Glossary: from A to Zest

1   "Deep Fat Frying and Food Safety." USDA Food Safety and Inspection Service, USDA, June 27, 2013, https://www.fsis.usda.gov/wps/portal/fsis/topics/food-safety-education/get-answers/food-safety-fact-sheets/safe-food-handling/deep-fat-frying-and-food-safety/ct_index. Accessed May 24, 2017.

Index

Underscored page references indicate sidebars and tables. An asterisk (*) indicates that photographs appear in the color insert pages.